GARBAGE IN POPULAR CULTURE

Garbage in
Popular
Culture

Consumption and the Aesthetics of Waste

MEHITA IQANI

SUNY
PRESS

Cover image: *Cape Mongo* (2015) by Francois Knoetze.
Courtesy of Francois Knoetze.

Published by State University of New York Press, Albany

For information, contact State University of New York Press, Albany, NY
www.sunypress.edu

Library of Congress Cataloging-in-Publication Data

Names: Iqani, Mehita, author.
Title: Garbage in popular culture : consumption and the aesthetics of
    waste / Mehita Iqani.
Description: Albany : State University of New York Press, [2020] |
    Includes bibliographical references and index.
Identifiers: LCCN 2020001181 (print) | LCCN 2020001182 (ebook) |
    ISBN 9781438480176 (hardcover) | ISBN 9781438480190 (ebook) |
    ISBN 9781438480183 (pbk)
Subjects: LCSH: Consumption (Economics)—Social aspects. | Refuse
    and refuse disposal—Social aspects.
Classification: LCC HC79.C6 I63 2020 ; (print) | LCC HC79.C6 (ebook)
    | DDC 306.3—dc23
LC record available at https://lccn.loc.gov/2020001181
LC ebook record available at https://lccn.loc.gov/2020001182

10 9 8 7 6 5 4 3 2 1

CONTENTS

The academics, artists, environmentalists, writers, musicians, entrepreneurs, and critical thinkers I am lucky to have in my life and call my friends, students, and colleagues have shaped this book more than they know. There are too many to name, but I am deeply grateful to everyone who talked with me about the subject matter in this book; helped me shape my thinking and arguments; shared material, case studies, and ideas; encouraged me to start and stay with the writing; or inspired me in some way or other to capture into words the ideas in the pages that follow. A special thank you to my friends (or should I say, family) at Breezeblock, my neighborhood café in Brixton, Johannesburg, where I wrote and edited huge swathes of this book, buoyed by excellent coffee, food, sunshine in the winter, and what felt like a bottomless well of kindness from Keke Mamaleshoane and Azwi Netshirembe, in particular.

I participated in the "Sugarman" workshop on Toxicity and Detritus, which took place in Durban in 2016, organized by colleagues at the University of the Witwatersrand and the University of Michigan, where I presented some early work relevant to this book.

I was privileged to have had the opportunity to work on the manuscript for this book during academic writing residencies at the Bellagio Center of the Rockefeller Foundation in 2018 and Makerere University in Kampala, Uganda in 2019, through the American Council for Learned Scholars' African Humanities Programme. I am grateful to staff and fellow residents at both institutions for their support and intellectual generosity during my time with them. I am also grateful to the South African National Research Foundation for funding support during the time of writing this book.

I wrote a significant part of this book in Lamu, Kenya—a place that generously gave me both much inspiration and many new friends. I hope that somehow the work presented here can contribute in some tiny way to protecting places like it.

I would like to thank all the photographers, artists, activists, and public sector workers who gave explicit permission for me to include their images in this book, or who put their work into the public domain for fair use by researchers like me. Special thanks to Francois Knoetze for allowing me to feature his artwork on the cover.

I would not have been able to finalize this manuscript without the efficient and reliable assistance of Gabriel Shamu.

To David du Preez: thank you for being my Besten bester. Your love and partnership are constants in an inconstant world.

I dedicate this book to all out there on the frontlines working as best they are able for their fellow human beings in the quest to protect the environment.

1

Globalization, Consumption, and Media

Why Rubbish Matters

Most people on the planet have two things in common, both deeply embedded in the inescapably material nature of the human condition. The first is that we aspire to accumulate or possess things that, thanks to the power of market exchange in the global neoliberal economy, most often manifest as commodities. The second is that through our use, possession, and eventual utilization of those things, we produce some form of waste, which must then be disposed of. Wherever there is consumption, there is waste.

All people, from the most impoverished to the obscenely wealthy, through the day-to-day and often automatic decisions that we make, acquire things, use them, and throw what's left of them away. To date, much critical consumer culture theory has devoted attention to questions linked to the accumulation and use of things (be they defined in the material, virtual, or experiential sense). This book aims to understand the culturally shared meanings attached to the detritus that is left behind once consumption has taken place, and thereby to expand our critical thinking both about consumption and about rubbish. By better understanding the two in relation to one another, new insights will be gleaned into the futures of consumption and material culture, the latter increasingly defined by the waste that it creates. Scholars have deployed frameworks from a wide range of disciplines in order to understand what objects mean to people, how and why they acquire and exchange them, and how their consumption practices fit into the bigger picture of a world shaped by the economics of late capitalism. In previous writing, I have contributed to these understandings by revealing the role that media texts, discourses, and narratives play in shaping popular, often "taken-for-granted" ideas about consumption and the individual's place and role in the neoliberal economy. Some scholars have written about the ethics of consumption and questions of environmental sustainability in relation to consumption (Harrison, Newholm, & Shaw, 2005; Guido, 2009; Barnett et al., 2010; Smart, 2010; Carrier & Luetchford, 2012; Lewis & Potter, 2013), and others have written about the role of waste and garbage in material culture studies, media studies, geography and anthropology, and cultural philosophy (as the rest of this chapter explores in detail). However, not enough theoretical work has yet been done about the role of postconsumer trash in the neoliberal age, and specifically about how that role—or those roles—are narrated in such a way as to enter the popular imagination and shape and define cultural discourse.

This book aims to fill that gap. It focuses on the question of what waste means in relation to consumer culture. More specifically, it asks how popular media narratives about postconsumer waste create and share specific notions about consumption and neoliberal culture. Through this intellectual project, the book makes an original contribution to the areas of consumer culture studies, visual culture, media and communications, and cultural theory, through a critical analysis of the ways in which waste and garbage are visually communicated in the public realm. Although building on and speaking to much important work in a wide range of disciplinary and interdisciplinary spheres of knowledge, this book is the first to explicitly link media discourse, consumer culture, and the cultural politics of garbage in contemporary global society. Each of these things has been written about individually at length, but the current moment in cultural theory and the politics of survival—which some theorists summarize as the age of the Anthropocene (Steffen, Crutzen, & McNeill, 2007; Smith & Zeder, 2013; Zylinska, 2014; Bonneuil & Fressoz, 2016; Wark, 2016; Dellasala & Goldstein, 2017)—calls for an attempt to bring together the big questions that scholars are asking about media, waste, and consumption into an exploration of how waste is mediated, and to what extent those media narratives connect consumer culture with the environment and the sustainability of the human species.

This chapter provides a review of key literature dealing with garbage from a variety of disciplinary perspectives, and makes the argument that there has been a lacuna in theorizing garbage from the cultural, media, and discursive perspectives. Although garbage dumps, recycling systems, and the various individuals and communities who live in and off them, have been studied in detail from sociological and anthropological perspectives, in media studies little has been written about representations of garbage, save the use of "trash" as a metaphorical category for analyzing issues of class, for example, in talk shows (Manga, 2003). Building on my previous work, which examined the mechanics of consumerist discourse (Iqani, 2012), and the complex meanings of consumption in the global south (Iqani, 2016), this book will continue to politicize consumption, in global and cultural context, by turning attention to what is left behind after consumption has taken place. In the context of rapidly dwindling natural resources and increasingly extreme attempts to extract the fossil fuels that remain in the earth and under the oceans, a global population that is projected to have grown by another two billion souls within the next twenty years, and the many, intensifying ways in which consumption is being centered in narratives of what development and the "good life" means, it is increasingly important to consider the "other" side of consumption: those material formations of waste, garbage, and trash that accrue once human actors have accessed, enjoyed, and disposed of the many commodities that they want and need in their lives.

Waste interjects not only into our material spaces and experiences, but also into our mediated lives and representational spaces. When we look around us, at the highly mediated cultures in which we exist, it may seem that narratives of production, wealth, commodities, and their consumption dominate popular culture narratives. But arguably, with an increase in environmental awareness, knowledge about climate change and the growth of what could be termed an apocalyptic mentality (often reflected in dramatic films, novels, and television shows imagining the world in some state of postcollapse), the materiality of trash is becoming less hidden and more visible. Admittedly, narratives about the waste created by consumer culture are not a particularly overriding theme in popular media. Our screens, retail spaces, and virtual experiences remain dominated by narratives of celebrity, sexiness, and a world of glossy artifacts calling out to us to own them and achieve happiness, no matter how fleeting. But still, through this clatter of consumerist discourse, constantly being shaped and reshaped by economic and political power, constantly being integrated and deployed in different ways in personal psychologies, lifestyles, and identity projects, we can easily find a number of narratives in which postconsumer trash takes the stage. It is these narratives—purposefully selected for analysis—that form the material explored in this work.

At the end of all commodities' lives (and therefore consumption trajectory) are obsolescence, abandonment, and waste: the trash heap. It is arguably impossible to consider a culture of waste apart from a culture of materialism and consumption. To what extent do narratives about the material detritus of overconsumption fit into—and disrupt—glossy, hyperreal neoliberal discourses about consumer culture? Increasingly, through lifestyles centered around ethical consumption, popular critiques of hyperconsumption, and the rise of green consciousness (at least among the middle classes that most media forms serve), narratives about waste are coming into the public domain through various forms of representation, from fine art to popular culture. Waste enters the public imagination through a number of media forms and genres, often closely linked with particularly moralizing discussions about ethical consumption and the sustainability of the planet. What other narratives link waste and consumption? And, what else can be learned from looking at different ways in which garbage and waste are visualized and narrativized in popular media and culture?

Through the focus on the mediation of postconsumer trash, this book aims to explore pressing questions about the sustainability of consumer culture and by extension the entire system of global neoliberal capitalism. This takes place through the examination of three discrete, yet interrelated, thematic realms, each dealt with in a separate chapter. The first asks about the possibilities and limits of individual agency and action in relation to sustainable modes of consuming, producing, and working with waste. To what extent is the "problem" of trash something that can be solved by individual attitudes and deeds? How do these possibilities and limitations shift, depending on the geographical, class, and social context of agency and activism? These questions are explored through case studies relating to media narratives about recycling and waste reduction undertaken by diverse subjects in diverse locations. The second theme asks how the waste produced by luxurious consumption and hedonistic cultures is both talked about and denied in popular communication narratives. In what ways is waste talked about and represented in relation to pleasurable consumption? This question is explored through case studies linked to pleasure-seeking entertainment and music festivals as well as tropical island tourism, specifically Western media narratives about beach cleanups. The third theme aims to explore the media aesthetics of wide-scale environmental devastation, asking how complicity and hope are integrated into narratives about oil spills and plastic islands in the oceans, and how these are related to ideas about consumer accountability or recklessness. To what extent are optimistic and pessimistic attitudes, along with invitations for imagining responsibility, affect, and scale, integrated into media narratives about these planet-wide issues? And in turn, how is consumer culture included or excluded from this bigger picture?

Together, the focus on these three themes—individual agency and recycling, hedonistic consumption and its aftermath, and huge-scale devastation and the shadow of consumerism—allows for a new set of arguments about waste and its place in the popular imagination and the media matrix of consumer culture to emerge. In each thematic chapter, a number of different case studies are selected, dealing with media narratives and discourses linked to each theme, ranging from stories of agency in relation to recycling, different ways in which waste is aestheticized when it is used as a raw material for art making, how hedonistic practices of luxury island tourism and festival going are narrated in relation to waste, and how fossil fuel-based forms of environmental devastation are visually narrated. These case studies are purposefully selected from a variety of global contexts, allowing the analysis to travel from New York City to Pune to Johannesburg, from the Tankwa Karoo in South Africa to tropical Indian Ocean islands to the pastoral hills of Glastonbury in England, and into unpeopled ocean-scapes littered with oil or plastic. What links these case studies is that they are in some way *mediated* (Silverstone, 2005; Chouliaraki, 2006a)—that is, brought into the public eye through technological forms of communication and mass dissemination—and that they in some way include garbage in their narratives. Through these case studies, this book offers a "tour" through some of the key ways in which garbage has been mediated in recent years.

At this point it is useful to address the methodological and analytical approach taken in the book. The work reported on here draws on media discourse analysis and an ethnographic sensibility in order to develop narratively grounded cultural theory. Rooted in a qualitative epistemology, and seeking to explore big conceptual questions, specific case studies of media representation were selected for analysis in each thematic chapter. These case studies were purposively chosen on the basis of their relevance to the themes of individual agency, hedonistic consumption, and the aesthetics of environmental catastrophe. The content of each case study—comprised of specific media texts drawn from specific publicly available media sources—was then interpreted using tools of visual, multimodal, narrative, and discourse analysis, and put into dialogue with one another. In general, it is worth noting that wherever possible, these analyses were socially contextualized, sometimes through my own lived experiences relevant to the particular case study (for example, in chapter 2, media texts about Afrika Burn and Glastonbury Festival are discussed, but I have attended both festivals and was therefore able to add a little observational detail to the analysis), but mostly by making links between the case study and the cultural politics of the society in which the case study is embedded. It is certainly not possible for qualitative analysis to be objective; arguably it is the very subjectivity of its approach, and its grounding in a reflexive sensibility, that brings much of its analytical power. Of course, it is inescapable that my own intellectual and social predilections will have had some influence over the analysis offered in these pages. Many of the case studies I encountered through my own lived experience, both social and intellectual, and indeed my choice to focus my academic efforts on understanding them represents an important opportunity for the theoretical and the personal to come together in a meaningful way. It is very difficult to write about consumption and waste without reflecting on what consumption and waste mean to one's life, person, household, and community. Precisely because this book theorizes and politicizes the mediation of waste through an analytical framework tied to big philosophical questions about the role of consumer culture in human life, and the concomitant role of human consumption in the devastation of the planet, it requires a degree of personal involvement. In the same way that consumption is inherently tied to ideas of agency and individuality, so too is the waste produced by consumption. No theorist or author can be considered apart from the topics of which they write, especially those that are so closely tied to notions of the self and its place in the world. These big questions can be hard to hold, both in terms of the multiple theories and philosophical traditions that they call up and in terms of the deep emotional anxiety they inevitably touch (about the futures of the planet, the human race, other species, our own families and friends). Although I cannot claim to have fully resolved these theoretical complexities and anxieties, in this book I have explored them as thoroughly as I am able to, by bringing the methods of media discourse analysis into dialogue with auto-ethnographic and reflexive sensibilities. My intention was to write as critically and honestly as I could about what the stories of waste that we tell ourselves in turn can tell us about what consumption means to the self and to the environment and to the relationship between the two. The work presented here is therefore at once reflective, analytical, and exploratory, and it is aimed at opening up new avenues of theory and discussion about the links between consumption, waste, and the environment.

The rest of this chapter is devoted to constructing a theoretical framework that offers philosophical orientation points within which we can position ourselves intellectually and ethically in relation to garbage, in both media form and content. The discussion is also aimed at contextualizing the case studies and analyses that follow, and making a broader case for the importance of including questions of mediation in intellectual work aimed at making sense of this critical moment in which humankind finds itself: the Anthropocene.

There are many words that are used to describe the leftover matter that marks human life and activity. As such, it is necessary to consider the terms that will be used in this book. According to Rathje & Murphy (2001: 9), in the American context the words "garbage," "trash," "refuse," and "rubbish" each have specific meanings, and are not interchangeable. In line with technical definitions used by municipal workers and council waste collection systems, *trash* is defined as dry waste (that is, any item that is inorganic, such as discarded packaging), while *garbage* refers to wet waste (that is, most often the remains of food as well as other kinds of organic detritus). *Refuse* refers to both wet and dry items (that is, a mix of trash and garbage), while *rubbish* refers to refuse that has been combined with construction debris. Although these precise terms are useful in a technical sense, they are most relevant to the bureaucratic systems designed to collect and dispose of various forms of domestic and industrial waste in urban environments. To the nonspecialist, the terms are likely used interchangeably in everyday talk. Users of American English are likely to prefer the terms *garbage* and *trash*, while users of British English are likely to prefer the term *rubbish* or *refuse*. Considered together, the "simplest definition of waste is discarded, expelled or excess matter," and "while terms like 'rubbish' or 'litter' describe the random by-products of daily life, 'waste' invokes a much more complicated set of meanings" (Hawkins, 2006: vii). *Waste* is often used to gesture back to the excess matter produced by various industries, such as nuclear, medical, or construction waste, whereas *litter* is often characterized as the individualized dropping of excess matter in public space (rather than a dustbin). In this book, at times the specific meanings of each term as outlined above will be deployed in relation to discussions of specific case studies. But in more general theoretical observations and explorations, the terms *rubbish*, *trash*, and *garbage* will be used more or less interchangeably, to mean in the general sense the excess matter produced by various forms of human production and consumption. After all, the aim of this book is not to describe in detail the technical processes and bureaucratic vocabulary deployed by those whose task it is to dispose of waste, but to think through the broader cultural and consumerist implications of how narratives about waste enter the public realm through media, and what this in turn can tell us about the current moment in the human condition.

MEDIA REPRESENTATIONS OF GARBAGE

This book focuses exclusively on media representations of garbage. As such, it is necessary to clarify how media representation is defined and deployed, and why media images and narratives of garbage specifically matter. Much important work has already been done, bringing together the realms of media studies and environmental studies in different ways. Some take a focus on matters of political communication in relation to risk and environmental pollution (Hook et al., 2017), while others focus on the impact of the infrastructures of media technology on the environment (Cubitt, 2005; Gabrys, 2013; Rust, Monani & Cubitt, 2015; Starosielski & Walker, 2016). Other works explore the ways in which media texts and technologies impact on and intersect with environmental activism and communication (Pickerill, 2010; Graf, 2016; Newlands, 2018). Another important link between media studies and environmental studies is work that looks at *greenwashing*—when corporations seek to make their brands seem environmentally friendly or aligned to sustainable values (often without a direct link to their actual practices and actions on the ground) (Greer & Bruno, 1998; Pearse, 2012; Bowen, 2014). Some companies use "tokenistic" eco-projects to improve their image to environmentally conscious consumers, and these corporate branding efforts need to be firmly theorized as a media practice. Furthermore, it is arguably important to consider practices of "greenwashing" and corporate social responsibility as linked to longer histories of paternalistic philanthropy and patterns of public relations strategies aimed at benefiting the bottom line (Littler, 2008: 57–60). As Jussi Parikki writes, media technologies themselves have a "geology," that is, were partly made from compounds extracted from the earth (Parikka, 2015), and leave behind on and in the earth very material, often toxic, remnants (Jucan, Parikka, & Schneider, 2019). It also worth noting that the term *media environment* is often deployed to mean the totality of mediated texts, technologies, and interfaces that surround individuals in their everyday lives, particularly in the digital age (Press & Williams, 2010). Of course, this specific correlation between the terms media and environment is not the one intended to be explored in this book, though an argument could be made that it is precisely in the all-encompassing media environment that representation about the environment can be said to matter more than ever.

This book concerns itself with representations of rubbish rather than actual garbage. It has been observed that "it would be a blessing if it were possible to study garbage in the abstract, to study garbage without having to handle it physically" (Rathje & Murphy, 2001: 9). This wistful observation comes from the leaders of a long-term research project based at the University of Arizona, in which they studied, quite literally, trash. The researchers systematically collected a wide variety of household rubbish and industry waste from the landfill, and took it to a specialized research site at the university in order to carefully comb through it to learn more about domestic habits, patterns of consumption and disposal, and what those things in turn said about the condition of humanity in the United States. The physical waste produced by human activities is very repellent: it is comprised of decomposing and rotting materials. Every manner of waste produced by us combines, over time, into one quite abhorrent materiality in the garbage dump. There, things decay over time: foodstuffs rot and give off foul odors, attracting rats, flies, and other vermin; metals rust and become toxic; papers and cards become soggy and disintegrate; and other materials, such as plastic, change shape and become dull and broken (although not breaking down into constituent matter for many hundreds of years). The approach taken by the Garbage Project was to look at, touch, smell, sort through the garbage that they collected, and to try to return the otherwise assimilated state of the garbage into clear typologies and categories in such a way that light could be shed on the scope of American material culture. This approach is not altogether alien to those researching and doing media and cultural studies. Indeed there was a time when paparazzi journalists would go through the bins of celebrities in New York city (Rathje & Murphy, 2001: 17), seeking clues for stories that could be written that would shed light on the hidden secrets of their private lives. Indeed, some became so adept at the "art" of going through the garbage cans of celebrities and finding "gold," such as a half-written letter from Bob Dylan to Johnny Cash, that they began to refer to themselves as "garbologists" (Weberman, 1980).

Although the Garbage Project researchers (Rathje, 1984; Rathje & Murphy, 2001; Lehmann, 2015) might consider it an extremely timid approach to developing critical understandings of trash, this study focuses instead only on rubbish in the abstract, that is, on representations of rubbish. This is not to say that studies of actual garbage are no longer relevant—indeed they are, especially in the current moment in which awareness about trash, and the fact that there is no "away" to which we can throw anything, is growing. Rather, it is to note that garbage is not only a material experience, but it is also something that enters very strongly into our popular cultures and shared social discourses. Theories of representation hold that forms of narrative and visual communication do not merely "reflect" the "real" world, but are deeply involved also in constructing it (Hall, 1997). In other words, a social constructionist theory of media representation requires an acknowledgment of the important role that communication plays in producing shared understandings of reality, the things that are "taken for granted" as "common sense" within cultures. From this perspective, the argument needs to be made that media representations of garbage are a key site in which the social reality, and therefore the cultural politics, of garbage is produced. The link that I am making here between garbage and discourse is not new: "Our consciousness is full of these stock images, symbols, and metaphors that form a kind of waste social imaginary. This imaginary provides a set of frameworks and ideas that operate in the background to our everyday practices [. . .] akin to the operations of 'discourse'" (Hawkins, 2006: 8).

In her important 2006 book, Gay Hawkins considers a range of cultural and media representations of trash, looking at case studies of images of plastic bags as well as documentaries about sanitation, as part of a project aimed at considering the ethics of waste, and how more public orientations can be introduced into private practices. Undoubtedly, "waste has become visible, a landscape in its own right" (Hawkins, 2006: 30). Some scholars of the Anthropocene have given a little attention to media narratives about waste. For example, Tim Morton comments on the animated film *Wall-E,* in which a lonely little robot is the last sign of life on a future earth overrun by garbage, to the extent that the humans exiled themselves to live on corporate-sponsored space ships (Morton, 2013: 23; 2016: 147). Brian Thill writes about the place of waste in science-fiction narratives, arguing that even though waste is aesthetically eliminated in most of the fantastical worlds constructed by authors and makers of television, in more postapocalyptic narratives, such as Neil Blomkamp's film, *District 9,* "waste serves as a useful counterweight to the genre's own longstanding interests in exploring the limits of those gleaming futures" (Thill, 2015: 47). Edward Humes claims that one of the "enduring effects" of "the golden age of television and mass marketing" was "helping bring about an American trash tsunami" (Humes, 2013); in other words, he argues that it is the consumerist messaging of mass media that contributed to disposable culture. Much attention has also been paid to various art forms constructed with waste, or commenting on rubbish (Vergine, 1997, 2007; Scanlan, 2005; Whiteley, 2010; Pájaro, 2015). Environmental activists usually consider media to be an educational or activist tool, which should be deployed in order to raise awareness about environmental problems among citizens, and pressure governments into creating better policies (DeLuca, 2012). These various existing perspectives on the links between media and waste are quite minimal, and more work needs to be done in order to explore the various ways in which rubbish is integrated into narrative and artistic forms. As such, it is necessary to pay more attention to the precise ways in which media discourses talk about and show garbage. This will allow the extension of the project of considering the ethics of waste and wastefulness as Hawkins argues we should, not simply as a tool for changing policy and educating people, but so as to be able to consider how very powerful discourses about consumption interface with those ethics and co-construct broader social understandings about the links between what we consume and rubbish.

It is also crucial to recognize that media texts and technologies themselves produce inordinate amounts of rubbish, from the mountains of unsold newspapers and books that are sent for pulping to the tonnes of obsolete electronics destined for specialized dumps, where they may be stripped and recycled—or not. As Jennifer Gabrys writes in her important book about the material and cultural formations of waste created by the disposal of obsolete electronics, or e-waste (Gabrys, 2013), the tools that we use to access and consume a wide variety of media content produce many types of material residue. Indeed, the media industries, broadly defined to include all forms of technological manufacture of the devices that we use to compute data and communicate and share information, in combination with consumer culture and planned obsolescence in production of tech gadgets, is a primary cause of material waste. This is perhaps one of the most poignant places at which the real and hyperreal intersect (arguably a key feature of the world according to media theory). Without the material devices that we use to download and upload; publish, share, and like; watch and stream; comment, troll, and interact; the "hyperreal" world of representation would not be possible. It relies on the material devices as well as the material networks of communications (the servers, cables, routers, transmitters, and power chargers) to exist. And in turn, without our growing dependence on mediated forms of culture, politics, and economics, and increasingly interlinked forms of textuality and communications, the mountains of obsolete and broken television sets, keyboards, monitors, tablets, and so on would not be accumulating on the surface of the earth.

Alongside this important understanding of the direct link between media and waste, this book makes the claim that it is crucial to consider discourse and representation in the study of garbage in contemporary culture, drawing on cultural and media studies perspectives on visual communication (Matheson, 2005; Machin & Leeuwen, 2007). It is necessary to center media narratives in the intellectual project devoted to explicating and forging an ethics of waste, rather than consider them peripheral or tangential to it, because a significant proportion of public life is socially constructed through a wide variety of media practices. This media-centric view is something that some scholars, particularly those working within the disciplinary frameworks of sociology and anthropology, may disagree with. But the number of writers from those disciplines regularly drawing on media-based material, without methodological rigor or application of media theory, reveals at best an unwillingness to engage rigorously with media studies and at worst disciplinary snobbery. Media representations, and practices linked to the ever-proliferating range of media spaces, platforms, and technologies, are inherently social and play an active part in the production of social, political, economic, and cultural systems (Silverstone, 1999, 2013; Couldry, 2000, 2010). As such, focusing on media discourses about garbage allows us to open a window into shared ideas about what they mean, and also consider how ideas about waste are collectively produced and disseminated. Rather than consider the media simply as playing roles of education (Rathje & Murphy, 2001: 5), in which trash is seen as a social problem and communications campaigns are seen as a solution to changing people's behaviors, it is crucial instead to think dialectically about representation and materiality. Waste is both real and represented, and the representation of trash contributes to its realness, and vice versa. As such, examining how rubbish is represented allows for the meanings encoded in those messages to be analyzed, and for insight to be gleaned into how broader social meanings about garbage are constructed and disseminated.

> History always tends to globalize reality into its own form, but as soon as the possibility of waste is taken into account, it seems that some sort of mediation becomes necessary, that some linkage and narrative desire are in turn produced. The result is a proliferation of stories, of narrativity without

linearity, multiple narratives within singular voices and without ultimate agency. (Neville & Villeneuve, 2012: 5–6)

The rest of this chapter offers a theoretical framework for analyses of media representations of garbage. This framework is constructed from a wide variety of scholarly work, drawn from multiple disciplinary sources. There are four aspects to the framework, which can be thought of as nodes in a conceptual network spanning from ideas of selfhood through to ideas about universality: materiality and morality, identity and individuality, toxicity and domesticity, and space and time.

MATERIALITY AND MORALITY

Linked to theories of the Anthropocene (Bonneuil & Fressoz, 2016; Wark, 2016), and revisiting theories that all human cultures are inherently material (Miller, 1994, 2010, 2013), a synthesis of work on garbage from the social sciences helps to sketch out the place of waste and trash in human societies writ large (Rathje & Murphy, 2001). In consumer culture studies, waste and garbage are flagged as indicators of the unsustainability of wasteful, Western modes of consumption (Littler, 2008: 1). Often Western-style consumption is held up as an example of the environmental and ethical dangers of consumer society, and much angst is expressed about the move of the global south toward intense industrialization and how consumer markets are growing rapidly postcolonial societies. Green or ethical consumption (Brown, 2013; Haenn, Harnish, & Wilk, 2016) centers a responsible moral position in relation to waste and is often held up as the most viable solution to overconsumption and the growing rubbish-islands in oceans and piles of trash on the peripheries of cities. As Jo Littler writes, ethical consumption runs the gamut from choosing "fair trade" products, to boycotting certain brands, to recycling, and it is necessary to explore how "radical" these forms of consumption actually are, or whether they offer a sop to the middle classes and a convenient new form of branding (greenwashing) for big corporations (Littler, 2008: 2). Littler's contribution to cultural theory allows us to see the direct link between environmental problems (including the mess created by waste) and consumption, and shows how various forms of ethical behavior or messaging are tied into to the existing political-economic structures of mediated consumer culture. Her work invites us to explore the extent to which individual actions and moral positioning can "solve" the problem of overconsumption in a world with finite resources. In particular, it begs the question of how trash can be morally positioned, and understood to be linked in different ways, to larger structures of power.

Rubbish calls up, perhaps most acutely, the material condition of consumer cultures. Although huge amounts of effort and resources are invested by corporate actors into creating glossy fantasy worlds and narratives of hyperreal commodity perfection, in garbage we encounter the detritus of the commodity. In the crushed plastic water bottle littering the street side, we see the truth of the object that the branding tried to obscure, claiming it to be pure and sourced from unblemished nature. We see an item, used once and discarded, perhaps to be recycled, more likely to sit in a rubbish dump without decomposing for hundreds of years. Similarly, in the wrecked carcass of a crashed car, we can recognize the inherent fallibility of that shiny object marketed to fulfill all dreams and transcend all limitations. Precisely due to its extreme materiality, garbage reminds us how important it is to center theories of material culture in our analyses of consumerism. The study of material culture is rooted in archaeology. Interestingly, archaeology is more or less the study of trash: "the discipline that tries to understand old garbage" (Rathje & Murphy, 2001: 10). "The creation of garbage is the unequivocal sign of human presence" (Rathje & Murphy, 2001: 10) and as such the study of garbage holds the key to past (Rathje & Murphy, 2001: 11). The material detritus left behind by past civilizations functions as data that can be analyzed in order to gain deeper insight into how those societies organized themselves and what daily life was like in a different age.

> As archaeologists and anthropologists have long recognized, material culture provides evidence of the distinctive form of a society. It provides this evidence because it is an integral part of what that society is; just as the individual cannot be understood independently of society, so society cannot be grasped independently of its material stuff. (Dant, 1999: 2)

Materiality then, is a key to unlocking the secrets of how a society is structured and what values it prioritizes. But, even though "material culture is never distinct from language or interaction," it "ties us to others in our society" (Dant, 1999: 2). Each human collective forges ways of being through the things that they make, use, exchange, and dispose of. In the same way that the contemporary archaeologist sifts through the leftovers of past civilizations in order to glean insight into their workings, our contemporary societies are also "always in the process of becoming the past" (Rathje, 2004: 406). "The archaeologist must work back and up from the material remains" (Knappett,

2011: 3)—but this raises the questions of how we work with those "remains" when they surround us in the immediacy of our lived present. Some scholars have considered these questions and have initiated studies on the archaeology of the garbage that lives on the dumps at the edges of our cities. For example, archaeologists have bored into the Fresh Kills rubbish dump in New Jersey in the United States (Rathje & Murphy, 2001; Melosi, 2016). The deeper they drilled into the landfill, the further back in time they went as each deeper layer of the dump revealed—like time capsules—items from the 1970s, then the 1960s, then the 1950s, then the 1940s ... What this shows is that archaeological methods focusing on material items, often discarded, can be examined in order to gain insight not only into times long passed but also into our current lifestyles. In addition, it reminds us that despite the constant focus we give to the aesthetic, psychological, and intellectual aspects of our lives, still they are ultimately constituted materially through the various objects that populate our everyday lives. How then can we theorize the materiality of trash?

> The things we call our waste exist in an interzone between two states of mind and two structures of feeling about the glittering, shattered object-worlds we have built around ourselves. These relics float between the poles of desire and discard. (Thill, 2015: 8)

The commonsense understanding of garbage is that it is the substance we usually want to remove from our sight. In contemporary cities, this equates to taking it away to landfills on the peripheries where the material is piled up, sometimes covered with earth, but more or less just left to slowly decay. But we did not always seek to have our detritus removed far from our sight, or seek to distinguish ourselves as moral, ethical, or radical consumers on the basis of much or how little waste we create. There is archaeological evidence that humans used to live with their waste—that is, simply leave it on the floor of their abode and when it became too much, it was simply covered it up with more clay, thus raising the levels of the floor surface (Rathje & Murphy, 2001: 35). In some cities in the world, trash is a daily visible presence (consider the perpetual piles of black trash bags on street corners in New York City, or the litter that patterns road verges in Mumbai). In other cities, any trace of detritus is systematically removed in an obsessive way, such that not even a scrap of paper is visible to the naked eye (e.g., in Singapore, where it is illegal to import and sell chewing gum and tossing a candy wrapper on the street can lead to a $300 fine). Precisely due to the bureaucratic, spatial, and technical systems that modern humanity has invented to remove garbage from our homes and cities, "contextual analysis of our material products will be extremely difficult for future archaeologists" (Rathje, 2004: 404). The taking away of trash from everyday life means that it is more challenging to use trash to understand it; and as such the impulse to examine media representations of rubbish becomes all the more compelling.

Rubbish presents not only an opportunity to understand material culture, but also to expand our theorization of it. To do this, we "need to review the relationship between mind and matter, between agent and artefact" (Knappett, 2011: 3). We need to recognize that "objects are routinely, mundanely part of everyday existence" and that in tandem with this mundanity is the capacity of "even the most commonplace object to symbolize the deepest human anxieties and aspirations" (Woodward, 2007: vi). Indeed, "to study the objects themselves, and people's relations with them, is an effective strategy for understanding modern consumption and indeed culture broadly" (Woodward, 2007: vii). This is arguably even more the case when considering the materiality of trash. "The age of these things and the very fact of their having been used may make them unattractive to others but does not mean that for us they are no longer useful" (Dant, 1999: 38). Trash can be put to use in order to help us learn more about our deepest anxieties and aspirations than can be made possible by analyzing the new commodities in their original forms, because it is in expenditure that the true emotive and material value of an object becomes known.

> With the rise of consumer culture we have come to live with an enormous number of things. [...] For all the talk about how we occupy consumer culture there has been a cavalier disregard for the all the wasted things that form an enormous part of this way of living. (Hawkins, 2006: 15)

A culture of disposability was one of the main legacies of the Industrial Revolution and the growth in middle classes and consumption opportunities particularly in the West (Strasser, 1999). Disposable culture originated in the nineteenth century (Rathje & Murphy, 2001: 41) and it remains to be seen whether it will persist into the twenty-first. The increasing visibility of trash, both in public spaces and in media narratives, means that there is also a growing awareness about the moral implications of that rubbish—that it links in very tightly with our accepted ways of life, and is not simply something that needs to be managed by urban and city bureaucrats but toward which entirely new collective and individual orientations need to be forged.

In other words, it is the very materiality of wasteful consumer culture that requires some kind of moral response. It is no longer acceptable or possible to lack consideration about the scale and type of waste produced by consumption, and it is crucial to "make sense of the distinct ethos of waste that underpins consumption, to acknowledge that how we eliminate things is just as important as how we acquire them" (Hawkins, 2006: 15). This new ethic has emerged partly thanks to the rise of environmentalism (Haenn, Harnish, & Wilk, 2016). Prior to this, waste was framed as a *technical* rather than a *moral* problem" (Hawkins, 2006: 29). But it has increasingly become framed as a problem that can be solved by individual consumer choices. As Jo Littler writes, ethical orientations toward consumption are one of the popular culture responses to the moral problem of, among other environmental problems, rubbish. While some consumers may seek to differentiate themselves from the problematic aspects of consumption through the choices that they make in relation to fair trade, the environment, recycling, and so on, they are still using "consumption as a means of self-fashioning" (Littler, 2008: 8), and thus remain embedded within the strictures of neoliberal consumer culture. And, while ethical consumption may indeed allow new ways to think about social responsibility, it also introduces questions about whether the labeling of certain forms of consumption behavior "ethical" empties out the notion of ethics entirely (Littler, 2008: 11). In the same way that certain consumption behaviors can be theorized within ideas of ethics and morality, as Litter shows, so too can certain behaviors oriented toward rubbish, be considered. And these need to be understood in dynamic tension with the materiality of trash itself, as it is its precisely overwhelming and apocalyptic materiality that forces the moral dilemma into consumer behaviors and identities.

Questions of materiality and morality are central to examining the different ways in which trash, and narratives about it, are made visible and invisible in different ways. Part of this project requires a commitment to dissecting the moral complexities inherent in that in/visibility. Precisely because "material culture ties us to others in our society providing a means of sharing values, activities and styles of life" (Hawkins, 2006: 2), thinking about materiality forces us to also think about morality in more concrete ways, because when the cause of the moral dilemma is material, then so too should be our responses to it. And this takes us toward the question of how to theorize the roles of identity and individuality, specifically forms of subjectivity and agency, in the mediation of trash.

How does the individual fit into the system of consumer culture and its inherent inequalities? More specifically, how does the individual fit into the economics of disposability and waste? And how, in turn, might identity be shaped and influenced by theorizing the cultural politics of rubbish?

Contemporary commercial and advertising discourses privilege the idea of newness, and encourage people to see themselves as supremely deserving of any and every pleasure for which they might find a whim (McCracken, 1990; Mattelart, 1991; Goldman, 1996; Nava et al., 2013). There is a strong sense in contemporary consumerist theory that commodities play a role of helping to define identity, and that individuals exercise agency when they choose which commodities and items they introduce into their lives. The processes of accumulation and consumption have been well theorized and explored in the literature in relation to identity (Du Gay, 1996; Slater, 1997; O'Dougherty, 2002; Iqani, 2012). In short, we are what we consume. In a similar vein, Gay Hawkins argues that practices in relation to waste also forge subjects: "what we want to get rid of also makes us who we are" (Hawkins, 2006: 2). If both of these propositions are true—that subjectivity is forged both through what we acquire and enjoy and what we use and dispose of—then we can find an important conceptual overlap between practices of acquisition and disposal. It is arguably our "ordinary encounters" with both commodities and waste that "are implicated in the making of a self" and that "mediates relations to our bodies, prompts various habits and disciplines, and orders relations between the self and the world" (Hawkins, 2006: 4). It is crucial, especially in the current moment, that studies in consumer culture and consumption integrate the materiality of waste into theories of consumer subjectivity, in a way that lets us get past moralistic arguments about consumption as the root of all environmental evil. Conscious individual choices are made not only in relation to which commodities and services to acquire, which brands with which to form relationships, which celebrities and social media influencers to follow or emulate, but also in relation to how we dispose of (or repair, reuse, gift, or recycle) the things we no longer have a use for. "Choosing a paper bag rather than a plastic one, composting, recycling, all indicate important shifts in our relationship to waste matter, how we manage it, and how guilty or righteous it can make us feel" (Hawkins, 2006: 5). The affect of waste—that is, the at once emotional and embodied politics of how waste makes us feel and our actions in relation to it—is also a key area in which new theories are needed, both in order to understand how to drive positive change at the individual (and ultimately collective) level, and to deepen our understandings about how the material worlds within which we are rooted shape our notions of self. Consumer-centered forms of activism have been theorized as "a form of affective citizenship, an ethos of egalitarianism and a shift in the political mindset from public to private spaces and actions" (Lekakis, 2013: 141). Conceptualizing rubbish as a materially part of, not apart from, consumer culture, requires an expansion of theories of affect in relation to rubbish to encompass not only disgust but some kind moral response.

Although neoliberal culture profits off the fantasy that accumulation can be limitless, and encourages consumers to center that idea in their relation to the many commodities on constant offer on the shelves, web stores and media representations—which I have termed the *world of goods* (Iqani, 2012)—there are only so many of each thing that a person can own. Extreme inequality means that many people are too poor to afford even the most basic necessities, which are increasingly privatized and marketized rather than made available through public services. Meanwhile, the one percent are so wealthy that they can afford to collect multiple versions of similar items, from shoes to cars (Dorling, 2015). And those in between find themselves in a constant effort to both climb the social ladder of accumulation and not slip down to a more precarious condition. There is a strong class association with consumption (Bennett et al., 2009; Baviskar & Ray, 2011; Brosius, 2012; Alexander et al., 2013), but we also need to theorize the class aspects of disposal. It is no accident that the rich rarely have to deal with their own rubbish, while the poor have to deal not only with their own but with everyone else's, too. As such, when considering the links between identity and garbage, we need to take into account social status; class; socioeconomic conditions, both historical and contemporary; and other social power structures that shape economic opportunity, such as race, gender, caste, religion, and sexuality. Speaking rather parochially of the American context, it is argued that "everyone seems to realize that we can't just keep consuming—and discarding—more and more commodities; everyone seems to realize that if the rest of the world were to follow our consumerist lead, we'd be in disturbing straits indeed" (Rathje & Murphy, 2001: 2). What is being alluded to here is a situation in which every human being on the planet consumes and throws away as much as the average American. The United States arguably taught the world that "more" is "better" (Smart, 2010: 224). The reality of the garbage-ification of American culture is not something that exists in a vacuum. Part of the reason that Americans have been able to create and dispose of so much trash with so much impunity has to do with the inequalities of the global political economy in which the wealthy West enjoyed the fruits of a consumer economy built on the exploitation and suffering of citizens in the rest of the world. If every country in the world evolves into a consumer-driven economy in which even modest aspirations for social mobility and the improvement of life are wrapped up in commodity and material cultures (Iqani, 2016)—as seems to be the case in more and more locations—then we are looking at future urban landscapes defined by growing garbage dumps, litter, and wildly unsustainable forms of consumption. As I have written about elsewhere, in the global south, increasingly a "better life" is being defined in public media spaces as one that provides full access to consumption opportunities (rather than, say, forging a society in which collective needs are provided for through good-quality public resources and institutions). This is not to suggest that all consumption is "bad," but, rather, to sound the call for the need to consider the geopolitical implications of endless growth in production and consumption. If the current trajectory continues, then we can conceive of a future in which every person on the planet has full access to middle-class style consumption. This means unimaginable quantities of waste. The more we consume, the more rubbish we create, and thus it follows that questions about what to do with that trash will become central to various consumer individualities and identities. This is not to suggest that it would be preferable for those aspiring to middle-class lifestyles to be denied the opportunity to fulfill those aspirations, which they surely deserve just as much if not more than those privileged by histories of exploitation, but to insist that as scholars we have a responsibility to retheorize what subjectivity, individual responsibility, inequality, and agency mean in relation to trash-based consumer cultures.

While some people are hoarders, and have a psychological block against throwing anything away (Humes, 2013: 13–15) and others, often the extremely rich, enjoy increasingly elaborate collections of stiletto shoes, sneakers, toys, clothes, or even cars, most ordinary consumers have a limit—financial and spatial—to how many things they can own. Production-oriented capitalism comes up against the problem of too much supply and not enough demand. The solution devised for this problem of overproduction was advertising—a sophisticated form of communication aimed at emotionally and psychologically manipulating people to believe that they wanted or needed certain items (Ewen, 2008), and to form relationships of aspiration with certain brands and products. In addition to this, strategies of built-in obsolescence (Zallio & Berry,

2017), especially in electronic and communication items such as music players, televisions, and mobile phones, has meant that the devices intentionally fail after a couple of years and need to be replaced. Alongside this, the creation of disposable products, for example, sanitary napkins (Strasser, 1999: 338), has also created mountains of contemporary trash that never used to exist. It is difficult to squarely place the blame on the shoulders of individual consumers who choose to regularly buy new versions of items they already own or disposable versions of products that could just as well be reusable, when there is a sophisticated and well-resourced system in place that aims to make sure that objects do not last as long as they could, to force them to buy new items when those they have already bought, which they expect will last for decades, stop working within two years, and when disposable products are pushed into the market, making reusable versions seem old-fashioned and obsolete. But at the same time, it would be patronizing to assume that individuals have no power to make choices thoughtfully and carefully about what they buy, whether to throw something away or replace it, and indeed how that item is disposed of. The rise of the fair-trade movement (Lekakis, 2013) shows that questions of justice, fairness, and the public good can also fit into individual consumer's identity projects and choices. It is therefore necessary to develop a dialectical way of thinking about individuality within the context of capitalist structures of consumer culture. Individuals are free to choose, but usually only within a set array of options, what has been termed a state of "conditional freedom" (Chouliaraki, 2008; Iqani, 2012). In relation to thinking about trash and how it is represented, it is necessary to consider what forms of action are possible, and how individuals find themselves empowered to make choices in ways that feel ethical without denying themselves the various pleasures that are enjoyed through consumer choices. Trash should not be used to vilify and undermine the individual importance that consumption holds socially and culturally. However, it should force us to theorize how new forms of identity should emerge from the project of facing up to the links between consumption and waste.

Although it can be argued that most people think more about the stuff they want to consume than about how to ethically account for the garbage they produce, it is worth considering whether and how the narrative might be able to shift. To what extent does witnessing "the detritus of urban life congealed in gutters or dumped on the street," whether it is in person or through media narratives, "destabilize the self"? And to what extent is it just "largely ignored" (Hawkins, 2006: 3)? Thanks to burgeoning theories of postmodern identity, it now widely accepted that "ethics revolve around embodied practices and micropolitics of self" (Hawkins, 2006: 15). These range from body modifications to sexual practices, to regimes of eating, to fashion and dress. From this perspective, the self is "grounded in actions and bodies rather than transcendent moral codes" (Hawkins, 2006: 15). As such, "styles of waste disposal then are also styles of self; in managing waste we constitute an ethos and a sensibility" (Hawkins, 2006: 15). Through various choices that are made in relation to waste—how to produce or not produce it, how to dispose of it, whether and how to recycle, what to buy in relation to its packaging, whether one buys new or secondhand, and so on—ideas of self-hood are built up and also communicated to others. It could be argued that these ideas are synonymous with various theories of consumer subjectivity, which hold that moral, aesthetic, and social narratives about the self are produced through various conscious and unconscious choices made about what is consumed and how.

In short, there is a strong overlap—precisely in the realm of subjectivity—between theories of self-management in relation to consumption and in relation to waste. They are two sides of the same coin—on the one side, we produce and acquire things, on the other, we consume and dispose of them. The two experiences are diametrically linked: *we must dispose of what we consume*. It was precisely "when commodity cultures redefined freedom as 'freedom to consume'" that is also came to mean "freedom to waste" (Hawkins, 2006: 29). How that "freedom to waste" is discursively constructed in relation to identity and individuality, keeping in mind the central place of inequality in that matrix, in media narratives is one of the key questions addressed by this book. This "freedom" also brings up questions of the rights and responsibilities that are arguably commensurate, as well where and how they are exercised. This leads us then, into a consideration of notions of civic duty and how it relates with the ways in which trash is linked to notions of the public and private.

DOMESTICITY AND CIVIC DUTY

Consumption has been theorized as existing at the interface of the private and public realm. A "world of goods" is made available and displayed publicly in various online and offline retail spaces, and individuals carefully choose which they will integrate into their lives, and take home to live with, eat, use, or gift to others. Although commodities are inherently public in terms of the discourses that they produce and are shaped by (Iqani, 2012), they are also inherently private in that they hold intensely personal meanings and populate domestic lives and spaces. The home zone, no matter how grand or humble, is a space in which commodities are domesticated and personalized: cleaning products are used up, sugar or salt run out, sporting equipment might be stored away and forgotten, art and designer ceramics might be proudly put on display, family heirlooms are treasured. Any home, no matter how humble or extravagant, reflects a collection of objects that are considered either useful or beautiful or both by their owners. In important ways then, objects and commodities construct and produce private spaces. Importantly also, the consumption and use that takes place in private spaces produce trash.

Rubbish is a form of materiality that crosses from the private into the commons. Every human culture in the world shares a certain orientation to dirt: that it does not belong in the home and needs to be removed. With the advent of industrial mass production, households produce more waste than ever. How that waste is managed and removed from the home speaks to deeper cultural orientations toward civilization, waste, and cleanliness. In even the dirtiest cities in the world—those that lack the infrastructure and political will to remove trash regularly and provide recycling and composting schemes—people typically maintain extremely high standards of cleanliness in their own homes. Even among communities that make a living by scavenging materials off garbage dumps, there is likely to be a commitment to keeping the space of one's own, even if it is just a corner under a bridge, tidy. In countries in which littering is not considered a heinous immoral act, and people are not ashamed to be seen throwing a plastic bottle out of a car window or along a hiking path in a spectacular mountain nature reserve, their homes and yards are likely to be fastidiously swept and no fallen leaf will be allowed to besmirch the appearance of the homestead. It is clear then, that trash takes on a different meaning depending on whether it is contextualized in private or public space. As Mary Douglas writes in *Purity and Danger*, all human cultures have ways of delineating between the clean and the impure (Douglas, 2013). These symbolic orderings function on many levels, most notably in service of delineating between private and public spaces. With regard to rubbish specifically, Douglas points out that pieces of waste go through two phases. In the first, they are recognized as out of place, "unwanted bits of whatever it was they came from, hair or food or wrappings." At this stage, she argues, these discarded items "are dangerous; their half-identity still clings to them and the clarity of the scene in which they obtrude is impaired by their presence" (Douglas, 2013: 161). It is only in the second phase—once these items have pulverized, dissolved, and rotted—that they lose identity, and enter "into the mass of common rubbish" (Douglas, 2013: 161). Perhaps the most common manifestation of public rubbish is litter. When people thoughtlessly throw the remnants of their consumption into public spaces, it is considered litter. Policy makers, researchers into human behavior and urbanists have given attention to the problem of litter, and thinking about how it can be best addressed from social and design perspectives (Reich & Robertson, 1979; Sibley & Liu, 2003; de Kort, McCalley, & Midden, 2008; Schultz et al., 2013).

In Western cultures, "that pride themselves on being technologically 'advanced' catching a glimpse of the brute physicality of waste signals a kind of failure" (Hawkins, 2006: 1). In other words, there is an expectation that modern society is meant to "protect us from our waste; to hide the disgusting and valueless"—in opposition to premodern and preindustrial European cities, in which "excrement would pile up on the streets" (Wiesner, 2013: 290). Indeed, big cities have elaborate systems of waste removal, for example, as documented in detail in Robin Nagle's ethnography of the sanitation workers of New York, a city that produces 12,000 tonnes of waste a day (Nagle, 2014). Through the construction of new sewerage systems and waste removal infrastructures, citizens became used to the "elimination of waste," which in turn very quickly "became a marker of civilised modernity" (Hawkins, 2006: 1). Even now in popular thinking, likely influenced by Freud's argument that cleanliness is linked to civilization (Freud, 2015: 73), there is a notion that cities that are "clean" (i.e., that have removed waste from sight) are more civilized than those in which the waste is in view. But in assessing how "civilized" certain public spaces are, we need to consider the global geopolitics of urban design and think about which political economies have benefited which city spaces. And we also need to think about whether the visibility of waste means there is more of it, or whether the obsessive removal of waste to out-of-sight locations means there is less of it. Although certain global south cities might be seen as "dirty" to visitors from the global north, evidence shows that global north cities are in fact producing more trash, which is swiftly exported out of view, either to the peri-urban landfill, or loaded onto a container ship and taken elsewhere on the globe to be processed as recycling. To take a pressing example, "e-waste" (defunct information technology equipment) is routinely "dumped" by rich northern countries onto poor southern countries (Lepawsky, 2014), where it is sorted and processed by hand.

> The disposal of electronics [...] follows a trajectory between developed and developing countries, where devices migrate from technology-rich re-

gions to those places with an abundance of cheap labor and a high demand for raw materials. While countries such as China are currently regulating against the importation of electronic waste, shipments continue to make their way to Asia, Africa, and other developing countries for recycling and disposal. (Gabrys, 2013: 91)

The "global recycling networks take things of rubbish value (often spent or end-of-life goods) and turn them back into resources in other places and production networks"; this process typically flows from the global north to the global south (Crang et al., 2012: 12). While rich consumers in the west replace their laptops and mobile phones every couple of years, poor workers in the global south have to undertake toxic and dangerous work to try and extract the remaining substances of value from those obsolete objects. Although the flow of e-waste is sometimes disguised as "donations" to poorer economies, this of course "does not contend with the dilemma that these machines will eventually become waste" (Gabrys, 2013: 92), adding to the growing piles of e-waste in key locations in the global south. The example of e-waste is instructive because it provides an anchor for thinking about the ways in which rubbish transcends the boundaries between public and private at both a local and global scale. Media devices such as smartphones and laptops can be considered an extension of the personal, and are usually used with a great sense of possessiveness. Once they get old, slow, broken, or outdated, they are replaced and the old devices then become public objects, either entering into a secondhand market (as would be likely in most African cities), and eventually ending up on an e-waste dump, where they become a public problem, as well as an individual problem for the worker tasked with burning away the plastic to get to the copper wire, for example. The moral questions created by post-consumer rubbish are at once personal and domestic, and public and civic, precisely because the rubbish extends into the public realm in material ways.

As Gay Hawkins observes, "Waste doesn't just threaten the self in the horror of abjection, it also constitutes the self in the habits and embodied practices through which we decide what is connected to us and what isn't" (Hawkins, 2006: 4). Although once intimately connected to its user, an obsolete mobile phone loses that connection once it is discarded. It is easy to shrug off responsibility for e-waste once the mobile device is no longer in the personal possession of the consumer, but what kinds of shared sense of common concern might be created, or not, by knowledge about e-waste, for example? Similarly, other forms of waste, such as plastics destined for recycling, were regularly exported from the global north to the global south. This is increasingly being revealed as a wildly unsustainable approach to the public management of waste, as China has shown by recently deciding to ban imports of plastic recycling from Western nations, leading to a pile-up of plastics in ports and depots in the West, while public servants tasked with managing recycling try to work out what to do with it (Freytas-Tamura, 2018). Various processes of disposal, from the domestic to the global, comprise how "we keep chaos at bay" (Hawkins, 2006: 4). But who is the "we" in this picture? Is it a public in which all people can participate? Or only implicitly "modern" subjects based in the global north and enjoying the fruits of centuries of modernization fired by colonial exploitation and imperialist expansion? And what is the chaos that "we" try to keep at bay? Is it a chaos that we once used to live with, underfoot, in our own homes? And why do "we" think it is acceptable to send "our" chaos to other people, other places? When "we" try to keep chaos at bay are we trying to send it away, without any willingness to accept that, in a global political-economy and a planetary environment, *there is no away?* What these questions force us to consider is the very status of civilization itself, the role that rubbish plays in how our sense of civility and public duty are organized, and indeed how material formations of waste force new ways of constituting a sense of the commons. It cannot be an acceptable answer that being "civilized" constitutes overconsumption and the exporting of trash to another side of the globe, as this solution is not sustainable politically, economically, or ethically.

As eco-critical media studies has argued, "we share the world in common with one another and with other non-human organisms and processes" and as such the notion of the "commons" is central (Rust, Monani, & Cubitt, 2015: 2). Just as certain environmental resources—water, air, the land—are part of the commons, so too are the material remnants of production and consumption, whether we like it or not. Rubbish is public; the challenge is to explore ways of using "commons sense" (Berlant, 2016) to deal with it in more just and equitable ways. New imaginaries of what it means to be public—on local, national and global scales—are required if we are to succeed in fully understanding our relationships—at once intensely domestic, personal, and supremely public collective—with the waste that we produce. And precisely because a significant amount of rubbish is produced through individualized, personal consumption, we cannot theorize the ways in which rubbish is a matter of collective concern without also thinking about how it is personal; how it is both public and domestic. Building on this exploration of the ways in which trash speaks to both domestic and civic concerns, it is next necessary to consider how that very same trash also forces us to renegotiate what consumption means in relation to experiences of space and time.

SPACE AND TIME

As many environmentalists have argued, "There is no away." What they mean by this is that the notion that we can just "throw away" our rubbish is incorrect, because due to the closed system that is planet earth, wherever we throw it, it stays with us in one way or another. Although it may no longer be immediately visible, it has not disappeared; indeed some of it can never go "away."

> We have colonized [the world] with our waste and the elaborate processes that produced it, creating human waste and wasted human lives all along globalization's dirty path; and now we must consider where these waste-products, living and dead, could go next; or what it means for us if there really is nowhere else to go. There is no path past the wastes we've made. (Thill, 2015: 4)

Rubbish occupies spaces and crosses time in ways unprecedented in human history. As Heather Rogers observes, one of the few man-made objects visible from outer space is the Fresh Kills Landfill (Rogers, 2006: 1). Trash occupies space. The scale of rubbish produced by capitalist consumption can be monumental. Landfills in big cities measure several square miles and can be as deep as hundreds of feet (Blight, 2014). These man-made mountains of waste, although often strategically placed on the outskirts of towns and cities in order to make them less visible to citizens, are visible in the extreme once they are seen or visited: towering mounds of festering and rotting garbage as far as the eye can see. The social semiotics of new precipitous landscapes created by the accumulation of trash begs interpretation. Although some might think that the hallmark of human ingenuity and engineering is captured in the architectural feats of towering skyscrapers in Shanghai, Dubai, or New York City, a counterargument could suggest that it is the massive garbage dump that more accurately reflects the moral condition of human achievement in the age of the Anthropocene. As Zygmunt Bauman writes, we are facing "an acute crisis of the human waste disposal industry. While the production of human waste goes on unabated and rises to new heights, the planet is fast running short of refuse dumps and the tools of waste recycling" (Bauman, 2004: 16). Though monumental, the space of the garbage dump is liminal in both the social and psychological sense. Well-heeled Western observers may shudder to hear tales of poverty-stricken men, women, and children making a living by scavenging landfills or working as informal recyclers in global south cities (Boo, 2012), or when they see photo-essays of the same in the news (Blight, 2014). Concerns may be raised about health and safety, about the toxicity of the dumps, about the safety of the workers. But often these issues will not be directly connected to the problems of overproduction and overconsumption that emanate from Western capitalism, having found expression of its ideologies and structures across the globe. How trash exists in and is removed from shared public spaces is central to any cultural politics of consumption. Waste "simply gets taken 'away,' and while we know where it goes, the invisibility of these places, their location underground or on the margins of cities, facilitates denial or active not knowing" (Hawkins, 2006: 16). Spaces can be defined as domestic or public, as civilized or uncivilized, depending on the presence or absence of trash. In some respects, trash is acutely local, for example when it characterizes a specific street, home, village or garbage dump. But in other equally important ways trash is global, as it crosses space in both material and representational ways. Before they become used and discarded, various commodities are already global in the sense that they are often produced in one location, then sold across borders in another. In the same way that almost every commodity is embedded in the global economy, so too is garbage. Although most commodities are used up in local settings, and disposed of in a similar way, some cities and countries have such an excess of garbage that their own landfill and recycling infrastructures cannot handle it. As already discussed in the previous section, some countries therefore export their trash (or try to) to other locations willing to take in the material for sorting, recycling, or other disposal. The image of a container ship coming from China full of cheap plastic products, and returning to China filled with plastic waste (often those same products, broken and thrown away) is indeed compelling, and highlights the ways in which trash has crossed space and transcended locality in the most material of ways.

There is arguably some similarity in the process of taking out the trash in the domestic sense and in the collective sense. At home, we clean our spaces and remove the detritus, either by flushing it away or placing it in bins, which are usually regularly cleared by the authorities, to whom we pay some form of tax or duty in return. In the city, a similar pattern is visible, in which the trash is "taken out" of the city to the landfills beyond. And globally, too, trash is removed from some countries and taken to others. Although there appears to be a shift toward a new international relations of rubbish in which those on the receiving end of these shipments are starting to exercise their rights and refuse entry, the legacy of this geopolitical and spatial pattern of global trash removal remains, not least in the material problem of what to do with the materials destined for recycling that can no longer be recycled in the locations that they once were (Schlanger, 2018). Because of the persistent inequalities in income and opportunity across the globe, it is reasonable to predict that despite the China ban, new markets will emerge for the import of recycling to countries in which high unemployment and low wages mean that there are many people willing to do the dirty work of processing materials for recycling, far from the eyes of those who originally created the garbage. For example, both Kenya and Uganda have seen the recent establishment of plastic recycling plants (Reuters, 2018), and reports have emerged that the US has simply redirected recycling shipments to "poor countries" in Southeast Asia following the China ban (McVeigh, 2018). The move of rubbish from domestic, often highly personal, spaces and situations into public, impersonal, and ultimately global sets of relations requires a dialectic way of thinking that encompasses both orientation points, and that considers the local, national, and global as interconnected spaces through which ideas, and rubbish, flow.

> [As] the processes of the commodification, commercialization and monetarization of human livelihoods have penetrated every nook and cranny of the globe, global solutions to locally produced problems, or global outlets for local excesses, are no longer available. Just the contrary is the case: all localities (including, most notably, the highly modernized ones) have to bear the consequences of modernity's global triumph. They are now faced with the need to seek (in vain, it seems) local solutions to globally produced problems. (Bauman, 2004: 16)

As with space, trash brings up deep existential questions linked to time. Media artifacts are already linked to deep time, because many devices that transmit media are themselves media made with rare earth minerals extracted from the earth, and formed by ancient geological processes (Parikka, 2015). And in return, the waste created by media systems persist, both the carbon emissions produced by the energy burned to keep huge servers running and in terms of the materialities of obsolete products (Parikka, 2015: 41). "Witnessing nature's demise reminds us of our own" (Hawkins, 2006: 12). Organic trash decomposes: although repellent to us during the time that it takes for maggots to eat through a piece of discarded food, we understand that the laws of nature will do their work and turn that matter into something that can again nourish new life and new growth from the soil. Not so with the artificial plastics that we humans have cunningly engineered from fossil fuels and chemical compounds. Plastic is the most postmodern of substances. Having no organic basis (unlike paper, tin, and glass), plastic also has no organic mode of decomposition (Freinkel, 2011). Plastic persists. Although it will over time and subject to forces of pressure and movement break down into smaller and smaller pieces, it can never entirely re-integrate into organic matter because it did not come from there; it came from laboratory and a factory. Although no one knows for sure how long plastics will last, scientists estimate that they will be around for 200, 400, or 1,000 years (Rogers, 2006: 6). Scientists have discovered micromolecules of plastic with-in fish and other tiny oceanic organisms. Not only does plastic not go away, it also enters the food chain: humans ingest microparticles of plastic that stay in the fish that they eat, which ingested plastic fragments in the ocean (Freinkel, 2011: 320). Furthermore, the many plastics that we surround ourselves with and use, from lifesaving medical treatments to those in which we store our leftover foods, alter the chemistry of the human body: "All of us, even newborns, now carry traces in our systems of phthalates and other synthetic substances, such as fire retardants, stain repellants, solvents, metals, waterproofing agents, and bactericides" (Freinkel, 2011: 200). The plastic water bottle that is thrown in the dustbin will spend more time on the planet than the human being who threw it there—this fact is irrefutable. Once that human dies—as we all will—their body will be buried to decompose or be cremated and reenter an organic cycle of life. The plastic water bottle will never do this. It is timeless, ageless, it lives forever. How ironic that we humans—who have through science and medicine and science fiction been working toward and dreaming of extending our own lives—succeeded in creating a substance that will live forever instead of us. This is a "disenchantment story" (Hawkins, 2006: 8) like no other: humans have mas-tered and alienated themselves from nature, while creating a substance that will be on the planet long after we cause (as some argue is possible) our own extinc-tion (Kolbert, 2014).

But trash also has another—slightly more optimistic—way of time travel-ing. Although some "items that slip from the useful to the useless status will be thrown away, perhaps to be recycled [...] Some things will be 'recovered' from their status as rubbish to regain value and re-enter the cycle of exchange" (Dant, 1999: 38). This can happen through a variety of ways—items can be recovered or repurposed, reclaimed, fixed and used once again, or the ma-terials from which they were made extracted and used to make new things, which once again have use and value to people. An entire genre of craft and art is predicated on using recycled materials. Craft markets in cities and towns across Africa are likely to proudly display beautiful items made from reused items: stylish sandals from car tires, mats, bags and baskets from reused plastic, jewelry from bottle caps, the list goes on. Many artists are also increasingly interested in using found materials and recyclable items to craft their sculptures and multimedia work. In this way, trash takes on a new life and enters new spaces as well as new times. Some objects gain value by aging—as with antiques—but with trash the opposite is usually true, the older it is the more likely it is to be associated as rubbish (Dant, 1999: 131). The passage of time, therefore, will partly contribute to new ways of defining of trash, but it also opens up possibilities for rubbish, particularly plastic kinds that cannot decompose, to be reimagined and redeployed in new ways. The ecobrick movement, for example, trains people to make bricks from plastic bottles and plastic rubbish, which can then be used in sustainable building (Inhabitat Staff, 2019). Although thinking through what trash tells us about space and time may take us in deeply pessimistic directions, it is important to also recognize the kernel of hope also present in innovative approaches to treating rubbish as resources with potential economic and cultural value. Rubbish presents opportunities for considering the reach of material and consumer culture across space and time, and arguably it should be theorized in relation to global as well as local spatiality, while also considering how it connects with the ways in which we understand the temporal conditions of existence and decomposition.

THE STRUCTURE OF THIS BOOK

Thus far, this chapter has explored important orientation points for theorizing the cultural importance and political significance of rubbish. It has argued that understanding trash is an important route into making sense of the human condition, everyday life, and macropolitical issues, in the age of the Anthropocene. The discussion has crossed four axes: exploring how materiality and morality collide in thinking about what trash means, considering the complexities that garbage introduces in our thinking about subjectivity, individuality and identity, reflecting on notions of the public and private in relation to the ownership of trash, and finally thinking through existential notions of time and space in relation to rubbish. These four pairs of ideas serve as a theoretical framework for the analytical work that follows.

To bring these ideas together, it is necessary to return to the idea of mediation, and to extend the argument that an examination of media representations of trash can help us to delve deeper into theories of morality, subjectivity, the public and time-space, just as those concepts can help us to understand why rubbish matters in human life today. "There is a garbage angle to every human activity" (Rathje & Murphy, 2001: 3). Increasingly, in both wealthy and poor nations, media texts and technologies are playing a role in all sorts of human activities, from the most personal (like finding sex or love through dating websites) to the most public (like choosing or resisting governments or participating in some kind of discussion about public life). It is curious, despite the fact that "garbage is among humanity's most prodigious physical legacies to those who have yet to be born" (Rathje & Murphy, 2001: 4), that we have yet to turn serious scholarly attention to the question of how, in our collectively mediated lives, we speak of garbage. This book argues—and implements this through the analyses that follow—that "if we can come to understand our discards [. . .] then we will better understand the world in which we live" (Rathje & Murphy, 2001: 4). Garbage is the "steaming detritus of daily existence" (Rathje & Murphy, 2001: 4); it is at once a material and symbolic object that is central to the workings of consumer culture. Although often ignored in daily life, it is beginning to enter into various forms of public discourse, as this book will show. The work here builds on existing important work that links media studies to environmental studies, summarized as research in "ecomedia" (Cubitt, 2005; Murray & Heumann, 2009; Rust, Monani & Cubitt, 2015; Starosielski & Walker, 2016). This scholarship emphasizes how "our love of media and technology has become part and parcel of our global environmental crisis" (Rust, Monani, & Cubitt, 2015: 1). This book shares this orientation and makes the claim that a specific focus on how public conversations about rubbish are shaped in media narratives will provide us with the resources we need to think about how to integrate explicit discussions about trash and consumption with existing debates about "ecomedia." And this in turn will serve as a key contribution to imagining and producing more sustainable, just, and humane forms of consumption in the future.

The rest of the book is structured as follows. Three thematically organized chapters introduce a variety of case studies of the media representation of garbage, and a synthetic theoretical chapter brings together the case studies into a concluding discussion. Each of the thematic chapters contains a discussion of key methodological approaches, and engagement with additional relevant literature not covered in this chapter.

Chapter 2 explores media narratives focusing on questions of agency and forms of action in relation to rubbish. These are organized along the subcategories of reduction, reuse and recycling. In relation to thinking about action in relation to reducing waste, the discussion focuses on New York City social media heroine, Lauren Singer, known as "Zero Trash Girl," who made a media project and career out of living her consumer lifestyle in such a way as to not produce any trash. In relation to the project of reusing waste, the discussion explores works by artists who work with rubbish as their medium. The multimedia work *Cape Mongo* by artist Francois Knoetze and a collaborative public installation called iThemba Tower are analyzed in relation to exploring new forms of value creation and the potential of rubbish to act as a medium of communication. Then, self-representations of the work of a cooperative of women recyclers based in Pune, India, are explored in relation to the labor of recycling, and new ways of considering economic activity in trash-centered occupations. Through these three sets of case studies, themes of agency (both individual and collective) and hope are explored. The possibility of moral action in relation to trash contributing to a broader change in culture is considered, and the optimistic potential of individual behavior change is put into context of the larger structural challenges also shaping the production and disposal of postconsumer trash.

Chapter 3 looks at two important forms of hedonistic consumption—expensive music and entertainment festivals and tropical island tourism—and considers how waste is examined in media narratives about the pleasures enjoyed by relatively wealthy consumers. Media coverage of the postparty landscapes of two entertainments festivals—Glastonbury Festival in the UK and Afrika Burn in South Africa—are examined. How these entertainment institutions narrate their own orientations to waste, and how the detritus (or lack thereof) of the postparty spaces are visually represented, are analyzed in order to make an argument about how forms of waste-making and removal are integrated into practices and narratives of pleasure and leisure-oriented consumption. Similarly, in relation to tourism, media narratives about trash on beaches in tropical islands are examined in order to get insight into how a clinical and persistent removal of trash is necessary in order to maintain the advertised fantasy of a tropical idyll untouched by waste and the destruction of the environment. Together, these case studies allow for the development of an argument about how global class politics impacts on the mediation of trash, but also interjects into social spaces defined by inequality. Most often, it is the poor who are expected to live uncomplainingly alongside garbage, while the rich expect it to be cleaned away for them. The chapter explores how traces of trash after hedonistic consumption practices blurs the boundaries of any sense of place, and asks to what extent a type of happy nihilism is present in media discourses lamenting the trashing of beautiful environments.

Chapter 4 turns its attention to media narratives about massive environmental disasters. It focuses on the devastation of natural environments through fossil-fuel based waste: specifically, oil and plastic. Film narratives about the Deepwater Horizon oil spill are examined in order to understand how the impacts—both human and environmental—of the huge spill were publicly processed in different ways. As well as this, filmic and visual narratives about huge-scale plastic pollution in the oceans are analyzed in order to attempt to map out the spatial and ethical dimensions of the global garbage problem as well as how various calls to action (or inaction) are encoded therein. The chapter explores visual narratives of the oil spill and so-called plastic islands in order to make an argument that the scale of the devastation that the human race has created is almost unfathomable to us, and as such it is incredibly difficult to capture the full sense of the problems we have created when we attempt to represent them. The argument is made that the "new" sublime is our own tiptoeing toward an edge that we ourselves have created, and the knowledge—increasingly unambiguous—that there is no coming back from that abyss.

Finally, chapter 5 brings together the various analytical threads explored in chapters 2, 3, and 4 in order to reflect on the moral positioning of the consuming and trash-producing human in the current age. The argument is made that rubbish is the most public of all objects, as such it insists on moral responses. The extent to which these are made possible by media narratives is considered, and the argument is made that there is potential for media discourses and communicative forms to contribute positively to new shared ideas (and perhaps then behaviors) about rubbish. The chapter also argues that it is imperative to retheorize subjectivity in the age of rubbish through the figure of Homo detritus, a new iteration of the human species, one defined by the trash we create. It argues that a collective, ethical orientation toward consumption and trash might allow for a new future to be imagined, and asks to what extent the inherently selfish and pleasure-seeking nature of Homo sapiens will triumph. The chapter also considers the longing that is produced by media narratives tracking the many ways in which humankind is destroying our planet, and argues that while there is a painful beauty captured in the huge-scale visuals that show the scale of destruction, there is also a sense in which it may be too late for us to fix the problems we have caused. The chapter concludes by sketching out some possible futures for the study of consumption, arguing that new moral orientations are needed that take into account the centrality of waste to material culture.

2

Agency and Action

Recycling Consumer Subjectivity through Waste

This chapter explores questions of agency, action, and optimism in relation to media narratives about forms of individual and collective action in relation to consumer rubbish. As the previous chapter set out, the presence of huge amounts of rubbish on the planet is symptomatic of the failure of consumer capitalism as well as the entrenchment of the age of the Anthropocene, and has implications for how we consider subjectivity and identity more broadly, and specific ways of relating to garbage as citizens and consumers. There is no turning back from the moment at which humanity has arrived, indeed, has brought itself to. As Bill McKibben writes in *Eaarth*, our planet is no longer the planet that it used to be, it no longer functions the way that we thought it always would (McKibben, 2010). Those of us who think that it can someday be the same again are laboring under an illusion. Through overproduction, overconsumption, and irresponsible disposal, humans have changed the planet irreversibly. The bigger picture of this new "eaarth" is climate change, deforestation, ocean acidification, and major shortages of water. Within this bleak environmental bigger picture are the massive piles of rubbish that exist in tandem with every human settlement. Can we still hope to save some part of the ecosystem of our planet from the growing amounts of waste that we produce? What kinds of environmental and consumer activism are required to do so? Or is there is little point in trying to save something that is beyond saving? Is there anything constructive that we can do with those huge piles of trash, things that might help us to help ourselves?

Recycling is one answer to these at-once existential and deeply pragmatic questions.

One key way in which trash has become a topic of popular attention in recent years is through a variety of creative approaches to working with or against it, sometimes in service of ideological self-branding, sometimes in service of job creation, and sometimes in service of politically inspired art. Each of these ways of narrating human actors' relationships to rubbish allows a rethinking of our collective relationship to the rubbish our societies have created. This in turn invites us to reconsider what individual agency and activity mean, including how they are enacted and represented through media narratives, in a world increasingly shaped and defined by garbage.

Does rubbish create entirely new forms of work and labor, both material and mediated, and if so, how can we rethink notions of value creation? Similarly, if the materialities of garbage are producing entirely new forms of work—in terms of self-branding, artistic labor, and the need to physically sort through waste—then how do we need to reconceptualize the ways in which our economies are organized, no longer defined clearly by practices of production and consumption, and perhaps moving toward the exchange of reusability? At the heart of all of these questions are practices of recycling, which entail the reuse and redeployment of waste into new forms of value. As the planet gets cluttered with more and more trash, it is possible that practices of recycling will shift from a sort of unusual eco-conscious set of choices practiced by people in the global north and people trying to make a living in the global south, into a more prosaic, postconsumer economy no longer defined by extraction, relentless production and overconsumption.

Inspired by the eco-slogan "reduce, reuse, recycle," which implores citizens to take all three strategies in relation to the rubbish they produce, this chapter considers three empirical themes. First, it looks at work done to reduce the amount of trash for which people are individually responsible. How can this result in new forms of eco-identity formation? The second considers how trash can be reappropriated as a material for art-making, with potentially wider political and aesthetic implications for consciousness-raising. How can this reuse help redefine collective understandings of the materiality of trash? The third looks at the kind of labor involved in recycling, and how that labor is discursively constructed in the self-representation efforts of recycling workers themselves. How can rubbish offer new ways of thinking about how value is identified and mobilized in the economic system? Together these three thematic elements come together to allow for a synthetic discussion about how media narratives about trash discursively construct certain ideas about agency, individualism, creativity, and labor. The discussion in this chapter will draw on examples from the global north and south, exploring the work done by an internet celebrity in New York City, artists in Johannesburg and Cape Town, and subsistence recyclers in Pune. The methodological approach taken across all three case studies is narrative and thematic analysis of the texts and images produced by those reworking the rubbish in different ways. Focus is given to the messages constructed by the texts, rather than the intentions or motivations of those who made them. What kinds of messages about rubbish in relation to its reduction, reuse and recycling are created and shared by those actively working in those ways with it, and how can those messages be understood to form part of new ways of imaging consumer agency in the current moment?

REDUCE OR SELF-BRAND? THE LUXURY OF WASTE-FREE CONSUMPTION

The notion of "zero waste" has received some attention in industrial and spatial design (Connett, 2013; Lehmann & Crocker, 2013), and increasingly in a subgenre of environmental activism aimed at reducing the scale of waste produced in ordinary middle class consumer lifestyles (Korst, 2012; Johnson, 2013; Su, 2018). Many institutions and local governments urge their members and citizens to work toward a zero-waste ethic in an attempt to forge progressive refuse management strategies in their locales. The emergence of such discourses hints at a new argument about the extent to which consumers need to take personal responsibility for the waste created through their consumption of necessities and luxuries alike. Waste reduction campaigns have become visible, for example, encouraging consumers to refuse disposable plastic straws in restaurants (see #RefuseTheStraw on social media), or to leave behind excess plastic packaging in the supermarket when they buy their groceries (Finch & Smithers, 2006).

Perhaps the most extreme example of this idea of aiming for zero-waste consumption is when individuals work at reducing their personal waste-production to as close to zero as possible. Particularly notable is the career of a young woman named Lauren Singer, a New York City resident, who branded herself "Zero Trash Girl" and set up an online media brand called "Trash Is For Tossers!," through which she documents the various strategies she takes in order to consume less, reduce waste, and avoid environmentally damaging packaging. Through an intensely mediated campaign to reduce the postconsumer trash for which she is personally responsible, Singer has arguably contributed significantly to zero-trash discourse (Somerville, 2015). A college-educated, middle-class, twenty-something New Yorker, Singer took it upon herself to change her lifestyle in order to avoid producing trash and documented her efforts over two years with the aim of showing how a low-impact lifestyle is possible, even in the most consumerist of urban settings. She famously produced so little waste over four years that what was left (e.g., items that could not be composted or recycled) fit into a glass mason jar (see fig. 1). Her efforts were exhaustively documented in a YouTube channel, social media profiles, personal website, and a range of spinoff media appearances and features in mainstream publications, including TED Talks, the *New York Times*, and the BBC. As a social media personality—some have even called her an internet star—Singer is a quintessential media-savvy millennial, expertly using online platforms to narrate her journey toward a zero-waste lifestyle and the related businesses that she set up as a result. One, the Simply Co, makes zero-waste organic detergent; the other is an eponymous packaging free store in New York City. Through the various hyperlinked media platforms used to promote both Singer herself as well as her services and products, in addition to the proliferating mainstream media coverage about her, she has created a successful brand that is firmly rooted within an environmentalist, eco-conscious—but still deeply consumerist—mentality. On her website (TrashIsforTossers.com), Singer details her personal journey toward a zero-waste lifestyle, which she defines as not sending anything to landfill and not tossing anything in the trash can. Instead, she composts and recycles, and if she cannot do either of those things with an item that she wants or needs, she will not buy it. The waste footprint of every item in her world has been carefully considered in advance. She avoids buying any products in packaging that cannot be recycled, and goes so far as to make her own toothpaste, laundry detergent, skin and hair-care products rather than buy these items in single-use plastic containers. She chooses glass, bamboo, and wood products and packaging instead of plastic. She chooses to shop at farmers' markets where she can buy produce without packaging, rather than at supermarkets, where single pieces of fruit often come overwrapped in Styrofoam and plastic.

Singer is often pictured in a minimalist, stylish, and modern apartment, with pristine kitchen surfaces and undecorated walls, capturing the simple, almost austere, lifestyle that she has chosen, and which she is promoting as

Figure 1. In a portrait shared on Instagram in April 2019, Lauren Singer shows four years of trash in a mason jar. Image reproduced with kind permission of to www.trashisfortossers.com and www.packagefreeshop.com.

the more moral consumer option for viewers. Singer fits the mainstream idea of attractiveness—she is white, slim, has long, dark hair, a pretty face, and is extremely photogenic. She is stylish and fashion-conscious, always dressed well (she emphasizes that her clothes are vintage, secondhand or reclaimed rather than purchased from "fast fashion" stores), and immaculately turned out. On her website and Instagram profile, she is regularly featured at the center of many images, for example, those that illustrate articles on a waste-free beauty routine, trash-free gift ideas for Valentine's Day, or where to buy the best reusable water bottle. The aesthetic of the website "Trash Is for Tossers" is professional and clean-looking, reminiscent of a high-end designer brand. In it, Singer describes her main motivation in starting on the zero-trash journey as wanting to lessen her personal environmental impact, and to align her values with her actions. As she writes in the caption to the Instagram post shown in fig. 1, "I set out to align what I care passionately about with how I live my day to day life," "I am aware of not just the world around me, but my impact on it," and "I believe in taking responsibility, so I did." As these phrases show, Singer is making a strong moral argument for individual responsibility for consumption and its effects, and also emphasizing the link between awareness and action. Being aware of the problem of excess trash in the world requires action to be taken to reduce it. The logic is clear: if my throwaway packaging is adding to the landfill, I can change that by not throwing away that packaging. And the way to do that is to not buy the thing that requires the packaging to be thrown away, and choosing instead another thing without packaging. What this translates to is a different type of economic agency. Instead of, as the "free-market" system would have it, consumers making choices purely on price and without external judgment, we see "alternative considerations of what constitutes the role of economic activity in people's lives" (Brown & Timmerman, 2015: 26). The message of Zero Trash Girl is that choosing to buy, or not to buy, something should be based not only on individual pleasure or desire, but on macrocollective questions to do with the environment, and whether the purchase will cause harm outside of the lived experience of the buyer. It is notable that Singer does not advocate a cessation to all consumption as a solution to the trash problem. Instead she encourages a new form of "ethical shopping," which "requires that we positively act to alleviate suffering through refusing to buy 'unethical' products and through the positive promotion of their ethical counterparts" (Fagan, 2006: 131). Extending the parameters of ethical consumption beyond questions of fair trade and the exploitation of workers to the domain of detritus, Singer argues that her choice to radically reduce the amount of trash she produces is a matter of taking responsibility and caring.

Let's pause for a moment to consider why, in the age of late capitalism, consumer-based neoliberalism, a trash-filled planet, and climate change that is being ignored by most governments, individuals believe that making decisions based on personal choices and taking individual actions are the most appropriate ways to act?

It is important not to undermine the significance or importance of what Singer has achieved. It is remarkable that through an individual social media campaign, one person could have succeeded in reaching so many people with a message of the need to reduce individual trash footprints, as well as with practical, doable, and sometimes affordable advice about how to achieve that goal. At the time of writing, Singer has over 210,000 followers on Instagram, over 16,000 on Twitter, and over 110,000 on Facebook. It is clear, therefore, that Singer's efforts to provide an example of how it is possible to reduce the trash created through consumption has indeed reached many thousands of people, and possibly inspired them to think differently about how they consume, why they consume, and how much trash they produce. Of course, it is difficult to measure how much that awareness translates into action. Furthermore, even if every single person in the developed world were to change their consumption habits to the extent that they are able to reduce the amount of trash they produce, would it be enough to halt the trashing of the environment? Arguably not, because by far the majority of waste and trash is produced by industrial production and the "rise of the petro-chemical industry" (Freinkel, 2011: 23). Most human beings need to consume in order to live (Korst, 2012: 580) and are at the "mercy of the manufacturers" in terms of how they package their products (Korst, 2012: 581). For many people, the added labor of trying to minimize their consumer waste might seem incredibly onerous, on top of the daily struggles of earning an income, looking after children and/or elderly parents, and maintaining a household.

Although it is worth thinking through how consumer activism can contribute to shifting the patterns of industrial production—that old chicken-and-egg question of supply and demand—it is also worth considering whether individualized activism such as that modeled by Singer is a sufficient response to the problem of trash, or whether it might be more of a strategy to make individuals feel less morally conflicted about their complicity in the system. As Jo Littler points out,

> Consciously reduced consumption is a practice pursued on the whole by those who could be more resource-intensive consumers if they chose to be: the practice arises primarily because they choose this path as a more 'enlightened,' satisfying or less guilt-inducing alternative. (Littler, 2008: 107)

Singer is an excellent example of a subject who has chosen to regulate and discipline her "personal practices in order to render the self more congruent with particular values like restraint [and] responsibility" (Hawkins, 2006: 32); in other words, "a monitoring and disciplining relation to the self" (Hawkins, 2006: 33). Crucially, these efforts at aligning her values and actions take place almost entirely within the sphere of consumer culture and the sphere of market exchange. As is the case for all citizens of almost every city and country in the world, Singer lives within the structures provided by economic and political power systems. Neoliberal culture prizes individuality; this is even more acutely the case for women (Gill, 2008). In some senses, Singer's highly controlled and thoughtful consumption reflects the success of neoliberal power, most famously articulated by Nikolas Rose as a form of governing the soul (Rose, 1990). Singer has, admirably, chosen to take personal responsibility for creating a less wasteful society, and has governed her own material and mental practices in order to actualize her ideal of moral consumer selfhood. This ideal consumer does not deny the self the pleasures of consumption, but presents an alternative, more ethical form of consumption instead. She still shapes her life by use of purchasing power (Rose, 1990: 103) and makes her life meaningful by selecting a personal lifestyle (Rose, 1990: 103), and she makes sense of her existence by exercising her freedom to choose (Rose, 1990: 103). As a "choosing self," she exercises her freedom but also produces herself as a neoliberal subject. Though an ethical consumer, a consumer still she remains; because it is impossible to function in neoliberal society in any other way.

Some radical environmentalists argue that individual actions—such as reducing waste, recycling, changing to low-energy light bulbs, becoming vegetarian, and not flying—are absolutely pointless as long as the corporate and industrial actors who have been facilitated by corrupt governments to desecrate and destroy and pollute the planet are allowed to continue to do so. They advocate organized struggle and "ecological warfare" to defend the planet (Jensen, McBay, & Keith, 2011). Does this mean that trying to live a zero-waste consumer lifestyle is totally pointless? This question—is individual environmental action meaningless?—is perhaps the most pervasive moral concern for global north consumers in the current moment. This book does not have the scope to explore this question fully, but let us consider it in relation to rubbish, and through the prism of this case study.

According to Zero Trash Girl, one of the ways to save the planet is to create less rubbish, which involves buying an alternative "eco-friendly" product, often available through her own website. For example, Singer recommends using stainless-steel airtight containers instead of plastic Tupperware, stainless-steel ice trays instead of plastic, beeswax food wrap instead of cling wrap, and so on. All of these items are significantly more expensive than the mainstream plastic options available in the supermarket, and are much harder to get ahold of. Although the eco-alternatives are better quality and will arguably last longer that the cheap plastic items, it is worth considering the extent to which they are luxury items that are difficult to access for those without the upfront capital needed to invest in more expensive (though longer-lasting) versions of these household items.

Through setting up her online and bricks-and-mortar Package Free stores, Singer is actively trying to make the more sustainable, longer-lasting, and environmentally friendly products more widely available. At no point in her eco-conscious media narrative does Singer suggest that the consumer economy is to blame for environmental troubles, or that the best solution would be to tap out of consumption entirely. Although she does strongly advocate buying less, she still advocates buying. Just buying different: choosing things that last longer and that do not come wrapped in layers of unnecessary plastic packaging. Although Singer does also give advice on ways to reduce waste that don't cost money, and offers recipes for relatively easy homemade cleaning solution and toothpaste, for example, which are likely to be cheaper than the commercial options available, even these solutions cost money, as the raw materials must be purchased. The question also arises as to how far back along the supply chain the zero-packaging choice can go. I could, for example, choose to make my own toothpaste, as Lauren advises, from coconut oil, essential peppermint oil, and baking soda, but all of those items come packaged from the supplier. I could try to source wholesale suppliers rather than buy from the supermarket, but the items would still come packaged somehow, albeit it in bigger packets, jugs, or jars. How can I be sure that the various forms of packaging further back along the supply chain were not plastic, or were properly recycled? And to what extent am I, as an individual consumer, responsible for that? Although making one's own toothpaste may be cheaper and less wasteful on the individual level, to what extent will that really reduce the amount of packaging that is being manufactured and used to apportion and distribute mass-manufactured toothpaste?

It becomes clear, considering the practicalities of the zero-waste lifestyle, that questions of class are central. The lifestyle that Singer represents through her media presence is slick, stylish and would not look out of place in the pages of a designer magazine. The interiors in which she is photographed—both domestic and retail—present an understated, minimalist taste, which reads as associated with an upper-class, wealthy aesthetic. The racial and class politics of the zero-trash lifestyle are unspoken, but come through implicitly in the visual narratives presented. Does one need to be white, rich, and privileged in order to live a zero-waste life? Is it expensive? It is accessible to low-income people? Would a single mom working two jobs and living in the Bronx have the time and energy to make her own toothpaste, or spend hours researching where she could source a more expensive stainless-steel alternative to the plastic Tupperware in which she packs school lunches for her children? In addition to class, gender seems central. Most of the consumption and waste-reduction practices on which Singer gives advice are centered on the home, still gendered as a space requiring women's work. "Abstract notions of care and management of the planet are linked to micropractices in the home, to instructions on how we should *be* around our rubbish: much more attentive, much more dutiful, much more careful than the culture of disposability" (Hawkins, 2006: 32). These forms of labor in relation to reducing waste are gendered, and linked to a postfeminist narrative of empowerment and self-actualization through consumption. As theorists of consumption have long argued, identities, relationships and moralities are mediated through choices made in relation to the objects we buy and exchange, and how we shape our worlds through commodities. Singer—though her own branded identity and through the exhortations to new forms of ethical consumption that her many followers are likely to be trying out—represents a fusion between an eco-warrior and high-end luxury consumer, where the argument goes that not only can the two identities co-exist but it is possible for consumption, at best, to be good for the planet or, at worst, not bad for it.

It is tricky to mediate between the argument that consumption is the cause of environmental degradation, and the converse that it can also be a solution to it. Does an attempt to reduce one's impact on the environment through consumption choices, whether they be modest (such as carrying a reusable bamboo straw in one's handbag rather than accepting disposable plastic ones in restaurants) or extreme (as in the case of Singer, where an entire lifestyle was radically overhauled to the extent that an entire year's worth of non-recyclable waste fitted in a jam jar), simply make the person in question feel more moral or contribute to solving the problem in a real way? The Trash Is for Tossers brand argues the latter. Zero Trash Girl shows that it is possible to also be a thoughtful consumer, to translate one's ethics into the choices and pleasures that characterize a material life. If everyone reduced their waste as Singer did, we might see the end of the landfill. To live thoughtfully and with care, to consider the impact that consumer lifestyles have on the environments in which we live, is laudable and worth aspiring toward. Nevertheless, the question remains as to whether such efforts—individualistic and embedded in the consumer economy as they are—are sufficient in the face of the environmental problems we face. At the very least, Singer's media narrative has brought this question into the public eye.

Through this exploration of one case study in narratives arguing for the reduction of waste through specialized ethical consumption, it has become clear the terrain is anything but clear. Rubbish is deployed as a symbolic resource to make claims about moral agency in relation to consumption, and the form of ethical consumption prioritized by the zero-waste ethic is linked to and shaped by gendered work and class privilege. To what extent might narratives about agency in relation to reusing trash offer a different set of ideas? To explore this, I turn to a different case study involving the reuse of rubbish.

REUSE IN ART: SUBJECTIVITY, SURFACE, AND COMMUNICATION IN RUBBISH ARTWORKS

Traditionally, garbage is considered the detritus of consumer and industrial practices. It is the stuff that is no longer useful, that we no longer wish to have in our homes or personal spaces, that we want to throw away. Perhaps precisely due to the proliferation of trash in material space, it has arguably also become a resource—something that has value and can be sold on at a profit. Artists—most often at the leading edge of rethinking materiality, value, and beauty—are among the first social actors to have taken seriously the possibility of reusing trash to make new things. Taking the discarded objects of others as found materials, many artists work with trash in order to create new aesthetic objects while at the same time making a commentary on the place of trash in the social and cultural world.

> Most of us have been at a gallery exhibition where someone is heard to remark, "that artwork is a piece of garbage." The remark is a metaphor—and a verdict. But in the late twentieth century it increasingly became possible to make the same remark and to mean it literally. Garbage art—pieces of colourful, creative eclecticism and beauty constructed out of what would otherwise have been thrown away—is today at the forefront of the avant-garde art world. (Rathje & Murphy, 2001: 1)

Much has been written by art critics and historians about the "turn to trash" in fine art practice (Vergine, 1997, 2007; Whiteley, 2010; Pájaro, 2015). Following Joanna Zylinska, I understand art to be "world-making rather than just representational" (Zylinska, 2014: 106). In line with a social-constructionist view of mediation as concretely contributing to the production and circulation of shared meanings which in turn construct relationships of power, this view of art sees it as a form of social action, which does more than simply comment on political, economic, and cultural happenings "out there" in the world, but partially constitutes the world through that commentary.

South African multimedia and performance artist Kai Lossgott combs streets or other public spaces, "hunting" and "gathering" pieces of trash that he finds there, no matter how small, and then assembling the scraps of paper, bottle tops, cigarette butts, and fragments of plastic into meticulous typologies (see fig. 2). By taking the random scatter of rubbish off the streets and putting them into some form of aesthetic order, Lossgott is both picking up litter, effectively tidying up the street, and inviting us to see the litter anew.

On an average walk down a street, most people won't notice tiny bits of litter, although they might be outraged by seeing an overturned trash bin or large pieces of rubbish thoughtlessly discarded. But cigarette butts, lollipop sticks, bottle tops, and scraps of paper blend in the urban landscape to the extent that they become more or less invisible. By ordering them, Lossgott makes them visible and, by reminding us that they are there, forces us to think why

Figure 2. *Hunter-gatherer,* Kai Lossgott, 2016. Production still from performance with wearable postconsumer plastic sculpture and found objects; 20 min., pavement outside Institute for Contemporary Arts, Zagreb. Photo: Boris Cvjetanović.

they are there, how they got there, and what role we might have played in that process. Further, through his process of "hunting and gathering," he encourages us to think about whether we too should be playing a role in picking it up. Lossgott's performance is a reminder about the trash we produce and the minute ways in which it surrounds us in everyday life, all the time. That there is no "away": tossing something might remove it from sight but it does not make it disappear. Picking up the detritus then arranging it artfully brings it back into sight, and that visibility forces a rethinking of what its presence means. By cataloging rubbish in the white space of a gallery or on his person in a video performance work, Lossgott makes a commentary not only about the pervasiveness of rubbish in our everyday lives, but on the politics of subjectivity in relation to trash.

In counterpoint is the worth of Thomas Hirschhorn. In his 2010 work, *Too Too-Much Much*, Hirschhorn fills the Museum Dhondt-Dhaenens in Deurle, Belgium, with huge piles of crushed aluminum soft drink cans, which spill out

Figure 3. Thomas Hirschhorn *Too Too-Much Much*, 2010. MDD (Museum Dhondt-Dhaenens), Deurle, Belgium. Courtesy Galerie Chantal Crousel, Paris. Photo Romain Lopez.

of the front door of the museum such that visitors had to gingerly climb over the mound to get into the exhibition. Inside the gallery, the installation took on monumental proportions, as the mound of crushed cans seemed to take on a life of its own, burying a domestic lounge scene, piled on top of computers and coffee tables, morphed into strange outfits on glass-caged mannequins, and even supersized into giant replicas nestled on a bed of their miniature doppelgängers. Literally filling the space such that the mannequins, mirroring the human observers, appeared to be wading through an ocean of trash which reached halfway up the glass fish tank windows of the gallery, the installation commented directly, starkly, on the extent to which humanity is drowning in the rubbish it has produced.

Eschewing the materials of paint and canvas or stone and chisel, these artists are reconceptualizing what artistic media are and what they mean while also commenting on the relation of humans to waste. Both hunter-gatherer and anxious adventurer are forced to navigate a new, treacherous terrain, which requires acknowledging the scale of the trash problem and its permeation of every banal space in everyday life. "It's not often that we experience rubbish as beautiful" (Hawkins, 2006: 22)—indeed, perhaps one of the key agendas of the artist who uses trash to make art is the mission to force the viewer to fundamentally rethink the material and social status of trash. No longer simply something that litters the street, trash becomes an object with value, which can be recontextualized into a thing of beauty and contemplation, horror and challenge, provoking a compulsion to look more closely at the fragments around us, or anxiety about the threat of being entirely overtaken by a tsunami of rubbish that we ourselves have thrown "away." Such art certainly requires the viewer to consider the relationship between consumption and trash. Living and working within urban cityscapes shaped by rubbish, it is no surprise that some artists are pushed into thinking about how those materials can be repurposed into things of beauty and social commentary. It is worth considering how consumerism shapes not only the availability of the materials used in such creative and thought-provoking ways but also the messages that they are able to construct. It is telling that in the detritus of consumer societies artists are finding materials with which to tell us stories about ourselves and our consumption. Of course, the most obvious message told in the story of trash being turned into art is that there is still some sort of value in materials that have been discarded. This functions as a radical change in meaning: that which was thrown away and considered worthless is in fact worth something. Consider the project by New York City–based artist, Justin

Gignac, who in a bid to prove the importance of packaging in selling a product, created designer Perspex cubes, branded and filled with trash "handpicked" from the streets of Times Square. The cubes are aesthetic objects that fill the palm, with smooth rounded edges and corners, the transparent sides showing off the contents inside, each curated by the artist: a used sales receipt, a fragment of a Coca-Cola bottle, a lost pair of cheap sunglasses, a plastic flower. Recontextualized in this way, with a clever commentary on the aesthetics of commodity culture, the trash takes on social and cultural value but also economic value: each cube sells for $50 and the website periodically states that they are out of stock. Interested buyers can join a mailing list to be notified when new NYC trash cubes are available.

In his 2015 work, *Cape Mongo*, South African artist Francois Knoetze, used rubbish to create wearable sculptures, which he then donned for filmed performances as a creature called Mongo, then integrated into multimedia video works. Mongo appeared in different iterations: as a tasseled monster made from the ribbon of discarded videotape clambering up the slopes of Signal Hill, as a multicolored huge parrot wandering along the backwater canal ways near the Table Bay harbor, as a jagged bottle-green beast constructed from old wine bottles contemplating the ocean, as a lumbering cardboard antelope wandering through a protest march, as a reptilian tin-can beast riding an elevator in a shopping mall. In a solo exhibition at the South African National Arts Festival in Makhanda in 2016, the Mongo sculpture-outfits were put on display as silent witnesses to projections of the short multimedia films made featuring each character. Exploring questions of obsolescence, memory, nostalgia, racism, and the uncanny, as well as the meaning of trash in an increasingly polluted urban environment, Knoetze's work reveals the huge creative potential that arises when rubbish is reappropriated as a material for making art. Arguably, it is the artist's eternal responsibility to consider the world around them not only in the subject matter of the art they make, but also with regards to the materials available to them to make it. The term *mongo* comes from the culture of dumpster-diving and freeganism (Whiteley, 2010: 3). Knoetze reimagines this to become something that can name not only objects but also subjects comprised of objects.

In Cape Mongo, there are multiple levels at which consumption matters, in the meanings of the artwork. In the performance and multimedia video featuring Plastic Mongo, the large cheerful rainbow-parrot interacts with various landscapes near the shore line of Cape Town harbor. The footage of plastic Mongo lumbering jovially around the concrete landscapes of the harbor, at times with Table Mountain in view in the background, seems to say very little obviously about consumer culture. But the coloring and aesthetics of the big bird itself are unmistakably the merchandise of commodity culture. As the product of a manmade, chemical process, plastic is produced in a wide variety of colors often quite hard to find in the natural world, and thus possesses a certain synthetic quality that is unmistakable. Fig. 4 shows a production still from the video. The big-bird plastic Mongo stands in a concrete trench with wings outstretched and its large quite beak angled forlornly downward. Around its three-clawed yellow feet we see scattered dozens of bright multicolored objects, which we could assume are tops from plastic bottles. The impression created by the scene is that the bright candy-like objects tumbled out of the wings of the bird and onto the gray floor. The colors are enticing, childlike, and speak to a cartoon-style aesthetic that characterizes the experiences of many Gen Xers and Millennials. In this scene, we are invited to witness the products of human ingenuity and industry. There are no two materials that quite summarize the impact that human beings have had on the environment as do concrete and plastic. As concrete reshapes natural landscapes, plastic litters it. Behind the seemingly cheerful demeanor of the big bird is a melancholic attitude. His gestures and postures seem to suggest that he is not quite sure how he ended up where he did. Reminiscent of the fabulous creatures that live deep in the rainforest, immortalized in magnificent wildlife photography and filmography, plastic Mongo's habitat is just as manmade as the feathers that adorn his wings.

Although it is seductive to engage with plastic Mongo as a character in its own right—a mute yet loudly Technicolor creature, a lonely-seeming yet vibrant being at once amusing and visually seductive—it is also important to remember that the creature is an elaborate mask that conceals a performer within. And that performer within is an artist seeking to comment on the ways in which plastic is increasingly integrated into our lived experiences and bodies. Knoetze has recounted his reasons for choosing an industrial oceanside location for parts of the performance for plastic Mongo. Recalling how the sculpture was incredibly uncomfortable to wear, because the plastic pieces would bite and scratch into his skin at every movement, Knoetze reflects on what the materiality of plastic signified to him in the decisions he made while creating the work.

Plastic is an interesting example. It's even becoming incorporated into human DNA. I don't know the exact science of it, but the narrative is like this:

Figure 4. *Cape Mongo* by Francois Knoetze, 2015. Photograph by Anton Scholtz.

there is all this microplastic waste that is discarded in the ocean, and a lot of it ends up in the bellies of fish and other sea creatures.... Then humans catch those fish and consume plastic-associated chemicals, and by eating it those microscopic traces of plastic become a part of our own being. So plastic is becoming part of the human condition in a very bodily, material way, it's no longer just material for packaging our lives and lifestyles. (Iqani & Knoetze, 2017)

In the same way that plastics and the toxins that they carry are being physiologically integrated into the bodies of human beings who eat fish, in Knoetze's artwork we see a human body assimilated into the heart of a plastic creature. A new kind of plastic-human cyborg emerges, and without "needing to know the exact science of it," the artist can explore the affect and aesthetic of a new kind of posthuman hybridity. By making plastic hypervisible through the construction of an attractive, mythical-seeming beast, and placing his own body of flesh and blood within in, Knoetze is inviting us to consider not only how plastic makes up the world around us but how it is evolving—if an inanimate object can be said to evolve—to consume us. The consumed becomes the consumer. The lifeless material is integrating itself into life—mingling with the microscopic plankton in the ocean and working its way up the food chain into our own fatty tissues. If we cut the plastic Mongo open, we'd find a human inside.

Taking this idea to its extreme, plastic Mongo represents a possible future for human life, one in which we are so integrated with this demon substance that cannot biodegrade that we turn into it, that our own flesh is obscured by the brilliant hues of various forms of synthetic material. "Most of today's plastics are made of hydrocarbon molecules—packets of carbon and hydrogen—derived from the refining of oil and natural gas" (Freinkel, 2011: 40). Most plastics are some variation of a polymer; when these meet the organic matter from which living beings are created, do we become poly-human?

The epic tragedy of the story of how plastic kills—and outlives us—is hinted at in the melancholy bearing of plastic Mongo character. This speaks to the now-famous photographs of decaying albatross corpses, their innards slowly rotting away to reveal the plastic material the birds ate while alive. Brian Thill (Thill, 2015: 8–10) writes about Chris Jordan's photographs of the decomposing bodies of albatrosses, which reveal the plastic in the stomachs that they had eaten. In these images, we see the tragedy of a single life lost, the story of a bird that mistook pieces of plastic for food, had a belly filled up with non-nutritious substances, then slowly and confusedly starved to death. More so, we see the evolutionary tragedy that a species hasn't had a chance to evolve to adapt to this new threat to its livelihood and to learn to differentiate between food and trash. Plastic has been on the planet for just over a hundred years, which is a mere millisecond in evolutionary time. No other species on the planet has had the chance to change its behavior and work out a way to survive in response to the trash-devastation that humans are unleashing on the planet. What the photos of plastic waste in albatross bellies give, is a sense that

> these nests of plastic [. . .] belong to us and yet feel apart from us, because they constitute the planetary debris field we have scattered so thoroughly and minutely that it's hard to find anything particularly spectacular or notable in it is. It is one of the many instances in which seemingly minor trash demonstrates its immense strength and durability, having reached every corner of our planet and troubled or killed so many of the things it touches. (Thill, 2015: 10)

From this perspective, humans are not subjects with agency who consume plastic objects. Rather, plastic is a monstrous substance, immortal, which over the long game of time, consumes the organic beings it touches. The sculpture of Plastic Mongo will outlive Francois Knoetze, the human. So, we move from thinking about consumer culture in prosaic terms—what have we made? what have we thrown away?—to thinking about consumer culture in apocalyptic terms—what will we leave on the planet long after our own bodies have decomposed, long after humanity has succeeded in ensuring the extinction of most species, possibly including our own? If humans go extinct, will there be giant plastic-rat hybrids scavenging in the ruins of unpeopled skyscrapers, huge floating plastic-jellyfish eating plastic-plankton? Although tempting to move to the realm of science fiction in this line of thinking, it is important to remember that scientific research is proving that microplastics are indeed showing up in fatty tissue of predators at the top of the food chain, not only in the bellies of animals a little lower down (Freinkel, 2011: 321). How these foreign materials will integrate—or not—with organic bodies is an open question for both science and cultural theory.

In contrast to the deep anxieties that surface when considering the meanings of an artwork like *Cape Mongo*, consider the public installation titled *iThemba Tower* (2016) by Johannesburg-based artist r1, who has created numerous street artworks using various found and discarded materials (see his website r1r1r1.net for a detailed documentation and portfolio). r1's approach to making public art is to take familiar items, such as chevron street signs, police tape, discarded CDs or plastic and paper waste, and to arrange them in geometric, often mandala-like patterns on building exteriors, store windows, or bus stops. Staying with this aesthetic, *iThemba Tower* is a 65.5-foot high art installation made with 7,000 recycled plastic bottles, each containing a message written by local schoolchildren and citizens from around the country who submitted their messages via a website. The project is described by its makers as a public art monument, and was documented in a ten-minute documentary, which is available on r1's website (see http://r1r1r1.net/ithemba-tower), as well as other platforms around the web. The documentary tells the story of the collaboration, which included local schoolchildren, street recyclers, a local engineering design firm, and the gallery on the grounds of which the communication tower stands. The documentary narrates how the idea for the tower came from r1's collaboration with Isaac, a homeless person and street recycler (who later disappeared, r1 was unable to track him down, since his last name never became known). r1 and Isaac struck up a kind of friendship, and eventually decided to collaborate on a project, and wrap one of the trees near Isaac's living space (under a bridge next to a highway in Johannesburg) with plastic bottles, as a visual message to the commuters, saying something about who was there and what they might be chucking out of their car windows (see a visual documentation at http://r1r1r1.net/interventions). This same technique was applied to the tower, which is located on the grounds of the Spaza Gallery, in Troyeville, a relatively low-income neighborhood to the east of Johannesburg's downtown. Once situated on public land just outside the gallery's grounds, the tower slowly became integrated into Spaza's sculpture garden. The old parastatal telecommunications tower became obsolete with the emergence of cheaper and more efficient mobile and internet communications services, and it stood silent in the sculpture garden, no longer sending out or receiving any signals, perhaps looked on by the many creative minds passing through the space as begging to be adorned somehow. As the documentary recounts, r1's idea to wrap it in plastic bottles, like he and Isaac did with the tree, evolved into to a full-blown community art project, which r1 spearheaded creatively and practically (in terms of organizing logistics and raising funds). The result is a simple yet effective sculpture that takes a piece of obsolete public architecture, wraps it in 7,000 plastic bottles, and thereby reimagines it as something new, a beacon of hope (which is the meaning of the isiZulu word, *ithemba*). The documentary features interviews with street recyclers who were employed to collect plastic bottles and provide workshops to local schoolchildren about their recycling work and lighting designers who got involved to install LED lights into the bottles, so that at night the tower could be lit up in a festive display. Seen in person, the tower seems taller than might be expected, and it juts out quite impressively from the single-story homes and structures that surround it.

Would those empty bottles have ended up in landfill? The *iThemba Tower* documentary suggests that they would have, featuring scenes of the major urban dump just to the south of the city. Nevertheless, recycling or "wastepicker" work (Samson, 2009, 2015; Viljoen, Blaauw, & Schenck, 2016) is becoming a more recognizable feature of the cityscape. The economy of Johannesburg, like many global south cities, is defined by a huge disparity between the wealth and poverty of its citizens. The city's huge numbers of poor are swelled by the influx of migrants from rural areas, as well as neighboring African countries, all looking for their fortune in the "City of Gold." And with unemployment high, as usual, it is no surprise that many people are forced to make a living by collecting recyclable materials thrown out as trash by the well-heeled middle and upper classes living in the city's leafy suburbs, hand-carting the materials up to fifty kilometers, and selling them at recycling centers (Sentime, 2011; Mamphitha, 2012). As such, the bottles that adorn *iThemba Tower*, resembling organic matter somehow, like a cluster of bluebottle jellyfish washed up on a beach, the perfect geometry of a knot of spider eggs or beehive cells, may not have been sent to landfill, and if they were, it is possible that they would have been collected by a reclaimer working the dump, and sold to earn a few Rands for the day. The South African plastic industry estimates that 43.7 percent of plastics are recycled in the country (Alfreds, 2018). The sculpture therefore arguably does take a significant number of plastic bottles off the streets and out of the landfill. But it is a different kind of reuse taking place, one that is quite different from the recycling of the materials into new plastic bottles.

One of the key characteristics of this artwork is that it was collaboratively made. r1 did not see himself as the ingénue inventing an avant-garde conceptual art sculpture, but as the driver of a participative process. As the documentary shows, he was at pains to pull different members of the Troyeville community into the project. In addition to collaborating with the self-employed recyclers who collected the plastic bottles from street-sides, as well as dustbins and suburban trash bags around the city, and raising money to pay them for the bottles they would have sold to recyclers, r1 developed an art-workshop program that he took to local schools. These workshops aimed to teach children about plastic waste and environmental responsibility, and asked each child to write a message of hope for the future. Each message was rolled up and inserted into one of the bottles before it was attached to the tower. Inside each plastic bubble, which will take hundreds of years to photodegrade and will never reenter the organic system, is the voice of a child expressing something about the world that he or she will grow up to inherit. From this perspective, the plastic bottles protect hopes for the future, while at once serving as a kind of time capsule. Public art projects need to be collaborative by definition, and intentionally situating art pieces in the public domain in itself sends a strong message about the purpose of creativity, which should be about more than indulging personal ideas and expression; rather, they should be commenting on matters that have something to do with all of us. In this sense, *iThemba Tower* (both the artwork and the documentary) draws attention to plastic pollution and recycling as issues that are of public concern and need to be deliberated upon collectively. It invites a minipublic sphere, and both explicitly and implicitly calls for conversation and dialogue about the issues.

iThemba Tower is aesthetically understated. Aside from its height, its "tower-ness," it does not seek to make a big splash visually or affectively. Its power is subtle, in the redeployment of the familiar into something new, and in the emotional appeal of the secret that lies at the heart of each bottle—the message from a local child or a citizen somewhere in the nation. Although sometimes

Figure 5. *iThemba Tower* in Troyeville, Johannesburg. Photograph by r1, reproduced with kind permission of r1.

lit up at night, for example, when there is a special event at the Spaza Gallery, most often the tower stands quietly, letting its new cladding speak for it. The result is an architectural sculpture that has become part of the urban land-scape of Troyeville. Here, instead of seeing human subjectivity consumed by plastic, as in *Cape Mongo*, we see a process in which human agency, collabo-ration, and communication come together to use the permanence of plastic to create messages of community and hope. The durability of plastic, its inor-ganic nature and the impossibility of its reintegration with the organic matter of the earth in this instance becomes the substance that allows for our ideas, our words, our feeling of connection, to be preserved for all eternity (unlike our bones, our flesh). It is possible to imagine a postapocalyptic cityscape in which that tower still stands, and within those bottles that adorn it the mes-sages in childish handwriting still protected, no matter what has happened around it. Whether or not this is a hopeful image is up for debate; neverthe-less, the point stands that it is thanks to the plastic from which those bottles are made that the message of hope will be preserved.

While *iThemba Tower* serves as a repository for messages of hope, it also functions as a message of hope in its own right. It serves as an example of how an inanimate material or surface can become a screen for communication. As Anna Feigenbaum writes, walls and fences that aim to separate can be used by human agents in different ways, most notably as surfaces for communication (Feigenbaum, 2012). Where the Mexico border wall, or the Israeli occupation wall, or the eight-foot-high walls topped with electric fences around the homes of the rich in Johannesburg seek to separate, all it takes is a person with a can of spray-paint to use those boundaries to say something else, and thereby to communicate across the separation and turn the barrier into a medium. To speak, to signify, to be seen or heard, and possibly understood: these hopes underwrite all forms of human communication. When we retheorize walls as surfaces for communication, as well as tools of separation and the exercise of power, it becomes possible to integrate a more hopeful set of possibilities into our understandings of material structures. Similarly, the creative and community-driven reappropriation of the broken telecommunications tower allows us to rethink what communication means, and how we share our thoughts, hopes, and ideas. As infrastructure, the broken tower, itself discarded and useless, has been appropriated for a new kind of public connection. What *iThemba Tower* teaches us is that postconsumer trash (both infrastructural and consumerist) can become a resource in more ways than one. As a material for art-making: of course. But also, crucially, as a medium for communication across time, from one generation to the next, as well as within the local geography of a community. From this perspective, trash is a cultural as well as economic resource, something that can be used to communicate as well as sold as a commodity. This means that the materiality of disposed plastic bottles can allow for new ways of forging connections and shared understandings.

The discussion in this section has explored how artworks made from trash are a key example of how reuse can function artistically. While almost all artworks using rubbish as found material comment on excess and wastefulness in the consumer economy, they also hold the potential to serve as surfaces for communication, and as evocative commentaries on how rubbish integrates materially and aesthetically with subjectivity. Garbage-art reuses waste rather than recycles it. What forms of agency might be enacted, then, through recycling and popular narratives about its importance and role in the economy? We now turn to this question.

RECYCLE TO EMPOWER? OWNING LABOR IN THE NEW ECONOMY

The work of recycling has been present, though less visible, behind the two media narratives that have been explored thus far in this chapter: reduce, reuse. Zero-waste aficionados rely on the existence of recycling programs in their cities to take care of a big portion of their personal waste. And artists using rubbish to create need to source it from somewhere; r1 explicitly collaborated with informal waste collectors to build *iThemba Tower*.

Recycling is often written about from a macro- and policy perspective, and key differences are highlighted between what recycling means in "developed" and "developing" contexts (Hall, 2004; Ferrell, 2006; Morgan, 2009; MacBride, 2011). As discussed in chapter 2, the global politics of trash has typically seen the global north sending recycling to the global south (while China has made bold moves to ban all plastic waste imports from the West, it is possible that other countries may start accepting it). Although global north countries and cities tend to pride themselves on their efficient recycling cultures and systems, global south cities can lag far behind. For example, Kenya's capital city, Nairobi, has an appalling track record of waste collection, with only thirteen garbage collection trucks servicing a population of four million in 2005 (Oyake-Ombis, 2018). Although many global south cities do not have publicly administered recycling programs, they remain at the heart of the global political-economy of recycling because of the work created by private industries that sort and recycle huge amounts of trash, either imported from the West or produced by their own elites. For example, in Mumbai, India, the slums are the center of a huge hand-powered recycling industry (Boo, 2012). Workers squat on the floor to handpick through giant piles of plastic, sorting bottles, tubs, caps, and unidentifiable fragments into color-coded heaps ready for processing. Others sweat in front of furnaces to melt down aluminum cans, ready to be transformed into new products such as cooking pots. In Accra, Ghana, the neighborhood of Agbogbloshie is the global capital of e-waste recycling. Shipping containers of "secondhand" computers, mobile phones, and printers arrive from the West and are added to the e-waste dump. Workers dissemble the electronics, and burn away plastic casings to get to the valuable metal components inside. Exposed to the toxic fumes released by burning, and many other hazards, the boys and men who work the Agbogbloshie e-waste dump consider it the only economic opportunity they have (McElvaney, 2014; Reid, 2014; Minter, 2016). In short, although some cities and nations in the global north may consider themselves to be leaders in cultures of recycling, it is in cities in the global south that the dirty, dangerous, and difficult work of the actual recycling takes place. And it is in those cities—so often negatively stereotyped by

Western observers as places of danger and dirt—that we can get some insight into what kinds of new economies, labor structures, and forms of value creation are offered by trash and its recycling.

To explore this in more detail, it is useful to examine a case study that gives some insight into what recycling work means to the people who do the actual recycling. A groundbreaking worker-owned recycling collection and processing organization is Solid Waste Collection and Handling (SWaCH) or, officially, SWaCH Seva Sahakari Sanstha Maryadit based in the city of Pune, India. SWaCH describes itself as India's first wholly owned cooperative of self-employed waste collectors. As in many global south cities, Pune sees many informal trash workers collecting waste to sell for recycling, in order to provide themselves with income to provide for their families. The SWaCH Co-op is unique in that it is made up almost entirely of women waste-pickers, who came together in 2006 in order to collectively organize their work and negotiate the terms of the service that they provide to their customers and to the city of Pune. SWaCH started in 2006 and has its roots in Kagad Kach Patra Kashtakari Panchayat (KKPKP) http://www.kkpkp-pune.org/. Instead of working individually and precariously, the SWaCH waste-pickers chose to organize in order to improve their capacity to generate income as well as their working conditions. Through owning their own cooperative, the women have been able to protect themselves from the economic and social risks of selling their labor and time to someone else.

The SWaCH collective has been held up by both the environmental and development movements as an example of what can be possible when workers' rights and environmental issues meet (Kilby, 2013; Chikarmane, 2016; Harshey & Sharma, 2016). The SWaCH collective, as well as excelling in the realm of self-organizing and profiting directly from their own labor, is also unsurprisingly very good at telling its own stories. On its website, it explains the structure and functions of the Collective, celebrates its achievements, and invites visitors to get to know the women who do the "dirty" work of collecting and sorting waste. The image on their website homepage, reproduced in fig. 6, celebrates the number of households covered (800,000), the number of waste-pickers integrated into the union (3,541), and the number of metric tons of waste they recycle annually. The co-op website explains how, using mostly handcarts (though the Collective also owns a small truck), the waste-workers collect refuse from homes in Pune, and then take it for sorting. Wet waste (that is foodstuffs and other organic matter) is separated from recyclables,

Figure 6. The portrait of SWaCH waste collectors included on the home page of www.swachcoop.com. Reproduced with kind permission of the SWaCH Cooperative. Photograph by Brodie Talbot.

which are further sorted into categories to be sent to paper, plastic, tin, or glass recycling depots). It is notable that the middle-class households in Pune serviced by SWaCH do not separate their trash before collection—sorting is part of the service provided. The SWaCH website also describes other innovative waste-related services they provide, for example, the delivery of bundles of "red-dot" bags made from recycled newspaper, which can be used for the disposal of used menstrual products (this service perhaps inspired by the unpleasant work of having to sort dirty sanitary towels from empty plastic water bottles), the collection and disposal of e-waste, and the generation of biogas from waste, and even school training programs to teach children about smart and ecological attitudes toward waste.

On the SWaCH website, a page is included titled, "Meet Sughandhabai," a waste-picker and cooperative member. Narrated as "A day in my life," the article tracks the work of a co-op member from when she awakes at 6:00 a.m. to see to the needs of her family in her own home, to arriving at work to clock in, then to setting off on the waste-collection rounds.

From 9.00 to 1.00 pm she goes door to door and collects waste from citizens. In some places, she collects the waste at the gate. In others, she has to go from house to house, or up and down the steps in highrise apartment buildings. She segregates wet and dry waste as she collects it. (https://swa-chcoop.com/sugandhabai/)

The handcarts converge on the co-op truck, where the waste is collated, and after a lunch break, the workers once again get busy, this time with sorting the waste that was collected that morning.

Here, she sorts waste into several categories—like plastic, paper/cardboard, cloth, leather, metal, etc. Each of these categories gets further sub-divided according to its recyclability and the use it will be put to later—and you have to be an expert to do this fine sorting! For example, let's take plastic. The plastic we throw away is carefully divided into:

- Main: All kinds of coloured plastic bags.
- Kadkadi: PET bottles, Bisleri bottles, plastic jars, ice creams cups, etc.
- Phuga: dirty/broken plastic bottles, low grade plastic, broken plastic toys, Parachute oil bottles, Head and Shoulders shampoo bottles, etc.

Each is kept in a different pile to be later sold to the scrap dealer who offers different rates for different kinds of waste. (https://swachcoop.com/sugandhabai/)

This narrative of the day-in-the-life of the waste-pickers is very matter of fact. It is bookended by comments about how Sughandabhai, before and after the full day of hard physical labor she undertakes, also has to do labor at home—filling water, preparing food, seeing to the needs of her children. This narrative is echoed in a thirteen-minute film included on the website as a link, *Amhi SWaCH/We, SWaCH* (Amit Thavraj 2010, Marathi/English), which "documents the door-to-door collection work of the collective" (https://swachcoop.com/resources/).

As these various narratives included on the SWaCH website show, the collective's many innovations and income-generating activities linked to recycling are evidence of the huge amount of dignity that can result from a sense of ownership of one's labor. But of course, the labor of recycling needs to be considered in context. In the case of SWaCH, the cultural and social context within which the co-op members work is a historical legacy of caste, and a contemporary reality of huge income inequality and limited employment opportunities linked thereto. The social system of caste historically predetermined the kinds of work a person could do and remains powerful in the organization of economic opportunity in India. As Arundhati Roy writes, searingly, it was caste that categorized some human beings as only fit to carry away the shit of others (Roy, 2016: 36), and in today's India, Dalit (so-called low caste) people remain marginalized, discriminated against, and excluded (Still, 2015). Dalit women, in particular, perform "under-paid, often degraded work" in the informal sector, which "remains unrecognised and undervalued" (Gopal, 2013: 91). There are very few people who would choose to work with waste. In all cultures, dealing with rubbish is seen as less auspicious, as a "yardstick of social status" (Frayne, 2015). In the context of the unique form of neoliberalism characterizing contemporary India, the labor and time of poor women is treated as a commodity for sale for the lowest possible price. Some Dalit women are employed in order to clean types of human excrement, such as soiled menstruation products, from the households of privileged women who can afford to outsource that work to someone else. In both the global north and south, it is typical for middle-class women to outsource various forms of domestic labor, from childcare to cooking to cleaning and waste management, to poorer migrant (international or domestic) or local women (Anderson, 2000; Momsen, 2003). The SWaCH waste-pickers are caught in this gendered global political-economy, yet they succeed in determining their own futures, and producing conditions of work in which their value is both recognized and deployed for their own benefit. As well as providing an inspiring model for thinking about how human innovation, passion, and creativity, as well as collectively organized action can deal cleverly with both systemic economic oppression and waste in ways that support humans to reach their full potential, the SWaCH collective also provides an example for thinking about practical possibilities for employment opportunities linked to waste collection and recycling.

The politics of class and caste, gender and domesticity in this case study are clear: the women who are part of the collective are up against a number of social forces that place them into positions of service, to their husbands, families, and their upper-caste clients. Nevertheless, it is clear from the self-representation of the SWaCH collective that they do not consider their work to be in any way less than respectable.

This is most likely due to the full sense of ownership that they have over their own labor—studies of women's cooperatives in India have found that they can broaden their social inclusion and empowerment (Datta & Gailey, 2012) within an awareness of their limitations (Mayoux, 1995). Although marginalized members of a society in which their lesser worth has been crystallized over centuries into a seemingly unchangeable system that allows little prospect for self-development or work other than at the lowest end of the social spectrum, the SWaCH workers nevertheless refuse to be humiliated or denigrated by it. Although the choices open to them are limited, they still approach their work and income generation with a full sense of agency and choice. To some extent, this could be the result of a certain pragmatism. They live in a highly unequal society, with very limited employment opportunities for people (low-caste women in specific) who have been systemically excluded from education and other forms of social privilege; this society is characterized by high levels of consumption by the middle classes, resulting in large amounts of trash. That trash needs to be dealt with, and collecting and recycling it is a viable form of income generation. Choosing dignity and self-actualization in that work is the only way to stand tall and command respect: one may as well own one's own labor if this is the only form of work available. This shows that even in highly exploitative systems—and with India's history of caste exclusion and oppression combined with the huge inequalities exacerbated by the expansion of neoliberal economics since the 1990s—it is possible for marginalized subjects to claim agency and have control over their lives. As this case study shows, it is trash that made that possible.

> In an era of economic rationalism [...]: waste only matters when it can be made profitable. But how can the economic value of recycling be separated from its ethical significance? Especially when one acknowledges that recycling is only possible due to the voluntary contributions of households, to the ethical commitment of people to sorting their waste out of concern for the environment. In the case of recycling, economics and ethical values depend on each other. (Hawkins & Muecke, 2003: x)

In the case of the self-employed recyclers of Pune, economic need combines with the ethic of entrepreneurship to make recycling a viable stream of income generation. Although they are structurally limited by the kinds of work that they are able to do, through their agency and activism the SWaCH women have turned rubbish into a resource from which they can claim dignity and independence; they have also chosen how they tell their story. Though some might see the recycling work that they do as low-status, the self-representational work of the SWaCH women makes the claim that they are experts, "trashologists," akin to the highly educated researchers at the University of Arizona's Garbage Project, who also spend their days sorting through trash and obsessively assigning each piece of litter from the garbage bag into one of

"150 specific coded categories" (Rathje & Murphy, 2001: 21) and "transforming raw garbage into data" (Rathje & Murphy, 2001: 22). Their intricate knowledge of the detritus of consumer culture—the various objects and materials that are thrown by a rich person into a trash can then forgotten, which once having exited the suburban homes of Pune become a kind of public property (Rathje & Murphy, 2001: 23)—allows them to cleverly transform it into an object of value that not only earns them income but also buys a kind of freedom. This insight into the economic opportunities made possible by overconsumption is far ahead of the thinking of most privileged subjects, who remain trapped in the tunnel vision of consumption: buy, consume, discard, repeat. In this wasteful process, it is not only material rubbish that is produced, but also forms of value that are lost. If there was a deeper knowledge and understanding not only of the damage being caused by trash but its actual economic value— how many rupees per kilogram—it is possible that the people throwing away an object might think twice before they do. Perhaps the middle classes need to become trashologists and learn to pay close attention to the trash created, how to recycle it, and seeing what it says about society, if we are to aim for a world in which we survive what, by all implications, will be a very dire future. As we have seen from looking at the narratives of self-employment shared by the SWaCH women on their website, recycling work puts individuals into direct contact with rubbish in ways that can be economically and socially empowering. Although the work might appear distasteful to middle-class observers, it is honorable, and deserves to be recognized—as the women demand—as a crucial economic activity in the age of waste.

Like artists who reuse waste, and eco-consumers who seek to reduce their waste footprint, the SWaCH recyclers also contribute in significant ways to a radical rethinking of human work and activity in relation to rubbish. To bring the discussion together, the remainder of this chapter considers how these forms of waste-action contribute to theories of labor, subjectivity, and moral agency.

WASTE-WORK AND WASTEFUL/L SUBJECTS

Up to this point, this chapter has explored different examples of subject-making through trash. We have met an upper-class New Yorker who has built a brand around her ability to reduce the scale of trash for which she is personally responsible; we have met artists who turn trash into the raw materials for works of art that challenge ideas of beauty, explore social responses to environmental issues, and destabilize subjectivity by reminding us of the links we have to the world of rubbish objects; and we have met innovative entrepreneurs who have produced income and a certain degree of autonomy through their work with garbage. Notably, all these forms of waste-related agency have been narrated and self-represented through media forms, from social media profiles to websites to artworks to short films. What all of these forms of action in relation to consumer waste share is an orientation that privileges labor. The existence of waste requires some kind of work whether to eliminate, remove or sort it. Waste therefore produces labor. As a shorthand, I would like to refer to these various intersecting forms of labor required by rubbish as *waste-work*, which I define as any type of material or aesthetic labor produced by the existence of waste in the world. Waste-work brings together subject and object in increasingly significant ways. Some critics, including those on the green left, denigrate consumption and the crass materialism of avaricious consumers, hungry for short-lived pleasures such as fast-food packaged in disposable plastic, as the source of many of the planet's ills. In this narrative, the blame for waste is placed on consumers and their lack of self-restraint, their lack of care for anything beyond their own pleasure, their own homes, their own families. Consumers are characterized as the worst of the worst: selfish, small-minded, individualistic, wasteful. As creators of trash, they are the ultimate litterbugs, desecrating shared public space with no thought to the consequences of their short-lived pleasures. In contrast, waste-work offers a new, more optimistic, narrative about how rubbish can forge subjectivity: through creativity, entrepreneurship, and a pragmatic relationship to the potential, not only the pitfalls, of trash.

A significant part of waste-work is material. The SWaCH workers and street-recyclers in Johannesburg who helped create iThemba Tower spend many hours a day collecting, hauling and sorting trash produced by other people, using their bodies for hard manual labor and being proximate to unpleasant and hazardous items. They become intimate with the contents of their customers' rubbish bins, and literally touch each piece of garbage as they sort it into wet and dry, plastic and paper, compostable and recyclable. The people who threw them away no longer think about the used menstrual pad, the dirty handkerchief, the mango peels or chicken bones, the empty tube of toothpaste. Like other forms of unpleasant domestic labor (washing clothes, scrubbing toilets, peeling potatoes) those who have thrown away the items have outsourced to someone else the work required to decide how to dispose of those things. This outsourcing of unpleasant work from the upper and middle classes to the lower classes mirrors the outsourcing of recycling from the global north to the global south. While middle-class subjects in Pune pay someone else to do the dirty work of recycling for them, upper-middle class subjects such as Zero Trash Girl and the fine artists who work with trash as a medium are deploying their own time and energy into these tasks, instead, as a statement of moral responsibility. Lauren Singer spends her productive laboring time into making careful decisions about what items to buy and what not, in service of her ideological commitment to not produce trash that will be sent to the landfill. But as her incredibly successful social media presence shows, perhaps even more of her time goes into the aesthetic and communicative work required to create and entrench her brand, and produce a consistently appealing and inspiring narrative on social media. Like other internet celebrities or social media influencers, Singer is required to put time and effort into her communications and to consistently innovate in terms of ways to monetize the influence and reach that she has built up over time. Like the SWaCH women, she is an entrepreneur who is taking charge of her own body and labor and using it to generate an income for herself. Similarly, artists like Francois Knoetze, Kai Lossgott, and r1 are deploying their aesthetic labor and artistic sensibilities (as well as their bodies through the performance and making processes) in order to at once produce new ways of thinking and making with trash, and new stories about how trash fits into our societies. Through creating fantastical creatures from waste and inserting their bodies into them (in the case of Knoetze) or using their bodies as tools for the collection, cataloging, and display of the little bits of trash crushed into the corners of streets (as in the case of Lossgott), artists who work with trash make explicit the unbreakable links between material objects and human identities. Human beings are comprised of the matter that we consume, even when we throw it away. Consumer subjectivity does not end at the trash can, it persists way beyond it into work done in the recycling plant and for and by the aesthetic narratives that we produce and share.

Both Singer and the SWaCH women insert their bodies into the heart of the trash narrative in gendered ways. Sughandabhai and colleagues by using their physical strength to haul and sort, Singer by putting her face and body in the center of the visual narrative organized around her zero-waste efforts and messages. A young, white, attractive woman, Singer uses portraiture and self-portraiture (in true millennial style), often showing off her slim body and pretty face, to promote the appeal of the trash-free lifestyle. This kind of communicative labor is increasingly common in the highly mediated, social media-driven consumer economy of the global north. Young women choose to share images of themselves on social media, and use that self-representation, which usually is successful because it conforms to some sense in which women are valued by the capitalist patriarchy, to generate income streams. It is notable that both forms of labor—the physical labor of the SWaCH women and the aesthetic labor of Singer—are gendered. The SWaCH women are forced by both caste and gender to work with trash, and their low status as women waste-pickers to some extent motivates their defiant self-organization. Singer, although not limited by race or class, remains obedient to heteronormative gender and beauty standards, because it works for her self-identity and the brand she is building. Because she is attractive in the sense valued by consumer culture and patriarchal power, she is able to exploit that system in a way that benefits her, by establishing her own brand and monetizing the attention she has accumulated in different ways, for example, through advertising revenue on her YouTube channel, sponsorships from various eco-brands, and promoting and selling the products and services that she offers on her website. Although limited and constrained by existing power relations in different ways, what the SWaCH women and Singer share is that they each are in control of their own labor. Rather than being alienated in the classic sense—in which individuals are forced to sell their time and energy for a fixed hourly wage to an employer who profits from it, and in which they are not able to tangibly connect with the outputs of their work, like the production-line worker who over and over screws a certain bolt onto the chassis of a car but never gets to drive the finished product—both the SWaCH women and Singer have direct control over the outputs of their work. Sughandabhai and her coworkers set their own working conditions and negotiate the prices for which they sell the recyclables directly with the scrap dealers, and they are free to come up with and implement ideas for new income streams. Likewise, Singer is able to manifest her vision and control how she spends her time. Both trash-workers are also in charge of how they are represented in the media, and each devotes significant time to communicating with the broader public about their trash-work, as well as setting the agenda for how they will be portrayed and perceived.

Both the SWaCH women and Zero Trash Girl show us that waste-work is central to the production of subjectivity. "The shifting and contingent meanings for waste, the innumerable ways in which it can be produced, reveal it not as essentially bad but as subject to relations. What is rubbish in one context is perfectly useful in another" (Hawkins, 2006: 10). Whether the work required by the presence of trash is the result of a pragmatic need to generate income or an ideological need to align practice with morality, senses of self are produced through forms of income-generating action related to trash. Because the forms of trash being dealt with by these women is postconsumer, it is necessary to acknowledge the emergence of entirely new forms of consumer subjectivities in the relation of self with waste.

I summarize these new subjectivities as *the wasteful/l self*. Like the individual in consumer culture, this self is constituted by relationships to material objects, only this time those objects are the remnants of commodities rather than the commodities themselves. Up to this point in consumer culture theory, consumers have been conceptualized as "wasteful" selves—largely self-interested actors who make decisions in relation to the world around them in ways that allow for the expression of identity, the forging of relationships, and the seeking of pleasure through consumption, oblivious to or uncaring of, the garbage that results from it. What happens after the consumption takes place falls outside of existing theories of consumer subjectivity. The rise of environmental awareness has transformed the consumer notion of self-hood into one that is malicious and wasteful; that privileges the various operations of self over the destruction that is caused to the planet after the consumption is over and the trash thrown away. In contrast to this wasteful self is the waste-*full* self. Waste-full subjects are not alienated from the trash they produce, or that is produced by others, and have forged productive strategies for dealing with, indeed profiting from, it. Although Singer has zero-trash in her life in the material sense, in the discursive sense her life is absolutely full of trash, indeed it is entirely organized around it, just like the SWaCH women's lives are organized around waste. In the waste-full self, new forms of trash-centered subjectivity emerge, which when enacted through media narratives provide examples of how work and self-identity can be productive and empowering aspects of global and local economies in the age of the Anthropocene.

How then does this wasteful/l subject, occupied with these different forms of waste-work, morally orient herself toward the condition of the Anthropocene? The next section explores how waste-work and wasteful/l subjects narrate what trash means in an existential sense.

INDIVIDUALS IN THE TRASHOCALYPSE: WORKING WITH HORROR OR HOPE?

Many have written about the horrors of the age of the Anthropocene, from the slow violence of climate change (Nixon, 2013) to the looming environmental and social devastation that will result (Zylinska, 2014; Bonneuil & Fressoz, 2016; Morton, 2016; Wark, 2016; Dellasala & Goldstein, 2017). Although many have also written about trash—its presence, its aesthetic, its politics, its economics—it is necessary to pay more attention to the question of the role that garbage plays in our understanding of what the Anthropocene means. Humans are affecting the geological and climactic structures of the earth in ways that are irreversible. Trash is possibly the most visible material trace left behind by the operations of capitalism and consumption. In rubbish we see evidence of what we do to the world around us—both individually and on an epic collective scale. In this sense, garbage makes manifest the apocalyptic vision of a future world devastated by huge-scale social and environmental problems of our own making. Such scenes are routinely captured by photographers at landfills. In October 2014, *The Guardian* published an interactive online photo-essay, documenting the largest and most toxic garbage dumps in the world, including infographics of their size (represented by symbols of football fields, showing how many each landfill would cover) and photographs of the spaces peopled by individuals who work the dumps to scavenge recyclable materials (Blight, 2014). The images of the garbage dumps are bleak indeed: although dotted at different points on the map of the world, they share in common an unmistakable aesthetic. Smoking or burning piles of garbage tower over the men, women, and children working the dumps, sometimes accompanied by dogs, cows, or pigs foraging for food. Garbage trucks dump yet more, on top of mountains of broken and decaying materials.

This vision of a world colonized by garbage in which other forms of life and society are lost, buried under the waste, a future scenario in which we are no longer able to feed ourselves, and the few human survivors that are left must resort to picking through the smoldering remains of garbage dumps can be summarized as a *trashocalypse*. It cannot be denied that these huge garbage dumps exists, and that they are growing. As such, they represent one tangible possible future for human experience, especially near urban centers. Is humanity destined for a world that, as the Comaroffs suggest, will evolve toward "African" modes of precariousness and survival (Comaroff & Comaroff, 2012)? Will the wealthy north have to resort, like "most of the Third World," to "a slopping-and-scavenging system" (Rathje & Murphy, 2001: 40), or perhaps more realistically, *when* will this need to happen, and *who* will do the physical labor that will be required? Is thinking about how we need to work with rubbish apocalyptic, or is it part of a set of pragmatic and moral responses to cleaning up our mess and forging a closer relationship to material culture, both in terms of what we acquire and what we throw away? As the discussion in this chapter has shown, existing structures of privilege shape the moral responses that people have to the problem of trash. Privileged consumers may, as they develop awareness about the scale of rubbish, adjust their consumption behaviors and come up with innovative and creative ways to lessen their waste and ultimately, the landfill. Various communications and artistic campaigns may in turn contribute to a greater public awareness of the looming trashocalypse. But those who are forced by history and circumstance to exist at the many precarious edges of capitalism, such as the SWaCH waste-pickers and the many human beings eking out a living on rubbish dumps around the world, have no such privilege. Theirs is not a sanitized set of options to reduce, reuse, or recycle; they have to scavenge what little value they can find at the dump in order to survive another day.

The supreme injustice of waste-work is that it is the wealthy—some of whom are now valiantly holding up recycling as a solution to the trashocalypse—who have put all that rubbish on those dumps. And it is the poor who not only have to cart the stuff there, but pick through it once it has arrived. Through no choice of their own, the poor are engaged in forms of work that mitigate the damaging presence of rubbish, while at the same time being most at risk from it. Most economically underprivileged people already exercise a "zero-waste" lifestyle by virtue of the circumstances of their existence. If we accept that the poor consume less and therefore produce less trash, should we not argue that it is precisely the responsibility of high-income and privileged people to take on zero-waste work, in order to start to make some amends for the disproportionate share of trash that they have created through their high-impact lifestyles up to this point? While all humans bear some moral responsibility for dealing with waste, arguably those that have been privileged due to the exploitations of the global economic system bear a greater proportion, and should work to become more conscious about the waste they produce and how they dispose of it. Various types of recycling offer tangible strategies to raising this consciousness and changing everyday consumption and disposal practices of well-off people. Upper- and middle-class consumers, and even those who aspire to climbing the social ladder through consumption, are morally required to consider the extent to which their consumption creates the mountains of trash that our indigent fellow humans are forced to pick in order to make a living. The narratives of agency and action in relation to waste-work explored in this chapter make a significant contribution to that agenda of consciousness-raising.

In the various forms of postconsumer subjectivity produced through forms of work and cultural production centered on trash, we also see the seeds of an optimistic narrative about how humanity can reengineer a relationship with waste. In the arc of long time, the period that we have collectively spent turning the planet into a trash heap is a mere few seconds. Although, media narratives are drawing attention the scale of the trash produced by global capitalism and consumer culture, as it fills up not only the landfills hidden on the outskirts of cities but also formerly pristine natural environments, we still as a species need to come to terms with what it will take to clean up our mess. The waste-reduction and transformation efforts that have been looked at in this chapter hint at the emergence of new forms of object-centered subjectivity. This can be incredibly empowering for those spearheading those practices. But at the heart of the hopeful narratives, the pragmatic and doable strategies that we see enacted by role models working toward a less wasteful future, we can also identify a kind of horror. It is impossible to consider the positive potential of recycling subjectivities without also acknowledging the scale of the problem that humanity has created. This problem is at once the product of and complicit in the machinery of global neoliberal capital, which has driven the production and overproduction of billions of single- and short-use commodities, and in the process created a culture of disposal that sometimes seems irreversible.

How many zero-trash girls do we need to stem the growth of landfills? How many self-employed and collectively mobilized Sughandabhais in every city in the world? Is it inevitable that trash will always need to be collected and taken away, that middle-class households will always be able and willing to pay to outsource that dirty work to people of a lower social status? Will trash always be in our lives? Of course, the answer is yes, because the one thing that humans always produce is some kind of waste. The question is, therefore, one of scale—how much trash will be in our lives and how will we deal with it? If the world continues to be organized as it is—around industrial extraction of resources, relentless production, the distribution and overconsumption of commodities across borders, and the proliferation of gargantuan landfills—then it seems that the outlook for better management of rubbish remains relatively apocalyptic. It will take a major consumption revolution to change things: consumers will have to become so voraciously moral in how they spend their money and which commodities they choose (in terms of how they are packaged, whether they are recyclable, and of how much waste was produced in the process of manufacture), that a collective movement is formed that forces the supply side of the chain to radically change how it does business and how much waste it produces. Would it be pessimistic to predict that the chances of this consumer revolution happening seem quite slim? It is relatively privileged subjects—like Singer, like professional artists—who seem to have the social and cultural resources to think deeply about the meanings of waste in their personal lives and immediate social environments, and who have the economic wherewithal to afford eco-friendly alternatives. Everyone else probably aspires to fully entering into the consumer economy and dreams of being able to load a shopping cart with the various products available, chucking away what is left over without worrying about where it goes. Yet, entering into the consumer economy as a full participant also means entering into the trash economy as a full participant. Whether or not the growing middle classes of the global south will be able to leapfrog the landfill approach and enter straight into the recycling economy will be a matter not so much of individual choice and conscientization, but a matter of government policy and regulation.

This is not to say that there is no role for individual agency and the media narratives that provide new options for people to think about their role in consumer culture. Artists are particularly important actors in this matrix, because through their creative works they are able to invite a level of engagement and response that touches humans in their hearts, through their aesthetic sensibilities. Similarly, media celebrities like Singer also work to inspire and offer role models for new orientations toward trash and consumption that could help to shift ideas about what is and is not possible, what is and is not necessary. Within these mediated subjectivities, all reorganizing their senses of self in one way or another in relation to trash and the threat that it offers our survival as a species, are invitations to have hope, and to contribute in tangible and positive ways to changing the status quo rather than simply accepting it in a fateful manner. But perhaps the most inspiring message of hope comes through in the work of the SWaCH collective, which remind us that not only is it possible to deal with trash cultures in ways that are sustainable and that create real economic opportunity for marginalized people, but that trash has *value*. This means that if our attitudes toward trash shifts, we will be able to identify ways to make trash work productively for the economy, preferably to the benefit of all rather than only the benefit of some. This will require a radical overhaul of our attitudes toward the economy, such that we prioritize opportunities for individuals to own and benefit from their own labor, and also so that trash becomes seen not as "worthless rubbish, but [...] potential resources" (Hawkins 11). On a practical level this means composting and recycling in every home, and self-owned waste redeployment collectives operating in every neighborhood. We need to strive toward a balance between collective solutions and individual actions. Media narratives invite "the waste-making subject [...] to change his or her mind about the status of rubbish and then voluntarily transform his or her actions" (Hawkins, 2006: 11), but this needs to go hand in hand with systemic, institutional changes to how garbage is handled collectively. We need to address both garbage elimination as an "art of existence" (Hawkins, 2006: 24) and find ways to encourage and support the emergence of organized responses to the wasted economic opportunities buried in the piles of trash smoldering on the edges of our cities.

As this chapter has shown, reducing waste, reusing trash, recycling garbage all afford huge opportunities for narratives of agency and hope, positive action by individuals and collectives in the service of imagining, and working toward, another possible world. Although media representations of individualized forms of waste-work might not achieve this independently, they play an important role in sharing inspiring new ideas about how consumer subjectivity and agency, in relation to rubbish, really matter.

3

Hedonism and Luxury

Waste and Its Traces in Narratives of Pleasure

Pleasure is perhaps one of the most obvious themes that come up in the scholarly examination of consumer culture. Indeed, it is this notion—that we all desire and deserve pleasure—that animates most of the commercial communication efforts powering the engines of global cultures of consumption. Consumers are constantly told by brands, advertising, and lifestyle media that they deserve to indulge and gratify their every wish, and that the accumulation of objects and experiences will make their lives more beautiful and pleasurable, will produce happy selves, families, and relationships (Iqani, 2012). Trash and waste exist at the other end of this continuum entirely. There is little that is pleasurable about garbage. Most of us try to remove trash from our lives as quickly as possible. The trash can, the garbage heap, the landfill—these are places of decay and rotting, places that humans only go if forced to scavenge in some way for survival, rarely through choice. While it may seem strange to claim that we need to find a way to theorize the relationship between pleasure and garbage, pleasure-oriented consumption is arguably one of the key causes of the planetary garbage crisis.

This chapter explores different ways in which trash interjects into media narratives about highly pleasurable aspects of consumer culture, and aims to open up new avenues for thinking about how the physiological-emotional affects and material effects of consumer culture are intermeshed. Luxury is often equated with excess; some moral orientations equate pleasure seeking itself with wastefulness (Adams, 2012). Further, luxurious and pleasurable consumption produces material formations of waste: think only of the crates of empty bottles that need to be carted away after any party. It is worth reflecting on whether luxurious consumption is always wasteful and waste-producing, and how it differs from other forms of material culture. Arguably, it is also necessary to specifically theorize the kinds of waste produced by luxury consumption. The pursuit of pleasure almost inevitably produces waste; questions then arise regarding both moral orientations toward that waste and whether and how it comes into the public eye. In order to develop this avenue of exploration, this chapter examines case studies in which media narratives about putatively hedonistic and pleasurable consumer practices and experiences focus, in one way or another, on garbage. How the rubbish is dealt with, materially and narratively, within these luxury consumption cultures forms the key focus of the discussion. Case studies examined are media narratives about luxury tourism on tropical islands and hedonistic festival culture. These facilitate a discussion of the themes of excess, responsibility, and moral orientations toward the trash produced by pleasure-oriented consumption. In particular, the chapter will articulate the ways in which trash-traces produced by the pursuit of pleasure are made visible in popular culture, and how discourses about postleisure waste are socially constructed in public narratives. In turn, these will allow for a deeper understanding of the links between hedonistic consumption and waste to emerge.

The pursuit of pleasure produces waste: after champagne has been imbibed, a bottle needs to be recycled. Luxury holidays require jet flights, which in turn require more and more oil to be extracted from increasingly inaccessible places, processed into jet fuel, and burned to power the travel. It is important to note that most luxurious consumption that takes place globally is enacted by the middle and upper classes, which form a small percentage of the total global population. Most human beings living on the planet are not voracious consumers, pursuing pleasure at any cost. While the 99 percent struggle to feed and clothe their children, the 1 percent enjoy champagne parties on yachts (Dorling, 2015). It is the well-off and wealthy in both the global north and south who are the main consumers of nonnecessary commodities and who produce the largest amounts of waste. These are the consumers who replace their smartphones, tablets, and laptop computers every couple of years, who thoughtlessly throw away a couple of disposable coffee cups or soft drink cans every day, who take holidays that require air travel. This minority of human beings produce the majority of waste present on the planet. It could be argued that coming up with new social and cultural formations for dealing with that waste is therefore disproportionately their responsibility, rather than, say, the responsibility of the poor and economically precarious. If you don't know where your next meal is coming from, or when clean water will be delivered to your community, and you suffer under a lack of delivery of basic public services such as rubbish collection, recycling is unlikely to be a top priority. And the pleasure of enjoying a rare can of Coca-Cola will become politicized in ways that do not apply to those who simply grab yet another can from their own fridge. In other words, it can be argued that it is precisely because the rich are responsible for the mountains of trash on the planet that they should be at the forefront of strategies to address it for the betterment of all. This argument parallels the kind of claim made by global south nations in international talks about climate change: if we didn't cause the mess, surely, we shouldn't have to take equal responsibility for cleaning it up (Böhm, 2015)? Of course, no one is emotionally capable of thinking constantly about the collective problems we face. Most people want to live their lives more or less selfishly, looking after their own needs and the needs of their families, and alongside whatever work is required to survive, to have a good time as often as possible. It is worth, therefore, looking at the ways in which people seek pleasure, and considering what relation that holds to the cultural politics of rubbish.

> When [...] we see images of mountains made of garbage, nature is framed as dead or definitely on its last legs, it's difficult not to feel a sense of despair or grief. While the political intention of these stories might be to shock us into action, their impact is often overwhelming and immobilizing. They can perpetuate the very relation to nature they seek to challenge: alienated distance and disinterest. When the exploitative force of economic power and human destruction is so overcoded why bother contesting it? You may as well just keep shopping. (Hawkins, 2006: 9)

Shopping *and* partying *and* traveling. And sometimes shopping for parties and holidays. One thing the global consuming class is exceptionally skilled at is having a good time—indulging in the pleasures of tourism and related forms of entertainment, from clubbing to music shows and festivals. The global middle class subject is very good at taking the time and space to seek pleasure—new experiences through traveling, relaxing in the sun on putatively untouched tropical beaches, heading off to escapist entertainment festivals to get drunk and high and try to forget about everything that is wrong with the world. How does waste figure—if at all—in the picture of global middle class consumption, and what can that tell us about both the politics of trash and the politics of mediated consumer culture in the age of the Anthropocene?

Garbage is usually associated with poverty. In South Africa, the oppressive racist apartheid government forced the majority black population to live in "townships" far from the "white" cities and towns—close enough to commute to work, but far enough to be deprived of public services (Swartz, 2009). In the "townships," which have by and large remained under-resourced despite almost three decades of democratic government, basic garbage collection is one of the services that were historically not provided, and this legacy still defines the urban landscape in some townships (Bonner & Segal, 1998). Similarly, in Cairo, poor neighborhoods are characterized by an excess of rubbish and pollution (Kuppinger, 2018). In cities in which public infrastructure and services have not been prioritized by their governments and in which citizens are too economically disadvantaged to demand better, it is common to see litter and rubbish on the streets. In contrast, towns and neighborhoods inhabited by well-off, demanding citizens and characterized by privilege and well-resourced, well-run public services are typically cleaner. An incorrect way to read the "messier" appearance of poor areas and the "cleaner" appearance of rich areas would be to ascribe the qualities of dirt and cleanliness to conditions of poverty and wealth, respectively. Rubbish is visible in poverty-stricken communities because they are spatially and socially marginalized, and underserved by their governments, while the rich have the resources to demand and pay for collection services. Rich people don't have trash around them because they typically pay poor people to take it away from their sight. As such, they get to enjoy the privilege of living in beautiful and trash-free environments, which likely skews their entire sense of the world and how much trash is actually in it. This extends to their leisure activities. Rich people like to have a nice time, to enjoy the finer things in life. This is true for most people, but the wealthy have the resources to actualize it. Precisely because the middle and upper classes are the main cause of excess waste, it is necessary to examine how the practices that cause that waste are publically imagined and visualized. To what extent do popular media narratives make the connection between the pleasures that the well-off get from consumption and the waste that it causes? In order to pursue this line of questioning, then, it helps to start with the pleasure and see where it takes us, waste-wise.

This chapter explores two key leisure activities enjoyed by the global consuming classes: entertainment festivals and tourism. Through a discussion of how waste comes into media narratives about both, the argument is made that middle-class pleasure-oriented consumption practices can no longer be theorized without putting rubbish in the picture.

AFTER THE PARTY: THE LITTERSCAPE POST-GLASTONBURY AND OTHER FESTIVALS

There are hundreds of entertainment festivals that feature in the arts and culture calendars of the middle classes around the world (Gilmore & Proyen, 2005; Robinson, 2015). Organized around different cultural economies, these festivals are major sites of mass consumption of the entertainment being offered and the various commodities and services on offer in relation to the performances. Festival culture provides an opportunity for middle- and upper-class people to "escape" from their everyday lives, their jobs, their responsibilities at home and in their communities and to have fun. In Europe and North America, huge music festivals attract up to hundreds of thousands of fans, who camp in fields for days on end to hear their favorite bands play, to socialize and party. Festivals are big business, responsible for bringing about £4 billion into the British economy in 2017, according to one study (Ellis-Petersen, 2017). Festival culture, especially in Britain, is closely tied to the cultural economy of music and youth culture. Tapping into the rebellious spirit of youth and their desire for pleasure, fun, and parties, festivals provide a ready-packaged experience of freedom, usually promising an "anything goes" hedonistic culture within the boundaries of the event, and an escape from the "real" world.

One of the most famous music festivals in the world is the Glastonbury Festival of Contemporary Performing Arts, known colloquially simply as Glastonbury, which happens annually on Worthy Farm in Somerset, England. The festival attracts around 200,000 revelers every year, and is usually broadcast live on British television and radio, covering the performances of all of the biggest music stars of the moment. At Glastonbury, "unbridled hedonism fizzes from every corner" (Hutchinson, 2015); the event overall and the many curated spaces within the festival attract famous DJs and performers from around the world, who play music designed to transport revelers into ecstatic dance all through the night and past sunrise. The following discussion of media narratives about the waste left behind after Glastonbury Festival is synthesized from various news articles, the festival organizer's website (https://www.glastonburyfestivals.co.uk), and contextualized by my personal experience of attending the event once, in 2007. The account offered here is not ethnographic, but pieced together from publicly available media texts, with the analytic discussion accentuated, where relevant, by observations drawn from personal experience.

Alongside the mainstream music program playing at the various huge stages, zones within the festival offer other forms of creative and sometimes radical subcultural entertainment. Perhaps most legendary was the "anarchic" Lost Vagueness, a "festival within a festival" that featured "an ironic pastiche of a Las Vegas strip with casinos, theatrical bars, naked burlesque, even an "unholy" wedding chapel and a boxing ring" (Walker, 2018), which was a central feature of late-night Glastonbury decadence from the early 1990s until 2007. With drag shows, burlesque, and ballroom dancing giving way to "hedonistic anything goes parties" (Walker, 2018), Lost Vagueness remains to many the ultimate symbol of pleasure-seeking party culture at Glastonbury. The southeast corner of the festival has since been replaced with Shangri-La, where all-night raves are punctuated by increasingly spectacular installations. For example, a thirty-foot fire-breathing, aerial-circus-hosting monster-spider, called Arcadia, has since 2009 become emblematic of the unbridled party-culture of more recent years at Glastonbury, and hosted a new stage called Pangea in 2019 (Krol, 2019). Underneath this mechanical creature that towers over ravers, the Shangri-La zone (Shangri-La, 2017) hosts an ever more creative set of art installations doubling as party zones, featuring supposedly subcultural aesthetics designed to speak to the rebellious spirit of the youth, and offering stages modeled each year to mimic reality TV shows, squat parties or circuses, burlesque clubs, or high-rise towers (Britton, 2016). To many conservative onlookers, festival culture is synonymous with drug culture. Although festival organizers are usually at pains to explicitly point out that illegal substances will not be tolerated on the premises of the event, and that police will be present and will be making arrests for possession or dealing, there is no doubt that many revelers use festivals as an opportunity to get high, and combine their appreciation for the music and art on offer with recreational drug use, the two forms of entertainment melding seamlessly one into the other. Reflecting on his drug-fueled attendance of Glastonbury throughout the nineties, one anonymous reformed-festivalgoer writes, "I remember watching, entranced, as a young man bursting with entrepreneurial joy stood by the path and called out relentlessly like a melodious songbird, "Weed! Speed! Guaranteed!" (Anonymous, 2017). It is no surprise, then, that Glastonbury has been theorized as a "commodified hyper-experience" and a "modern cathedral of consumption" (Flinn & Frew, 2014: 418).

Of course, when 200,000 people gather together in an area of around three square miles, and drink, take drugs, and party hard for five days, one of the main challenges for the organizers of the event will be setting up the infrastructure to deal with the various forms of waste that are produced in great quantities. The event is a hedonistic affair, with revelers drinking alcohol, eating from takeaway food carts, and taking various other substances in pursuit of enjoyment, and as such there are millions of disposable food and drink items, and other forms of waste, that need to be thrown away and disposed of every day over five days. Media coverage during the festival tends to focus on the scale of the gathering, with television coverage of the headline acts zooming out to show the scale of the effervescent crowd. Playing Glastonbury's Pyramid Stage is considered by many artists to be the peak of their careers, as there are very few other platforms on which they can play their music to such huge crowds—usually around 120,000 people for the headline act.

In addition to the intense media attention paid to the event itself, for some media outlets, equally newsworthy is coverage of what the farm looks like *after* the party. Without hiding its perpetually sneering tone, and its critical perspective on youth culture and hedonistic forms of material consumption, British tabloid the *Daily Mail* presents a photo-heavy review of the litter-strewn landscape left behind once the festival is over (Baker, 2015). Images show one or two dazed-looking campers hauling their stuff through muddy fields strewn with litter: thousands of plastic bottles, crushed beer cups, lost Wellington boots, broken umbrellas, empty bottles, abandoned broken camping chairs, and plastic bags strewn across the muddy green fields in front of the famous Pyramid Stage. The article reports that festival organizers employ around 800 people each year to help clean up the farm after the party, and they get their ticket prices refunded if they work a certain number of shifts. During the festival, attempts are made to encourage attendees to put their trash in color-coded recycling bins. But despite this, a huge mess is left behind. The litter-strewn fields left behind by partygoers after the festival could be considered a material manifestation of the giant hangover that is most likely experienced in the bodies and emotional landscapes of those same festivalgoers.

Media images of the aftermath of Glastonbury Festival have a historical trajectory and counterpoints from elsewhere in the world. The first large-scale music festival was Woodstock, in Upstate New York in 1969, and images of the aftermath of half a million people partying in the rain and mud in a "previously untouched alfalfa field" (Robinson, 2009) were documented by photographer Bill Eppridge, who took pictures of both party and aftermath for *Life* magazine in 1969 (Estrin, 2009). It reportedly took three weeks to clean up after Woodstock; the fields were left strewn with abandoned sleeping bags and piles of rubbish (Robinson, 2009). Similarly, the huge street Carnaval in Rio de Janeiro leaves behind a huge mess that takes the city days to clean up (IB Times, 2014). Media attention is often pointed toward the aftermath of other public street parties, such as Mardi Gras in New Orleans, first celebrated in the early 1800s in the city, and now an annual carnival attraction that sees the city hosting over a million revelers. A series of historical photographs on the official Mardi Gras website show cleanup operations removing tons of trash from the streets over the years (Mardi Gras, 2017), and it is estimated that each year the party creates over 600 tons of garbage (which inevitably gets sent to landfill) (Evans, 2018). Reflecting on an ethnography of Mardi Gras, one writer notes,

> Its 2 am and I've been awake for twenty-four hours. I'm sitting on a curb surrounded by broken beads, trash and puke, looking at the street littered with scraps of paper that read "Made in China" as dangling beads drape the trees above the gutter next to me. (Redmon, 2014: 86)

While the problem of a litter-strewn landscape appears to be common to many huge parties around the world, back at Glastonbury, there is also the pervasive problem of campers who leave their tents behind. It is estimated that each year around 175,000 people camp in the fields reserved for accommodation at Glastonbury. The festival is famously muddy, as the hundreds of thousands of festivalgoers hike all day and night through damp fields from one festival zone to the other. Made damper by the perennial rain that usually defines the British summer, festivalgoers quickly churn up the mud that lies just below the surface of the grass.

After five nights of hard partying, likely not sleeping well in campsites filled with the noise of others chatting or playing music late into the night, walking miles around the festival site, moving from one performance to another, from one party area to another, it is no surprise that many festivalgoers feel very tired at the end of it all (this I can report from personal experience; I attended Glastonbury in 2007, a year fabled for extreme muddiness). The result of this exhaustion most likely combined with significant hangovers, and faced with the prospect of a walk of a couple of miles schlepping their stuff to the bus stop or train station and onward toward home, means that many festivalgoers choose to leave their tents and other camping items behind (in 2007 I did not, though I considered it for a minute, and was talked out of it by a sensible friend). Instead of packing up their camping gear, many tired and hungover festival attendees will pack only their personal effects, and leave the rest behind. The wetter the weather, the more "extreme" the camping conditions, and the more likely that tents will be left behind (Smith, 2017).

To some extent it is understandable that a drunken reveler might throw an empty beer cup on the ground, especially if the dustbins are full. But it is less easy to understand why someone would leave behind a valuable item such as a tent—which if cared for could last tens of years and be used for numerous holidays and festivals. "According to festival organizers an estimated 11 tonnes of clothes and camping gear were abandoned in 2015 including 6,500 sleeping bags, 5,500 tents, 3,500 airbeds, 2,200 chairs, 950 rolled mats and 400 gazebos" (Smith, 2017). The scale of this litter can only be made evident in long shot visuals, in quite a similar style, if not tone, to the ways in which the scale of the shared cultural experience of attending a mega-event is communicated through long shots of blissful crowds. Some media outlets (e.g., the local newspaper *Somerset Live*) publish aerial photographs of the abandoned tents in the Glastonbury camping zone. The images are compelling, showing patchworks of pale squares of grass indicating sites where tents were removed, and squares of red, blue, yellow, and gray nylon and polyester testifying to the number of tents that were left behind. This postfestival "blight" on the rural beauty of the farm takes several weeks to clean up, and reportedly costs the organizers almost £800,000 annually. Some charities have arranged to collect the left-behind tents, and donate them to people in need, such as refugees. However, as the festival's Infrastructure manager explains in a 2011 interview, most tents don't get recycled or donated because "quite a lot of them have either been ripped or actually used as toilets. So, no one wants to recycle those" (Peake, 2011). As such, they end up in landfill. Most tents are manufactured from various synthetic fibers (plastic) and as such are not biodegradable. If they end up in landfill, that is where they will stay for hundreds of years.

On the official Glastonbury website, the advice for camping includes the mild request, "Love the farm—please do not leave any kit behind when you leave the farm" (Glastonbury Festival, 2018). The 2019 Festival web page urges guests to "take it, don't leave it" in the quest for a "greener" Glastonbury that "leaves no trace."

As part of our Love Worthy Farm, Leave No Trace campaign we are trying to raise awareness of the terrible state that Worthy Farm is left in when everyone goes home after the Festival. Abandoned camping equipment and rubbish blight the beautiful green pastures of the farm. It really is very sad.

Please do your bit when you leave, take all your camping gear home and put all your rubbish in the bin bags provided by your campsite stewards. Even just five minutes of effort from each person at the Festival would make a HUGE difference (https://www.glastonburyfestivals.co.uk/information/green-glastonbury/take-it-dont-leave-it/).

Despite, or perhaps because of, this admittedly balmy communication effort by the organizers of the festival, the problem of abandoned tents persists. As such, Glastonbury festival, as well as being emblematic of hedonistic party culture, also functions as a powerful symbol of the culture of disposability. Although the generous interpretation of the practice of leaving stuff behind is that campers are too overwhelmed by hangovers to pack up and carry their stuff home, it is also important to consider the possibility that many festivalgoers purchase items before the festival that they never had any intention of packing up to take home with them: umbrellas, Wellington boots, camping chairs, and tents. With many commodities cheaply produced in China and other manufacturing hubs in the global south, and priced low in the very competitive consumer marketplace of Britain, it is perfectly affordable for a middle-class consumer to buy a cheap tent for one-off use. This is especially the case considering that festival attendance is expensive, with tickets alone priced at around £240 per person at the time of writing, and the high costs of eating, drinking, and buying mementos over the five days. With all of these costs taken into account, the thought of leaving behind a tent may seem a sunk cost, and worth the possibility of lightening the load home for an individual to carry. The cumulative costs of this disposable sensibility are immense. The material accumulation of discarded items translates into a mountain of trash that revelers leave behind to become someone else's problem: the festival organizers; the teams of volunteers working to earn back the cost of their ticket; the paid litter-pickers, the entrepreneurs who claim, fix, and sell or rent the tents; the charities that try to redistribute unbroken items to those in need, or the municipal workers who cart what remains off to the dump. At Glastonbury, we see the culture of disposability in full swing: instead of each festivalgoer buying one tent that they will use over and over again for many years, we see many festivalgoers buying a tent for each festival, which they throw away, much like the packaging from the takeaway meal purchased from the food vans in-between band performances.

Looking at the post-festival littered landscape allows us to see that there is a very close relationship between hedonistic consumption and trash. Quite simply, the former produces the latter, in intensely condensed spaces and over short periods of time. In the context of party culture, trash comes across as a necessary evil: the thing that results from a lot of people having a very good time, it is the yin to the yang, the downer to the upper. While festivalgoers themselves appear unconcerned with the trash they leave behind, photographers and journalists have taken note of the extreme amounts of rubbish created at Glastonbury and other festivals and street parties in which hundreds of thousands of revelers gather. In addition to this, the festival organizers themselves appear to have taken heed of the problem of plastic waste, announcing in 2019 that they have banned the sale of plastic water bottles on the festival site (Marsh, 2019), and funding new art installations made from recycled plastic bottles (BBC Cornwall, 2019) in order to help raise awareness of the waste problem among attendees. There is an attempt here to make a connection between the experience of feeling free from societal norms and celebrating life, fun, youth, and pleasure and an awareness of the kind of ruination that results therefrom. As much as contemporary hedonistic consumer culture requires huge numbers of commodities and commoditized exchanges in order for the feeling of fun to be produced, so too will it create mountains of trash that need to be dealt with—and one cannot count on those who produce the trash to help dispose of it after the party. As the Shangri-La website notes, in 2017, in relation to its theme for that year, "Environ-mental," "Only the waste from last year's Festival remains. All the things you left behind. Giant Towers of Trash now dominate the Shangri-La skyline. Structures have formed from the scrap, dwellings made of detritus, art from the embers" (Shangri-La, 2017). Just like it might only be you and a couple of close friends or family members cleaning up your home after your birthday party, so too it falls to those who profit from the hosting of Glastonbury Festival to accept their role in tidying up after everyone else.

The discussion so far has shown how large-scale entertainment events such as Glastonbury, produce huge amounts of waste. Visual documentation of the postparty litterscape exposes how one of the direct results of hedonistic party culture is stunning quantities of rubbish, to which those who caused it often seem to have no ethical connection, although this may indeed shift as public awareness about plastic waste grows. The next section of this chapter further explores the theme of the mess created by middle-class consumers in their pursuits of pleasure by examining a different case study: luxury tropical island tourism and media narratives about the pollution of popular white-sand beaches.

Tropical islands are iconic locations of luxury tourism, where people go on honeymoon, for rest and relaxation, and to experience five-star tourism. Much has been written about the economic and ecological impacts of tropical island tourism (Gössling, 2003; Scheyvens & Momsen, 2008; Meyer-Arendt & Lew, 2016; Sivaperuman et al., 2018). Notably, tropical islands are particularly at risk due to climate change (Belle & Bramwell, 2005; Sivaperuman et al., 2018). Many tropical islands rely on income from tourism, and local economies are set up to serve the desires and interests of tourists, who are typically short-termist and pleasure-seeking. Whether couples come on honeymoon, seeking the perfect setting for romantic beach photo-shoots at sunset, or are groups of friends seeking sea- and sun-soaked indulgences, what is clear is that tropical island holidays represent a particular kind of luxury consumption. Indeed, most of the tourism-driven island states actively aim to attract "high end, luxury tropical island tourism based in resorts" (Hampton & Jeyacheya, 2013: 2). In Mauritius, for example, in the early 2000s "the destination went through an extensive upgrading of existing hotel facilities, especially at the luxury end of the market" (Carlsen & Butler, 2011: 161). Tourists expect certain things when they arrive at their tropical island holiday destination: the postcard-perfect white-sand beaches, clear turquoise waters, and opportunities for beach-based lazing with cocktails and ocean-based adventures such as snorkeling or coral-reef diving. What they do not wish to see is rubbish. Trinidad has been noted as struggling to attract luxury tourists because "homeless people continue to squat, […] feral dogs roam the landscape […] piles of garbage litter the landscape […] and used paper cups and plates, plastic bags, bottles and other detritus litter some of the beaches" (Carlsen & Butler, 2011: 122). In the tropical island tourist imagination, luxury is equated with a lack of litter.

Many tourists come from cold countries, and seek sun and relaxation away from the gray skies that characterize their winters (and sometimes, summers), or want to escape the stress; the hustle and bustle of city life; the crowded buses, subways, and highways; the noise and social pressure produced when millions of people live in close proximity with one another. On the tropical island paradise, in the luxury beach-side accommodation, tourists can pursue absolute leisure: they can relax their bodies on recliners in the sun or periodically immerse in warm waters; they can enjoy cocktails at any time of day and read their novels, looking out to the horizon and daydreaming under the shade of a coconut palm. They can leave their worries behind. "Tourists are consumers [...] focused on self-pleasure [and do] not pay attention to much beyond the cocktail in their hand or the view from their hotel room" (Dodds & Graci, 2012: 61). In service of these expectations, the hotels, guesthouses and lodges that provide accommodations and entertainment to tourists are likely to invest resources into keeping their particular patches of the beach clean. This means employing staff to rake up things that are considered unsightly, such as kelp that washed up on the beach at high tide, or more likely, the plastic trash that also washed up overnight. Hotel beaches are regularly swept or raked clean in order to meet the expectations of tourists to experience a piece of an "untouched" tropical paradise. In the Caribbean, climate change has caused the "massive influx of Sargassum seaweed, [which] has rendered many beaches unpleasant" and led to "dramatically increased daily costs for removal and beach clean-up" for hotels (Honey & Hogenson, 2017: 200). Beaches have, partially through the political-economy of tourism, been "domesticated into leisure zones swept clean of detritus and emptied of fisher-folk" (Samuelson, 2018).

Along with their expectations of spotlessly clean beaches, tourists are typically intense consumers of local resources. For example, in Zanzibar, a study has shown that the present levels of water withdrawal from the island's aquifers to serve tourism is unsustainable, and that, as a result, the local population experiences water deficits (Gössling, 2001). While on holiday, tourists drink out of plastic water bottles, which are then thrown into the trash bins in hotel rooms, and are taken away by cleaners and sent to the dump through the usual processes. In Gili Trawangan, Indonesia, "[m]any tourists are not aware of environmental issues" and "still consume water in [plastic] bottles and contribute to the very growing waste problem on the island" (Dodds & Graci, 2012: 127). In Indonesia, for example, beach litter was measured to have quintupled between 1985 and 1997 (Willoughby, Sangkoyo & Lakaseru, 1997). To sum up, tropical island tourism, although an important source of income generation for local and national economies, relies on the maintenance of "clean" beaches for tourists, who conversely are a significant part of the problem of trash creation in the first place. Sustainable strategies of solid waste management, including recycling, are problematic on tourist-destination islands because "waste management technologies and policies have not kept pace with the increase in waste production" (MacRae, 2012: 72). The waste infrastructures that exist in many tropical island destinations are privatized, and entail beachfront hotels investing in keeping their stretch of beach clean in order to meet the expectations of their guests, and not investing much in keeping the landscape clean outside of the boundaries of their own property. What does this practice of removing unsightly waste from the view of tourists indicate about the place of rubbish in the popular imagination about luxury holidays? The question here is both about the invisibility of waste on tropical beaches, but also on the question of what happens when the processes that seek to render that waste invisible are made visible.

The labor required in order to keep the beach looking clean is hidden from the gaze of the tourists. A closer look at the substance of the beach also reveals much about the extent to which trash is integrated into—and perhaps made invisible by—the landscape. Every beach, even those newly born due to volcanic activity, is comprised of microplastics (Gibbens, 2019). The fabled "long walk on the beach" enjoyed by many tourists can allow one to look a little closer. Perhaps while scanning the surf-edge for a special shell to pick up, to scrutinize and appreciate for its delicate geometry, one might notice that also pressed into the billions of grains of sand that make up the beach are other bright fragments. "Ruination lies latent here, like a harbinger of the planetary future itself. Like the plastic pellets that wash up on particular currents and swells, it is a lurking reminder that, while we may dispose of things, nothing is ever thrown 'away'" (Samuelson, 2018). These are pieces of plastic, which have broken down and washed up onto the shore, mixing in with the organic matter. How long until beach sand is comprised of as many plastic fragments as bits of shell and quartz? Although the larger bits of trash may be successfully removed from beaches, there is no escaping the presence of rubbish on beaches as it becomes integrated with the very stuff from which the beach is made.

The Maldives are a famous luxury tourism destination in the Indian Ocean. Made up of an archipelago of 1,000 coral islands and atolls situated southwest of Sri Lanka, the Maldives market themselves as the ultimate experience for those seeking a classic "white-sands" experience. With hundreds of resorts, many of them featuring clusters of thatched stilted bungalows hovering over the aqua ocean, offering accommodation and entertainment to the estimated 1 million tourists annually since 2013, and the remote situation of the atolls, it is no surprise that trash management is a major challenge for the local and national authorities. Tourists to the Maldives reportedly produce around 3.5 kilograms of rubbish per person per day (Evans, 2015). Where does this rubbish—around 3.5 million kilograms of it annually—go? Land space in the Maldives is extremely limited. The largest atoll in the system is over 1,988 square miles in size, but only 38,2 square kilometers is land area. With literally nowhere to put the rubbish produced by tourists, in 1992 the government

Figure 7. Thilafushi, Maldive's Rubbish Island. Image by Ibrahim Asad, licensed by Wikimedia Commons.

decided to deposit all of the trash in a location called Thilafushi, which used to be "a shallow lagoon composed of coral reefs" (Atlas Obscura, 2018) but over time, as the rubbish dumped there built up, became a man-made island: Rubbish Island. According to a 2011 report by the BBC, the scale of rubbish on Thilafushi had become so bad that boatmen had to wait up to seven hours to unload their rubbish, and the island featured "vast piles of rubbish and perpetual smog and smoke" caused by open incineration of waste (Haviland, 2011). In 2015 the *Financial Times* reported that the mountains of waste on Thilafushi rise 49 feet above sea level (in contrast to the average altitude of 6.5 feet above sea level for other islands in the archipelago), and details both the source of the excessive trash (the many tourist resorts), the rhetoric from local politicians about the urgency of dealing with the problem, and some of the steps taken by some of the resorts to lessen their trash footprint (Evans, 2015). It is intriguing that the presence of a rubbish dump—which is effectively what Thilafushi is—in a tropical island archipelago should have received such media attention. Perhaps it is the specific visibility of the dump—within eyeshot of the capital Malé—that has provoked it. What is the "rising price of prosperity" (Evans, 2015) brought about by a very successful tourist economy? From the perspective of the *Financial Times* writer, the price of prosperity is a smoldering 49-feet-high mountain of trash in what used to be an untouched tropical paradise. Ironically, it is the hope or dream of "touching" that paradise, combined with more affordable travel made available by globalization, that has been the cause of the destruction of the "once-pristine lagoon" (Evans, 2015). Journalistic commentary focuses on tourists as the cause for the accumulation of trash, but also, significantly, on the failure of local government to deal effectively with trash: to offer recycling schemes, to find ecologically sound ways to deal with the trash in a way that keeps it out of the line of sight of the tourists. There is an expectation that one of the key roles of government in an economy dependent on tourism (reportedly 30 percent of the Maldives' GDP) is to keep trash away from the tourist gaze. Nevertheless, precisely because of the huge influx of tourists and their curiosity to see more than simply the pristinely curated beaches of the resorts, the presence of huge amounts of trash in the Maldives is becoming better known.

In 2014 the UK Newspaper the *Daily Mail* carried a photo essay about Thilafushi, featuring a number of photographs by filmmaker Alison Teal, mostly featuring herself at the center. The images show Teal undertaking holiday activities, like carrying her surfboard or going for a swim, but all in the surroundings of the rubbish island rather than the pristine white-sand beaches that tourists would normally inhabit and see in promotional material about the Maldives as a holiday destination. The photo shoot features Teal, a young, trim blonde woman (a favored cover girl of the *Daily Mail*) wearing a bikini or swim gear (similarly, a favored dress code for women featured in the newspaper), carrying her surfboard through the mountains of rubbish on Thilafushi, or paddling it through blue waters crammed with floating plastic debris. The article is image heavy and carries only minimal copy. Each photograph features Teal wearing bikinis and beach wear, mostly in bright pink, and showing off not only the problem of the rubbish but also her body.

The *Daily Mail* feature effectively lifts its content from Alison Teal's own website, which promotes her as a media personality, "the female Indiana Jones," an exhibitionist eco-adventurer who spent a month "naked and afraid" on a Maldives island for the eponymous reality TV show for the Discover Channel. On her website the series of photographs are filed under a feature titled "Plastic Fashion," where she explains that the intention of the photo shoot was to raise awareness about the problem of plastic waste on tropical beaches by promoting a particular brand of bikinis (Odina Surf bikinis), which are purportedly made from fibers recycled from plastic bottles (though this detail is lost in the *Daily Mail* feature). Teal describes the aim of the shoot as to "rather see plastic in bikinis [. . .] than strewn across the beautiful beaches of the Maldives." By modeling the bikini in the Maldives rubbish landscape, Teal sought to raise awareness about the problem of waste and how ethical consumption (choosing a bikini made from recycled plastic) can offer one solution. But of course the images also seek to promote Teal's own brand as a media personality. By juxtaposing the signifiers of luxury island tourist—the sun-bleached long blonde hair, the toned and tanned physique, near nudity, bikinis—with the signifiers of wasteful consumption and thoughtless disposal, Teal attempts to make a statement about the links between the practices associated with luxury tourism and environmental degradation. By using her own body to attract the viewer's attention, to titillate them by presenting herself in a way that will satisfy the patriarchal gaze (as the uptake of the images in the famously sexist *Daily Mail* testifies), Teal manages to smuggle in an environmental message: that it is the people in the bikinis and swim trunks, visiting the islands on holiday, that are causing the very trash that is causing their moral outrage.

In Bali, Indonesia, Western visitors show similar concern about the presence of rubbish on what used to be pristine beaches. British newspaper, *The Telegraph*, reports on "worrying" beach cleanup trends in the popular tourist destination: instead of removing the trash altogether, some hotels are simply burying it in the sand to hide it, and of course when the tide comes in the trash is unburied again, only for the process to be repeated as dutiful cleanup staff rebury it the next day (see fig. 8). As such, British travel groups have been "forced" to organize beach-litter collection drives (Knapton, 2017). The article goes on to detail how trash management initiatives by local authorities are virtually nonexistent in Bali and that the practice of burying trash under beach sand is widespread. Illustrated with photos taken by an environmental film maker, the article also notes that tourism is one of the main causes of the littered beaches and suggests that holiday makers can help by making use of reusable water bottles rather than disposable ones.

Also in *The Telegraph*, it is later reported that Bali has declared a "rubbish emergency" as a tide of "plastic has buried its beaches" (Oliphant, 2017). The article is illustrated with numerous images of heavy machinery on the beach about to front-load piles of plastic rubbish, which the article goes on to explain, have washed in from the "heavily polluted Java Sea." Putting the cleanup operation into the context of campaigns by high-profile sportspeople, such as pro surfer Kelly Slater, who warns that the islands' famous beaches might soon become unsurfable because of the trash, and renowned television environmentalist David Attenborough, the article also devotes significant space to examining the inadequacy of efforts by the Indonesian government to control

Figure 8. Sanur Beach, Bali, at dawn in 2018. The two figures are beach sweepers, removing trash before the tourists arrive. Photograph by Mike Dickison. Image from Wikimedia Commons.

the problem. It further explains that most of the rubbish that arrives on the tourist beaches of Bali gets there from other heavily polluted, non-tourist-destination islands that form part of the Indonesian archipelago. "Indonesia is the second biggest maritime plastic polluter in the world after China. The river of Citarum in West Java has been described as the most polluted river in the world with detritus dumped in it by nearby factories" (Oliphant, 2017). This fact is presented in order to provide some context to the problem of trash on Bali: it is not simply caused by irreverent tourists and incompetent local officials. The problem of trash washing up on beaches is an inherently systemic problem because the oceans connect the entire planet (a theme that will be explored further in chapter 4). When trash ends up in the ocean, it becomes public property and a global problem. It can no longer be pinned to specific individuals, institutions, or governments: it is arguably only something that can be properly handled through collective international efforts. This attitude is hinted at in the concluding sentence of the article, which reports, "The [British] Department for International Development is considering proposals to direct aid to help clean up particularly polluted rivers in Africa and Asia that are believed to contribute disproportionately to plastics in the oceans"

(Oliphant, 2017). Although it is fair that some critique is directed at tourists as one of the sources of the problem, and local and national governments as the institutions mandated with dealing with matters of public affairs, arguably both of these critiques need to be contextualized within the pressing cross-border, collective, and global nature of trash.

Media coverage about the problem of trash in luxury tropical-island holiday destinations serves two purposes. The first is to inform prospective tourists about some of the ramifications of tourism, and try to raise some awareness of the impact of importing "Western" styles of consumption to local landscapes and economies. There is an element of schadenfreude in the coverage, where readers who may not have the financial means to enjoy luxury tropical holidays get the chance to voyeuristically pierce the veneer of pleasure and leisure to see what lies beneath the veil of the dreamy marketing of those destinations. Arguably, a kind of class commentary is at play, in which those wealthy and privileged enough to enjoy luxury beach holidays in the tropics are being called out as responsible for spoiling the very landscapes to which they celebrate having elite access. As the lower-middle and lower classes—unable to afford a holiday to the Maldives or Bali—might have long suspected, the upper-middle and upper classes are selfishly both claiming *and* destroying beautiful parts of the world. There is an element of poking fun in the coverage, a satirical unveiling of the double standards of the rich, who demand pristine clean environments, on the one hand, but destroy those same environments, with the other. But there is also a sense of class rage, in which the sense of entitlement of the wealthy is critiqued. Alongside this class politics coexists—quite uneasily—a global politics of competence and responsibility. There is a tone traceable in the coverage, which suggests that local authorities—the Maldivian and Indonesian municipalities and governments responsible for the disposal of trash—are somehow failing in their duties by not taking proper care of the waste produced by tourists. From this perspective, the actors who are at fault are not only the thoughtless, selfish tourists who toss away plastic water bottle after plastic water bottle, but also the local authorities who do not provide the necessary infrastructures that would allow for more ethical, community-minded behaviors on the part of the tourists. Here, the suggestion seems to be that it is the responsibility of local authorities to ensure that the reality of their destinations matches up to the promises made in marketing materials: and that tourists who hop on a plane expecting to find untouched, pristine white-sand beaches should not be forced, once they arrive, to join litter drives picking up plastic bottles from those very same beaches. Such expectations might seem reasonable to the individual tourists, who have certain hopes about their expensive holidays and who need someone or something to blame if those hopes are destroyed. But in the bigger context of the global nature of the problem of trash, and the extent to which it most often ends up in the oceans, it would seem quite unfair to place the sole responsibility for cleaning up the world's floating rubbish on a small, relatively poor island nation like the Maldives, which is most dramatically threatened by climate change (Gagain, 2012). What are the governments of the nations from which the majority of tourists emerge doing about the problem of trash on the beaches, much of it thrown there by their citizens? Arguably little. The hypocrisy of media attention paid to the problem of trash on the beaches on tropical islands is revealed: the concern with cleanliness, while to some extent attributable to the rise of global environmental awareness, is also likely rooted in a self-interest about how "worthwhile" certain holiday destinations are for tourists, and whether they will be able to fully immerse themselves in the fantasy of the untouched tropical getaway precisely at the same time that their "touching" of that place is contributing to its destruction.

Thus far, this chapter has explored two types of hedonistic consumption that create monumental amounts of rubbish—music festivals and island tourism—and considered some of the key themes that come up in media coverage about that trash. Disapproval of the wasted landscapes produced by hedonistic partying at Glastonbury, and beaches destroyed in part due to indulgent holidaying in the tropics, is clearly communicated in visual narratives about the wasted landscapes. But as the following section will show, there are other models for thinking about what hedonism means, and how pleasurable entertainment experiences can be enacted in ways that are less exploitative of disposable culture and the outsourcing of the cleaning up to others. The remainder of this chapter turns its attention back to festival culture, and explores an alternative narrative that also focuses on rubbish, this time in terms of how responsibility and civic duty in relation to rubbish can become central to pleasure-seeking events.

LEAVING NO TRACE? ETHICAL TRASH EFFORTS AT AFRIKA BURN

Every year at the end of April, around 15,000 people, many of them international tourists, gather in the middle of the Tankwa desert in the Northern Cape of South Africa, for a participatory creative festival called Afrika Burn (Atkinson & Ingle, 2016). A regional offshoot of the Burning Man Festival

(Gilmore & Proyen, 2005; Gilmore, 2010), which takes place every August in the US in Nevada, Afrika Burn is presented by its organizers as a hub of creativity, art-making, self-expression, and hedonistic partying in a remote context far from the norm of urban city life (the venue is approximately a five-hour drive from Cape Town, along one of the worst rutted dirt roads in the country). The following discussion of narratives about strategies relating to waste and ethical orientation toward it in the event are synthesized from the extensive communications provided by the event organizers on the Afrika Burn website (www.afrikaburn.com) and their monthly email newsletters, and contextualized by my personal experiences of attending the event six times between 2012 and 2018. As the event organizers describe on their website, its aim is to create a space outside of the "real world" (or as "Burners" call it, the "default world") consumer economy, and those who attend the event are considered part of a community that voluntarily adheres to key guiding principles (Afrika Burn, 2018). After buying their ticket and paying whatever costs are required to travel into the desert (not an inexpensive feat) and buying in advance whatever food and drink they'll need (including all the water needed for cooking and washing), participants arrive into a cashless economy where "radical self-reliance" and "gifting" define all interactions. As the material on the Afrika Burn website explains, once through the gates, the only thing that can be purchased for cash is ice, and as such those attending can put away their wallets, credit cards, car keys, and other indicators of middle-class consumer citizenship. They can share what they have with friends or strangers, or simply look after their own needs if their resources are little. All participants are encouraged to contribute something to the event, whether by helping to build large-scale collaborative art projects, such huge art sculptures or pieces of architecture for everyone to enjoy, or through gifting small items and experiences to one another, such as frying up pancakes for or offering organic lip balm to strangers. The event also encourages "radical self-expression," and there are no boundaries or social norms in terms of outfits or behaviors (beyond important issues of consent and sharing which the organizers are at pains to explain in detail in communications leading up to the event): nudity is normalized, consumption of alcohol and various illegal inebriants is tolerated, and dance parties happen all day and all night while participants wander about wearing weird and wonderful outfits or nothing at all, driving and pedaling even weirder and more wonderful "mutant vehicles" (scooters, buggies, or cars converted into moving artworks). Although certainly a product of the consumer economy, both in that is positions itself against it, and in that a huge amount of consumption is required in the lead up to the event, Afrika Burn and Burning Man are perhaps better theorized as "prosumption" events, in which participants both produce and consume their own entertainment experiences (Chen, 2012a).

The large sculptural artworks that are erected in the desert landscape are usually ritually burned (Gilmore, 2010) on one of the last three nights of the event, with most people at the festival coming together to be collectively transfixed by the spectacle of flames engulfing wood and sparks flying against a star-studded desert sky. The burning of the big sculptures has both a practical and emotional aspect to it. Practically speaking, the teams who have made the pieces release themselves of the administrative burden of dismantling the sculptures and taking the artworks back home, and, emotionally speaking, the burning allows not only for a beautiful aesthetic experience for those watching, but a ritualized form of detachment and letting go of the results of one's work. Materially, the ritual burning of the art speaks to the disposability of all the results of human creative efforts: we can make things, but they will eventually break down, degrade, or be destroyed by the forces of nature (Steele, 2015, 2017). Making a thing, displaying it for the pleasure of others, then burning it, is an expression of that process of making and unmaking and a willingness to accept the mutability and ethereality of all material forms that we may otherwise delude ourselves into believing are permanent.

One of the key organizational aspects of Afrika Burn is its insistence that it is a "leave no trace" event. This means that the expectation of all involved—organizers, volunteers, and participants—is that no visible impact on the landscape occurs as a result of the event. A couple of months before the party, teams go to the desert to build the infrastructure needed for up to 15,000 people: a "city" plan, roads, lighting, signage, and the open-air compost toilets. Participants are expected to leave no trace behind them: to take home with them every bit of rubbish that they produce, and to be responsible for leaving the patch of hard desert ground on which they pitched their tents exactly the way they found it. Due to the relatively harsh conditions of the Tankwa desert, in which a strong dust, rain, or windstorm might blow up out of nowhere, participants are given exhaustive instructions about how to deal with MOOP (or, Matter Out of Place) in advance of the event. These include reminders to ensure that toilet paper is put back into the lidded buckets after use so that it does not blow away, that loose items in camp are properly stowed away, and that revelers give thought to their outfit plans and avoid items that can easily come loose and fly away (such as sequins, glitter, and feathers), and that people avoid bringing disposable toys such as glow sticks. Although there are open camping areas, a significant part of the festival space is organized into theme camps, which are collectives of friends and acquaintances that develop a sense of community by working together to contribute some kind of artwork or shared space to the event. Theme camps are allocated spaces on the "city plan" for Tankwa Town and are expected to have MOOP plans in place before the event, and to ensure that they collectively arrange a trash-management infrastructure in their camp, to which all camp members are committed to adhering.

Experienced "Burners" put significant amounts of time and energy into planning their MOOP management strategies. For those who are allocated a theme camp—that is, a prebooked zone on the map, where they set up some kind of public engagement space—a huge amount of conversation about trash takes place in advance. Each theme camp community is required by the event organizers to allocate one team member as a MOOP officer. This person's job is to come up with a plan in advance that ensures that all those camping together in the theme camp have a shared understanding of how rubbish will be dealt with. Each theme camp's MOOP officer's job is to develop a MOOP management plan, including instructions on how trash will be separated and collected for recycling or composting, how the organic matter, gray water, and bags of trash will be taken away from the site. MOOP plans typically include instructions to leave unnecessary packaging at home (for example, the outer cardboard cover of a pack of biscuits should be left at home), requests for camp members to be conscious about which forms of packaging they bring along (for example, to bring soft drinks in tins that can be crushed and recycled rather than in plastic bottles), and details of how the camp will handle water left over from cooking, washing, and brushing teeth. In my own 2018 Afrika Burn community, our theme camp had a "MOOP Station," at which collapsible bins were set up for recyclables and nonrecyclables, a brick for crushing tins, and a Bokashi bin for collecting organic matter (though it should be noted that many camps might not use this approach, and would simply put all their mixed rubbish straight into black bags). Some camps also take the collecting of gray water very seriously, in order to fully actualize the "leave no trace" ethos of the event. This means that instead of tossing water left over from cooking and dish-washing straight into the desert, it is collected in various receptacles and transported off-site at the end. During the time of the festival, camp MOOP infrastructure is intended to not only keep the collective spaces clean and tidy and pleasant, but also to ensure that everyone

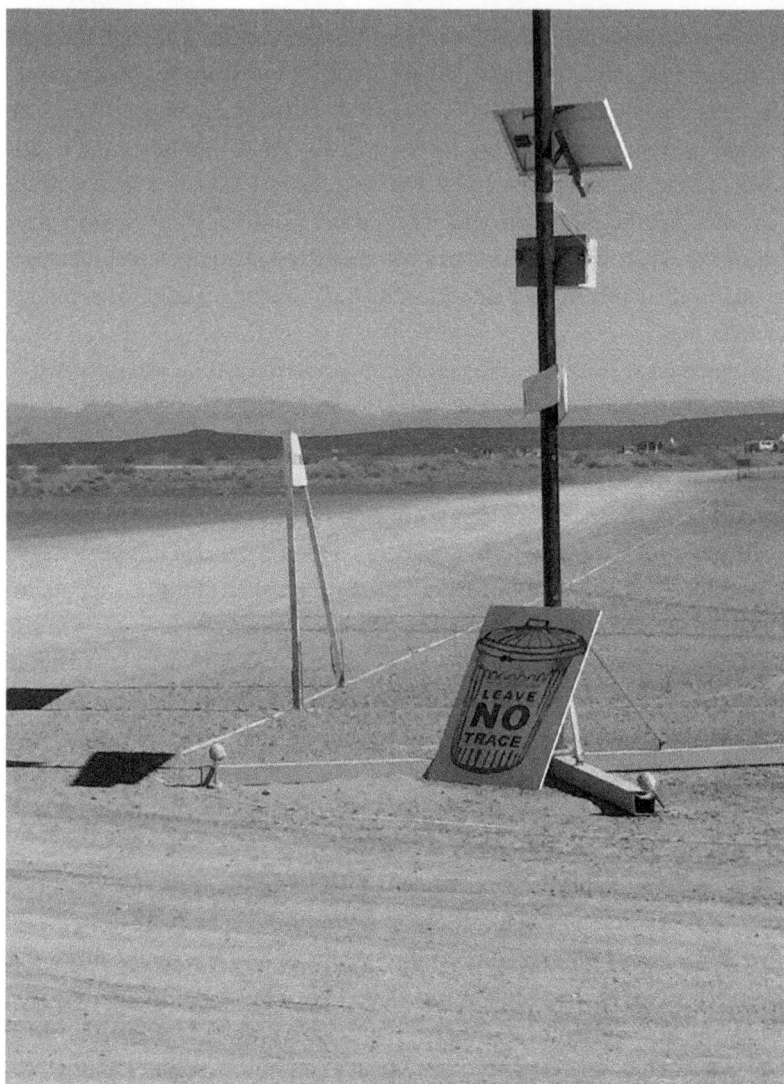

Figures 9a and b. (Left) A sign reading Leave No Trace reminds those arriving at Afrika Burn that they are responsible for their own rubbish. (Right) The last bags of MOOP from my theme camp in 2018. Photos by author.

in the camp is doing their fair share to make certain that the trash footprint of the camp is as light as possible.

Once the festivities have ended, participants pack up their own tents as well as the communal spaces they have created, and take back bags of trash and recycling with them in their vehicles to be disposed of en route home. Most important of all is the last "MOOP Sweep," where theme camp members scrutinize their allocated areas in order to pick up any remaining scraps of matter out of place (such as cigarette butts, threads, hairclips, or shreds of plastic). Various materials have, over the years, been identified as too MOOPy by the event organizers: glitter (though edible glitter is allowed), feathers of any type, Astro-Turf (the little plastic blades of grass get broken off and scattered far and wide by footfall). Although this doesn't stop all event participants from bringing them, in some theme camp circles a lot of conversation about these items takes place in advance, as more experienced participants seek to educate newbies about what substances cause more MOOP and how to avoid them. After the festival, each "theme camp" is reviewed by the Afrika Burn organizers, and the cleanliness in which they left their site rated on a MOOP Map. In other words, there is transparency among the organizers about which collective took their "leave no trace" responsibility seriously, and which did not. The event organizers explicitly state in multiple forms of pre- and postevent communication that there should be no impact on the natural environment of the Tankwa desert in service of the hedonistic self-expression that takes place.

There is something quite remarkable about the intensive attention shown to rubbish before, during, and after something that is, for all intents and purposes, just a huge eight-day party. Although some hardcore Burners consider Afrika Burn a space for radical self-expression and the invention of new communal forms of creativity, for many of the revelers who attend, it is a chance to cut themselves off from the real world, dance, drink, get high, and run around making new friends. Many people bring glow sticks, sequins, and glitter to the event though they have been told not to. Parties are times of pleasure-seeking and self-indulgence, which is precisely why they usually result in so much rubbish, as people let down their guards and allow themselves to follow their desires and pleasures, releasing the need to self-police or follow the usual social norms that direct their behavior in everyday life. As is evident from the discussion of the postparty litterscape of Glastonbury and other big parties, it is quite unusual for hedonistic pleasure-seekers to give thoughtful care to the waste that their indulgences might produce. Perhaps this is why some people who attend Afrika Burn religiously and fervently insist that it is not just another party, but a political movement that allows for the cocreation of new ways of thinking about the world. Although the space is "temporarily removed from the consumer culture that dominates in the default world" (Gilmore, 2010: 38), it is not removed from the material cultures of consuming things that create rubbish. It should also be noted that even though there is no market exchange at the event itself, a great deal of consumption takes place in the lead up to the event, as people buy the necessities and luxuries they will consume during their time in the desert. It would be unwise, therefore, to hold up Afrika Burn and similar Burning Man events as anti-consumerist simply because during the party a cashless economy is at play, and because most (but not all) participants make an effort to clean up after themselves (as though taking basic responsibility for the rubbish one creates is an impressive ascetic act).

The concept of "matter out of place" (MOOP) was first defined in relation to anti-litter campaigns in the late 1960s in Britain, in which activists represented litter as "morally unsettling, evidence of the collapse of civic obligation" (Hawkins, 2006: 9). The Burning Man and Afrika Burn ethos brings civic responsibility relating to MOOP into the heart of the party program. Does it put a damper on the party spirit to be thinking about crushing beer cans while drinking them, to be picking up worn-out glow sticks from the desert dust once the sun rises? Arguably not. Perhaps there is something gratifying about knowing that one is partying "responsibly," that one is not leaving one's mess behind for others to clean up. The extreme conditions of the party—its location way out in the desert, the need to bring your own water and food, plus the lack of any buying or selling—already create the circumstances for a sense of freedom from the systems and structures of everyday life. Taking responsibility for one's own rubbish is an extension of taking responsibility for one's survival and pleasure. In the context of events like Afrika Burn, defined by the "leave no trace" ethos of the Burning Man events worldwide, a new kind of collective civic responsibility, which is organized almost entirely around hedonism, arises in relation to trash. In the pursuit of pleasure and a sense of freedom, facing up to the material detritus that is produced in the process arguably allows participants to take a greater sense of ownership over their pleasure. It allows a person to have fun with less guilt (presuming that some people feel guilty about throwing down the empty can of beer once they have drunk it; doubtless many simply don't care). Smokers are entreated to keep their cigarette butts in a little container to dispose of later, rather than throwing them straight on the ground as they do in almost every other social setting. Some first-time Burners, joining eco-aware camps that recycle and compost, might feel enlightened and educated about rubbish, and able to take home new ways of thinking about how to manage garbage in their own homes. As such, the official messages about rubbish and personal responsibility persistently shared by the event organizers, encoded precisely within the "off-duty," fun times of an entertainment festival, arguably offer an opportunity for an evolved orientation toward personal hedonistic consumption and the waste that it produces.

Of course, this would presume that all Afrika Burn participants take on equal responsibility for the trash that they create, but as is equally the case in the "default world," not everyone is willing to make sure they put their trash in the correct recycling bin, or not throw their butts on the ground, or to compost their food waste. In the context of the Afrika Burn camp, MOOP, therefore, can also easily become a point of micropolitical tension. Who messes up the separating at source, putting nonrecyclable plastic in the recyclables bin because they are too drunk to think straight? Who has to fish a used condom out of the Bokashi bin? How many bags of trash are taken out by that car with five people in it and how many by the other car, with only two passengers?

Interestingly, although the experience of Afrika Burn is organized almost entirely around hedonism, creativity, and generosity, conflicts are certainly possible over how the waste is dealt with. Which collective members are the ones who take on a disproportionate responsibility for bringing bins to collect gray water, or taking home more bags of trash than they actually created, or doing the MOOP Sweep on the final day once most revelers have left? Who swoops into the party late and leaves early, forgetting things behind that need to be dealt with by others? Who has to take on the role of nagging camp-parent, reminding friends what item goes in which bin, and making announcements reminding everyone to keep adding the Bokashi powder to the bin? Considering the various ways in which trash is communicated about, before, during, and after the festival, it becomes clear that at the heart of hedonism lies the messy material realities of rubbish. And in the questions about civic responsibility that arise when considering how to deal with matter out of place, there is always the possibility of tension, both interpersonal and social. The project of "leaving no trace" is on the surface an admirable ethic, which seeks to connect a sense of broader social responsibility to hedonistic forms of release. But looking deeper into the messages about MOOP management, it also becomes clear that instead of leaving no "trace" (a euphemism for trash if there ever was one), what happens is that the trace is displaced onto other spaces and people, who then take on the burden of dealing with the rubbish left over after the party. In recent years, at the exit to the event, local farmers offered to take trash bags at R20 (20 rands, which is just over a dollar) each, loading up trailers with the waste, and presumably then carting it off to be at best taken to the local dump and recycled or at worst burned on a remote corner of their properties. Those who don't take the R20 option may carry their trash bags all the way to the nearest town, or all the way home with them, but then they will still displace their trash to a dump or recycling station. Once those bags of MOOP are dropped off at the recycling station in the nearest town, or taken for a fee by the entrepreneurial farmers at the exit gate, they are out of sight and out of mind. The Burners considers their work done, their trace not left behind, their civic responsibility fulfilled. There has been no trash left in the desert nature reserve that hosted techno music and huge bonfires just a few nights earlier. But the trash that the party created still exists somewhere, off-site. Trash never disappears, it is simply displaced. This raises the question of whether something that is out of sight is also out of mind. Just because the waste "trace" is not visible on the actual land on which the party took place, is that any guarantee that it has been dealt with responsibly, and that the overall trash impact of the event is less than, say, Glastonbury? Although most of the trash has not been left strewn across the desert floor (though, of course, some is, and it takes teams of volunteers weeks to pick it all up after the party), and it has been taken away by those who produced it, it is still effectively being outsourced for others to deal with.

Figure 10 shows an aerial photograph of the desert location in which the US event, Burning Man, takes place, twelve weeks after the 2014 event. Featured on the *Business Insider* website, the image is juxtaposed with a before image of Black Rock City (BRC) at its peak occupancy, with a nifty slider feature that allows the viewer to drag left and right in order to see the before and after images in overlay.

The two photographs are offered as evidence of the success of the cleanup operation after the event, and the power of the "leave no trace" ethic. And, of course, it is true that all the structures, habitats, and people present three months earlier are gone in the second image, and for all intents and purposes the desert has been returned to the form in which it was before the party. But precisely because of the juxtaposition of the aerial image of the party in full swing, it is also possible to see some faint traces of it on the cleaned-up landscape. Dark spots mark the position of the Burned Man and Temple and faint scars trace the lines and curves that mapped the roads of BRC. Up close, on the ground, perhaps this ultrafaint palimpsest of the temporary hedonistic

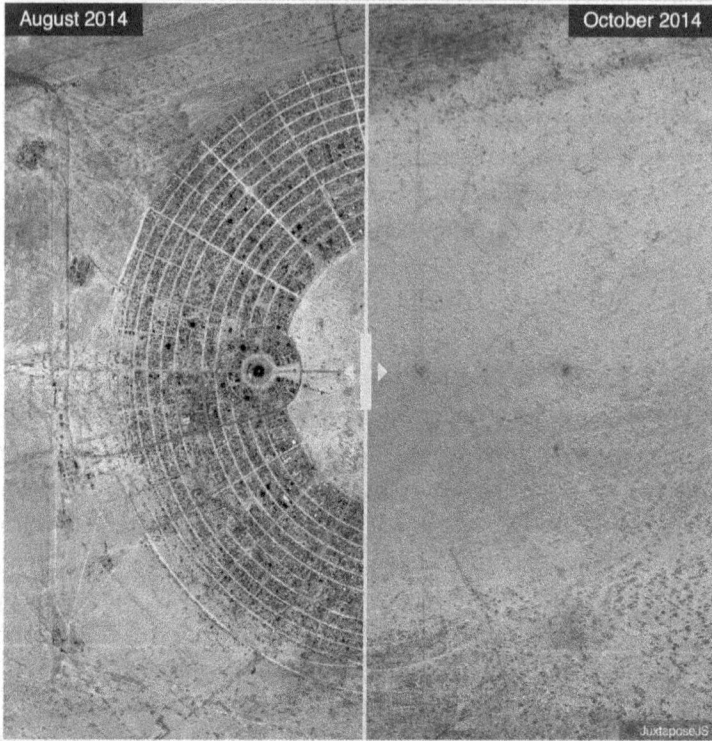

Figure 10. Before and after images of Burning Man festival in the Black Rock desert. Images reproduced with kind permission of Maxar and Digital Globe.

city would be harder to see, but from the air, and in contrast to the "before" picture, it comes into clarity. With the knowledge of what came before, it is possible to see the faintest remnants of it on the "after" picture. This is not to argue that the leave-no-trace aesthetic is a falsehood or misrepresentation, but to point out that there is an extent to which a trace is always left, no matter how intense the effort to remove evidence of the excess that took place on the site. There are no piles of burning garbage, as on Thilafushi, but there is a little visible evidence of what occurred. This visible trace of the hedonism, although explicitly absent of what we understand in the material sense to be rubbish, also functions as a kind of detritus. Although in one sense the traces are so minor as to be insignificant, in another sense it is precisely the presence of that palimpsest on the landscape that speaks to the pervasive impact that human activities have on the earth. In addition to this, the question arises about the invisible forms of trash that are produced by the event. The idea of MOOP is very biased toward visible, touchable items. What about things that cannot be seen or felt, such as the carbon emissions of the thousands of cars and vans that make the trek on desert roads to Burning Man and Afrika Burn each year, not to mention the local and international flights bringing revelers to the closest airport before they hit the road, and the smoke released by the burning of artworks? Is it really possible to leave no trace at all, in an annual event featuring tens of thousands of people? There is certainly a moral dimension to efforts to square up to the material items required for fun (the outfits, the inebriants, the music, and aesthetic settings) and also to the footprint that those materials leave behind once they are consumed and used. This said, it is also important to acknowledge the limitations of the "leave no trace" ethic. Although it is impressive, to an extent, that partygoers take their trash home with them (as opposed to simply leaving it on the field in front of the Pyramid Stage, as a point of contrast), does this really equate to taking full responsibility for its disposal? In a similar way that participants at Burning Man temporarily disconnect from consumer culture while still materially supporting the market (Kozinets, 2002), the disconnection from the "ordinary" relation to rubbish is likewise temporary.

Up to this point, this chapter has explored two diametrically different examples of hedonistic consumption and the place that rubbish is considered to have therein. Most typically, media narratives seek to expose how debauched entertainment festivals and indulgent tourism cause excessive amounts of waste. Less dominant, but nevertheless meaningful, are new narratives of alternative, trash-conscious forms of pleasure-seeking. Although not equivalent, both narratives bring into the public eye ways in which trash-traces are left behind, and raise questions about what they mean in terms of the civic duty of the consumer. In order to theorize this in more detail, the chapter now turns to a consideration of how postpleasure trash narratives complicate the idea of place, and a reflection on the moral costs of hedonistic consumption.

TRASH-TRACES: THERE IS NO AWAY IN PLEASURABLE CONSUMPTION

The discussion so far has taken us from the lush muddy fields of Somerset to the dusty desert-scapes of the Tankwa Karoo to the idyllic beaches of tropical islands. Although these geographical locations are quite different, and the cultures, politics, and societies that inhabit them are also extremely diverse, we see a kind of homogenization happening precisely through the medium of rubbish. Trash-littered environments look eerily similar to one another, as they cover and erase the landscapes beneath. There is a complex tension between private concerns and pleasures and public spaces and politics, which come into focus on the playing field of hedonistic consumption. People go to festivals and on holiday in order satisfy particularly self-centered desires to enjoy themselves, along with their close friends or family members. These arguably domestic concerns are projected into the shared spectacular spaces of entertainment and tourism. And the detritus of those private enjoyments become public through being left behind, tossed "away" (though there is no "away"). Mass consumption enacted in large entertainment festivals and beach tourism creates particular publics, in which the spectacle is centered, certainly, but so too is waste.

Hedonistic consumption, like other forms of consumption, fundamentally changes the physicality of the spaces where the pleasure is experienced. Sometimes the trash-trace is displaced and moved to another location, as with the MOOP from Afrika Burn, which is taken to a neighboring farm or the nearest town and the plastic waste removed from the vision of tourists at beach resorts in the Maldives, only to be piled high on a man-made island a few miles away. Although it may be out of sight of the partygoers heading home after leaving the rubbish bags at the dump and the tourist relaxing on the beaches that have been cleaned by hotel staff, the invisibility of it to those individual subjectivities does not mean that it is objectively erased. It is removed, displaced: not disappeared. The trash-traces left behind by various forms of pleasurable consumption always remain, and as such trash-trace requires an interrogation of how postconsumer trash fundamentally renegotiates our understandings of public and private space, as well as the politics of public and private action.

> The concept [of "world"] reaches zero when humans realize that there is no "away," that there is no background to their foreground despite the luxury holiday ads, a lack of a stage set on which world can perform, a lack that is evident in the return of culturally (and physically) repressed "pollution" and awareness of the consequences of human action on nonhumans. The end of the biosphere as we know it is also the end of the "world" as a normative and useful concept. (Morton, 2016: 46)

As Timothy Morton writes, part of the moment of ecological politics in the age of the Anthropocene is a fundamental reimagining of the world itself and our relation to it. Where people go to have fun, celebrate life, enjoy the pleasures offered by existence on this planet, what follows is a trail of trash. Sometimes that rubbish is acknowledged and efforts are made to deal with it in responsible ways, as is the case in the culture that has developed through the Burning Man family of events worldwide. No matter how effective those efforts are, it remains significant that they are at least being made, and in optimistic moments we might look to those efforts as the seeds of new forms of pleasure-seeking that could contribute to changing the world as we know it, and introducing new cultures of consumption that take greater care about the impacts made. On the other hand, more often hedonistic and pleasure-seeking forms of consumption produce momentous formations of detritus, which could hardly be summarized with the euphemistic word *trace*. The island of rubbish created by tourist consumption in the Maldives, the piles of litter in front of Glastonbury's Pyramid Stage: these are unavoidable pieces of evidence about the extent to which luxury and waste are connected and have a lasting impact on place as well as culture.

While most people keep their private spaces clean, many people are willing to despoil spaces that they consider public: be it the beach or the music festival field where thousands others are gathered. While in private, rubbish is typically ejected as quickly as possible from domestic settings (even the rented space of the hotel room or ocean-side bungalow), it takes more time and effort to remove trash from public places. And still the result is not a taking away, as there is no away, but a displacement of trash from view. Rubbish is always pushed to the edges of privileged places, away from the sight of the wealthy, by default despoiling the environments of those who are socially marginalized or who lack the economic power to complain. Trash is the ultimate object that transcends the boundaries of privilege, being moved until it comes to rest in the unsightly but ultimately public place of the trash heap (or rubbish island). Through media narratives that spotlight certain trash-soaked places typically ignored by, or hidden from, well-off consumers, new forms of visibility (and therefore a new politics of responsibility) are opened up.

Consumption always leaves a trace, and often that mark comes in the form of visible rubbish. I theorize the traces left behind by luxury consumption as *trash-traces*, which are not at all homogenous even though the materiality of trash can homogenize other landscapes through its presence. Sometimes the trace is extensive, like the rude pile of garbage left behind after Glastonbury the day after the party, and sometimes the trace is faint, almost invisible, like the Black Rock desert pictured three months after Burning Man, where every little piece of MOOP has been picked up and removed, despite the slight evidence of the temporary settlement that remains etched on the desert floor. The temporality of the trash-trace is important. Over time, it becomes fainter. Doubtless, Worthy Farm is also returned to its normal tidy, clean condition three months after Glastonbury festival, and Tanka Town is not perfectly pristine the day after most of its 10,000 temporary citizens leave: its take weeks and dozens of volunteers doing MOOP-sweeps to achieve the kind of cleanliness expected by the organizers. Some trash biodegrades over time—barring of course that perpetual material, plastic, which will outlive every creature alive this minute, human or not. The role of human effort in dealing with trash is highlighted by luxury excesses: and the class dimensions of this are obvious. The rich and privileged have the fun and create the waste, and the economically precarious clean it up. This is certainly the case for tropical island tourism and mainstream music festivals like Glastonbury. In the case of alternative, "radical" entertainment efforts like the Burning Man group of events, there is a more explicit public commitment to taking responsibility for the trash-trace (and although it cannot be guaranteed that all participants share that equally, collectively the cleanup is achieved).

That trash-traces are produced by hedonistic consumption should now be clear; these trash-traces cross boundaries of class and privilege, and although often displaced by wealth, they are never entirely removed. As such it becomes necessary to reflect on the moral costs of rubbish-producing pleasure seeking.

HAPPY NIHILISM? THE MORAL COST OF HEDONISM AND LUXURY

There are certain public duties carried by entertainment festivals that draw thousands or hundreds of thousands of participants: these involve communicating the civic responsibilities relating to waste that come along with being present in and enjoying the temporary shared spaces of entertainment. Likewise, it could be argued that the authorities responsible for encouraging and regulating tourism should require certain moral orientations from the visitors they court. But many festivalgoers and tourists might be turned off by overly didactic instructions from the places they go to have fun and feel free. Both Glastonbury and Afrika Burn festivals state publicly their commitment to environmental values and awareness of the impact of such huge gatherings of people focused on hedonistic fun, yet take quite different approaches to dealing with the waste produced. Glastonbury asks attendees to "not leave kit" in campsites and provides recycling bins, but more or less accepts that those requests will be mostly ignored and therefore puts into place cleanup teams to do the necessary work after the fact; while Afrika Burn insists on radical self-reliance and leave-no-trace as the responsibility of each participant, going so far as to give a report card on the cleanliness of the entire town map, camp by camp, after the festival. This serves to name and shame people in certain areas if they did not take responsibility for removing their trash. Is shame always the dark side of pleasure? In the same way that British newspapers name and shame the globe-trotting holidaying classes as those responsible for destroying the Maldives with trash, they also name and shame the hedonistic and irresponsible youth for not cleaning up after themselves after partying in front of the Pyramid Stage at Glastonbury. Pleasure is often twinned with pain or shame; in contemporary consumer culture it is arguably impossible to have one without the other. "To exist is to coexist. Yet this coexistence is suffused with *pleasure*, pleasure that appears perverse from the standpoint of the subject under the illusion that it has stripped the abjection from itself" (Morton, 2016: 129). Hedonistic consumption—which is oriented toward the pleasures of the flesh and spirit, aimed at prioritizing enjoyment and delight—despite possibly seeming perverse to outside onlookers, is always linked with misery, even if only in its own attempts to triumph over it. Rubbish provides a useful hinge-point for thinking through how joy and dirt are the material high and low, respectively, of consumer culture—linked like yin and yang, impossible to define without the other. Which is more perverse, the unbridled indulgences enjoyed at Afrika Burn, or the smoking presence of Rubbish Island in the Maldives? Which is more illusory, the fleeting moments of musical ecstasy in the fields of Worthy Farm or the idea that it is possible to leave no trace on a landscape after a week of self-indulgent partying? Timothy Morton summarizes "happy nihilism" as processes that "reduce things to bland substances that can be manipulated at will without regard to unintended consequences" (Morton, 2016: 52). In other words, if the environment is so fundamentally threatened that we cannot fix it, may we as well have a good time while it all falls apart? In reflecting on the material detritus of luxury tourism and indulgent festivalgoing, we need to consider once again how materiality and morality are intertwined. Are the participants at Afrika Burn and Burning Man more ethical subjects, because they carry their rubbish out with them? Or are they just as unethical as the revelers who drop their rubbish on the floor and leave their tents behind, in that they might be creating a similar amount of trash, anyway? To what extent are all consumerist spectacles inherently nihilistic, as Morton argues, in that they see no way out of the socio-ecological bind that has been produced by global neoliberal capitalism? In other words, seeing as this ship is going down (where the ship is Mother Earth, or more accurately human existence, and the earth will continue to exist long after we have made ourselves extinct, and it is sinking because of the multitude of man-made reasons for the destruction of life and the opportunities for survival), does it not make sense to try and enjoy the last minutes of the doomed voyage? While it might be a temporary balm on the wound to offer ethical perspectives on how to clean up our postparty and post-holiday messes, perhaps there is more honesty in a claim that there is logic in purging the horror of the coming trashocalypse by burying ourselves in pursuits of pleasure instead.

Many climate scientists and environmentalists agree that even if every consumer on the planet changes their behavior to become more ethical and to minimize the amount of waste (both visible and invisible) that they produce, it will not be enough unless massive changes are made to the ways in which big industry is regulated and the waste that they produce is radically reduced. As David Wallace-Wells puts it in his sobering *The Uninhabitable Earth*, "We won't get there through the [...] choices of individuals, but through policy changes" (Wallace-Wells, 2019: 169). With this in mind, is it more or less ethical to believe that individualistic actions (like cleaning up after oneself at Afrika Burn, or making an effort to not create extra nonrecyclable trash when on holiday in Bali) are contributing toward a solution? Would a more moral stance not be to put all of one's energies into lobbying governments to force change in industry, or even taking more radical direct action (Jensen, McBay, & Keith, 2011)? Arguably, it is a red herring to think that certain forms of hedonistic consumption can be part of a solution: this is the main critique of marketing attempts at branding certain commodities and services as green, ethical, or sustainable (Thomlinson, 2013). Can there be such a thing as green tourism in the Maldives, considering what we know about the infrastructure for dealing with rubbish there, and the huge impact that growing tourism has had on the fragile ecosystems of the archipelago? Certain moralizing discourses are attached to the narratives around luxury trash: on the one hand, a moral orientation that sees consumption as the source of excessive rubbish, and therefore as evidence of inherent evils of neoliberal capitalism; on the other hand, an optimistic sense that through thoughtful approaches to pleasure-seeking, the imprint of damage can be lessened or halted.

These questions speak to moral concerns, which have always animated debates about the meanings of consumption in contemporary cultures, and which are arguably heightened in the context of the purest forms of consumption for consumption's sake. There is a theoretical connection between the cultures of debauchery, fun, and pleasure and the piles of rubbish that they create as excess; therefore, there is an imperative to think through the moral dimensions of the material aspects of hedonism. Luxury items are often theorized as excessive (Kapferer, 2017) in that they do not serve needs so much as desires. What argument can be made that any human actually *needs* champagne, a weekend or week at an entertainment festival, or a holiday in the tropics? To the extent that these forms of consumption are outside of the ambit of needs and survival, they are excessive. This is of course a moral judgment: the boundaries of what is considered essential for survival and happiness are to an extent subjective. What is a luxury to one person may be a necessity to another, and vice versa. Parking for a moment the complexities of how luxury is defined and the importance of taking the relativity of the notion into account, the notion of luxury as excess is particularly useful in relation to thinking about its material culture aspects. Trash too, is excessive in its own way. Rubbish is what is left behind, what is no longer wanted or needed (Hawkins, 2006). And when cultures of luxury consumption and material culture collide, the one thing that is sure is that a mountain of rubbish will be produced. As this chapter has shown, the material trash-traces of hedonistic consumption force new, complex moral orientations toward consumer culture and drive an existential debate about the place of pleasure in consumer culture.

The next chapter turns its attention to forms of rubbish that are far from any pleasurable consumer experience, and instead of seeking the waste within explicitly consumerist culture, seeks the remnants of consumption within monumental landscapes of waste.

4

Devastation and Affect

Seeking Consumption in Oil and Plastic Trashscapes

This chapter focuses its attention on what, working with ideas from fine art criticism (Downes, 1992; Seegert, 2014), I call "trashscapes." Taking as a starting point the idea that, "garbage and sewage and industrial effluent are characteristics of a landscape we all help to make" (Downes, 1992: 17), the questions then arise: how has trash fundamentally changed the idea of landscape, and how have our moral orientations toward landscapes been changed by the eruption of various forms of waste and trash into those spaces that we used to consider, in some way at least, sacred due to not having been touched by urban sprawl, industrialization and mass agriculture? As Brian Thill argues, human industrial, economic and social activity has turned every landscape into a trashscape, indeed the entire world into "one vast and unevenly distributed trash heap" (2015: 4). This chapter considers the oceanic trashscapes created by oil and plastic waste, specifically how they are mediated. It asks whether, and if so where, ideas about consumption fit into the visual and filmic narratives of these trashscapes. How are the epic landscapes produced by oil and plastic waste communicated in popular media narratives, and what are the implications of those forms of communication for collective and individual moralities in relation to consumption and trash cultures?

The ocean has long been considered the ideal location for the disposal of waste—including, among many other things, treated and untreated sewage poured easily into the sea, the vast quantities of sand and earth displaced into continental margins by harbor dredging, and the irredeemable by-products of nuclear reactions secretly sunk. (Lavery, 2017)

One of the key colossal landscapes affected by spillage and trash is the ocean. Around 70 percent of the earth is comprised of saltwater. This chapter aims to explore how the pollution of the ocean by massive amounts of waste produced by human extractive and consumption activity comes into popular discourses about the environment. By focusing on narratives about how ocean-borne trash is mediated, and what invitations those narratives make for thinking about the scale of the rubbish and moral orientations toward it, the argument is made that the materialities and mediations of trash can affect shared consciousness in the age of the Anthropocene. Taking for granted the "real" existence of trashed landscapes on the earth, it is important to consider how narrative forms—often visual but also including other multimodal aspects including the textual—succeed in capturing the significance of that waste in nature. While there are many types of rubbish that end up in oceans, this chapter will focus specifically on oil spills and the accumulation of plastics, both of which have received significant media attention on account of their spectacular devastation, and both of which are linked in key ways to cultures of consumption.

Selected media narratives about each type of trashscape are examined in detail in this chapter, in dialogue with theoretical explorations on the themes of accountability, scale, and affect. Although touching on the "how" of visual representation, the discussion also explores what messages are sent about the power of nature and the moral positionality of human witnessing in response to huge-scale trash disasters. How have mediated trashscapes introduced a new sublime to the popular imaginary, one in which humanity is invited (an invitation that is likely to be declined by the audience on account of the intense anxiety that it produces) to come face to face with profoundly existential questions about the end of our contemporary civilization, and thus all who inhabit it? And what affective and emotional possibilities are made possible by the narratives, in terms of accepting or declining the invitations to know about, and act in response to, the existence of oceanic trashscapes of oil and plastic? Before turning to these questions, it is necessary to demonstrate how oil, plastic, and consumption are linked, materially and metaphorically, and thus require our attention in the project of theorizing the links between waste and consumption.

OIL AND PLASTIC: OCEANIC DETRITA AS PART OF
MATERIAL CONSUMER CULTURE

The oceans are littered with plastic, ordinarily, and are also the scene of extraordinary spillages of both plastic and oil, from time to time. Both wreak ecological havoc, both are incredibly expensive and time and labor intensive to clean up, to the extent that they are possible to clean up. And both materials, too, are deeply linked to the global consumer economy. Oil can be thought of as the urtext of commodity culture, plastic as its leftovers.

Oil is a primary commodity. As the fossil fuel that largely drives production and the accumulation of wealth in the global political-economy, it may seem perhaps a strange fit for a book that has thus far looked at case studies linked to postconsumer trash. Oil has been at the heart of some major wars and conflicts during the last hundred years. It is a finite resource, buried in the bowels of the earth and below the ocean floor that once pumped out and burned to produce energy fires the engines of every major industry operating in the world at the moment. There would be no motorized transport without oil, nor would there be large-scale mass production of any commodities. Also, crucially, there would be no plastic without oil. For oil not only fires the machines that produce the polymers from which the myriad plastic items (water and soft drink bottles, polystyrene packaging, toys, appliances, components of cars, frivolous throwaway party decorations) that populate our world are produced, it is also one of the key components from which the plastic compounds that comprise those items are chemically engineered (Freinkel, 2011: 26). If oil is a starting point, and plastic is an end point, on a chemical continuum that results in large scale formations of material waste, then it is impossible for us to think about the cultural meanings of waste or consumption without considering oil. A growing amount of critical attention is being paid to oil by scholars in the humanities and social sciences, including on the cultural politics of oil and media representations of oil spills (Parra, 2004; Mitchell, 2011; Looney, 2012; LeMenager, 2014; Silverstein, 2014). Research has been done about forms of environmental and social activism opposing the increasingly dangerous and destructive attempts to extract oil and government policies that allow it (McKibben, 2013), for example, from the Alberta tar sands in Canada (McCurdy, 2017, 2018) and in relation to the building of new pipelines across environmentally protected areas (Veltmeyer & Bowles, 2014). When a massively devastating oil spill happens, like that caused by the explosion of the Deepwater Horizon oil rig in 2010, there is typically a huge amount of media attention paid to the issue, testifying to the innately public character of such events. When oil is spilled at a rate of several thousand gallons per minute into the ocean, it is a matter of concern for all human beings, indeed all living creatures. Building on and contributing to these existing social and cultural lines of oil analysis, it is necessary also to consider how the scale of devastation—both social and environmental—is communicated in media narratives. Indeed, it is crucial to ask if it is even possible to fully capture the destruction caused by trash spills in natural environments, and if is not, what ideas are included and excluded from media narratives that try?

As oil is the origin point of plastic, so is plastic one of the end points of oil. "The continuous flow of oil fueled not just cars but an entire culture based on the consumption of new products made of plastics" (Freinkel, 2011: 26). Almost every item imaginable that is available in the consumer market is manufactured from or packaged in the stuff. Because plastic is manufactured from hydrocarbon molecules (Freinkel, 2011: 40), it is not illogical to think of plastic as a form of oil. From this perspective, oil is present in our everyday lives in multiple ways: it bags our apples, shrink-wraps our new technology items and forms their casings, we eat fast food off and with it, we feed our children milk through bottles and teats made of it, we store leftover food in it, and more. The throwaway culture that defines late capitalism means that there are billions (trillions?) of items that are manufactured with the intention of only ever being used once: plastic drinking bottles, plastic grocery bags, plastic drinking straws, cotton ear buds with plastic shafts, disposable drinking cups, plates and utensils, sanitary towels, cable ties . . . the list is almost endless. As well as these single-use items are those that are intended for use for only a relatively short time, such as plastic toothbrushes, cheap children's toys and party decorations. Furthermore, consider the many electronic items that are made from plastic, which are designed in order to become obsolete within two or three years and be thrown away and replaced. Taken together, this means that a monumental amount of plastic waste has been produced and discarded, is being produced and discarded, in late modernity. And a huge amount of this plastic ends up in the ocean, through direct littering and dumping on beaches, and through being transported there along the water courses that flow into seas. "Unless it's been beached or removed, every piece of plastic that has entered the ocean in the past century remains there in some form or another—an everlasting synthetic intrusion in the natural marine ecology" (Freinkel, 2011: 292). It is ironic, then, that although much oil originates from under the ocean floor, much of the plastic that it produces, once used and discarded by consumers, ends up floating on the ocean surface. Due to the powerful movement of "lateral and three-dimensional currents," both at ocean depths and surfaces and transoceanic air masses that influence the circulation patterns of water in the seas, a process that has been described as "drift" (Lavery, 2017), as well as the incredibly lightweight nature of plastic, the floating rubbish coagulates. Over time, plastics photodegrade, that is, break down into smaller and smaller pieces. But these plastic particles never biodegrade; instead they mix with microscopic creatures living in the oceans to create a kind of plastic-plankton soup. Scientists estimate that for every kilogram of plankton in the ocean, there are six kilograms of photodegraded plastic fragments (Moore, 2003). Both large plastic trash items and tiny plastic trash items collect in oceanic gyres to form huge dead zones in which very little life can flourish, and in which the life that is present is irrevocably impacted by the plastic (Freinkel, 2011: 302).

The contemporary age of consumer culture is best defined by the materials that respectively drive it and are driven by it: oil and plastic. These two materials also represent two important ends of the consumer economy continuum, the first extractive, the second discardative. Although oil is a primary commodity that is extracted through large-scale industrial activity, a consumer economy could not exist without it. And although plastic is manufactured by human ingenuity and profit-seeking industries, it is compounded from oil and comprises or packages, in one form or another, almost every other commodity traded on the open markets. Both end up creating scales of damage and destruction that are almost impossible to fully articulate. Both, also, end up in the ocean through processes that most people would describe as accidental, yet which can be immediately be understood as linked to the operations of consumer capitalism. Rubbish in the form of both leaked oil and littered plastic beg to be theorized in relation to one another in order to consider questions of scale, complicity, and affect in relation to the mediation of trashscapes. Up to this point, this book has explored, from the starting point of consumption, how trash is integrated into public narratives about the links between the two. The discussion turns next to case studies that start with waste—on epic scales—in order to seek the role of consumption therein. This is achieved through a thematic exploration of the ways in which oil and plastic trashscapes enter the public imagination through narratives of accountability, spectacle, and affect.

Figure 11. Nurdles litter a Hong Kong Beach in 2012. Photograph by Gary Stokes. Image reproduced with kind permission of Gary Stokes and www.oceanasia.com.

WHOSE FAULT IS IT ANYWAY? ACCOUNTING FOR "ACCIDENTAL" SPILLS

In 2012, a typhoon off the coast of Hong Kong caused a huge shipping vessel to overturn and three containers of nurdles—the tiny white plastic pellets used as a baseline material for the manufacture of many plastic items (Freinkel, 2011: 162)—were battered and broken resulting in billions of nurdles spilling into the sea. The nurdles littered the beaches near the typhoon-induced capsizing to the extent that they looked like they were covered with snow (DNews, 2012). Because, as fig. 11 shows, they look like fish eggs, nurdles are eaten by a variety of sea creatures, and have turned up in the guts of sea life. They have also littered beaches all around the world, carried great distances from spilled containers by ocean currents (Williams, 2015). In the immediate aftermath of the 2012 nurdle spills near Hong Kong, citizen and activist reaction was strong: people from all over the region went down to their beaches to try and help clean up the nurdle mess, literally sifting beach sand by the handful (Chen, 2012b).

In terms of accountability, Sinotec, the company that manufactured the nurdles, agreed to cover the costs of the cleanup (DNews, 2012). Much media attention has been paid in recent years to the issue of plastic in the oceans (which will be explored in more detail later in this chapter). What this nurdle spill speaks to, however, is the role that corporations play in polluting the oceans. Unlike discarded plastic products that have been thrown away by consumers, and which are carried by watercourses into the ocean, the Sinotec nurdles got there accidentally, and although citizens rallied to try to help clean up, the firm had to take a significant portion of responsibility for the mess. This mirrors, in some ways, the questions of accountability that arise when there is a massive oil spill.

As the global economy remains deeply reliant on fossil fuels and the onward march to extract them seems irreversible despite efforts by civil society and environmental movements to raise awareness about the dangers of extracting and burning more, major catastrophes such as the 2010 oil spill in the Gulf of Mexico bring the question of consumer and industrial reliance on fossil fuels, and the many-layered catastrophe of oil spilled on a mass scale, into public focus. The 2010 spill was caused by an explosion, itself caused by trapped methane and a series of technical malfunctions, on BP's Deepwater Horizon rig, situated in the Gulf of Mexico (Safina, 2011; Anderson, 2014; Boebert & Blossom, 2016). Eleven employees were killed in the explosion, which triggered a devastating oil leakage that saw an estimated 154-billion gallons of oil spilled into the ocean, devastating marine life and coastal areas for thousands of miles. The spill was widely reported on in the news media, because it was the hugest of its nature that had ever taken place. According to the Pew Research Center, media coverage of the oil spill represented a "different kind of disaster coverage," in which the "slow-motion" nature of the devastation meant that the Deepwater spill dominated headlines for one hundred days, much more than any oil spill had in the past (Pew Research Center, 2010).

The systems failure of the well and rig have been well documented by experts (Safina, 2011; Boebert & Blossom, 2016). The Deepwater Horizon oil rig was exploring a new well, which if constructed would pump oil from miles below the ocean floor. The technical specifications of the rig are widely available online, as these facts collated on the community-authored online encyclopedia, Wikipedia, note: it was capable of operating in waters up to 8,000 feet deep and to a maximum drill depth of 30,000 feet. Before commencing drilling in what became the site of the disaster, the Macondo prospect off the coast of Louisiana, United States, the Deepwater Horizon rig had successfully drilled the deepest oil well in the world. The rig was owned by a company called Transocean, which leased it to BP (Wikipedia, 2018a). The explosion took place on April 20, 2010, and according to facts reported in various documents summarized on Wikipedia, at the time of the explosion the rig was drilling an exploratory well, with the intention of opening an extractive well that would be 18,373 feet below sea level. Sources report that workers on the rig had safety concerns but were discouraged from reporting them, and that BP chose "riskier procedures to save time or money" and the blast was triggered when "methane gas ran up the drilling column and ignited" (Hoffman & Jennings, 2011: 100), in turn causing a huge fire, which burned for more than a day, with the rig sinking on April 22, 2010 (Wikipedia, 2018b). The leak in the exploratory well was discovered that same day, and over the next six months the unplugged oil well spewed an estimated 2,559,055 cubic feet of crude into the ocean. Several efforts were made to plug the well, but these only succeeded on September 19, 2010 (Wikipedia, 2018c). Coastlines were covered in oil, and the environmental impact of the spill is still being measured, but by all accounts is devastating (Beyer et al., 2016). Due to the scale of the disaster, a great deal of public attention was focused on the question of responsibility, with various actors being blamed (and blaming each other). A number of institutional and public cultures collided in the complex matrix of discourses that circulated around the disaster, as private companies worked to blame others and defend themselves, and with contextual politics affecting the ways in which those discourses were received and circulated (Hoffman & Jennings, 2011). News reporting of the disaster tended to utilize a number of frames, including those preferred by BP, and those that centered on the impact on animals and wildlife (Anderson, 2014).

Some scholarly attention has been paid to question of communication in relation to the oil spill. From one perspective, organizational communication scholars have reflected on how the companies involved in the crisis, particularly BP, succeeded in communicating effectively with the public, and attempting to repair their image, after the oil-spill (Bostrom et al., 2015; Walker et al., 2015). Precisely because "BP became the focus of media attention, resulting in wide criticism of the company's actions surrounding the crisis" (Smithson & Venette, 2013: 396), the success or failure (although regrettably not in much detail the ethics) of BP's communication strategy post-spill has been discussed by scholars working in management and corporate communications. Another perspective, arguably under examined, has looked at how public conversations about the disaster played out on social media, for example the study of how online Twitter users interacted with information about the oil spill and participated in discussions about how to help clean it up (Starbird et al., 2015). The question of how the disaster came into the public imagination in other ways through various forms of popular narrative requires more attention, and it is this project to which this chapter partially contributes.

News footage of the disaster was so prolific that the image of the burning oil rig—smoke pluming hundreds of feet up, flames licking the blue of the sky, while firefighting boats struggle in vain to quell the blaze with puny-seeming arcs of water—are seared into popular memory. News websites featured image galleries cataloging the scale of the devastation. For example, the CBS News website hosts a gallery of one hundred images of the Deepwater Horizon disaster, which includes shots of the burning rig from every possible angle, wide-lens shots putting the burning rig in the center of a seemingly endless silver-blue ocean, images of the rust-brown slick of oil from up close and afar, satellite images of the extent of its spread, images of politicians, family members, cleanup workers, photographs of wildlife rescue volunteers trying to save birds and other wildlife, images of dead fish washed up on beaches, and images of oil slicked coastlines and wetlands. Other news outlets also included blurry deep-water images of the devastating crack in the pipe itself and the surge of dirty oil pumping out endlessly.

In addition to the extensive news coverage that ensued, the event has also found its way in to other cultural narratives. For example, in the opening episodes of the first season of the television series, *The Newsroom* (2012), the Deepwater Horizon disaster plays an important role in presenting the news as a core pillar of social and environmental democracy. Starring Jeff Bridges and written and produced by Aaron Sorkin, *The Newsroom* focuses on the work lives of the news team of a fictional cable news show. The pilot episode, as well as introducing us to a plethora of complex characters (the anchor, played by Bridges, is charming and intelligent on-screen, but arrogant, vitriolic, and borderline abusive off it; the executive producer, played by Emily Mortimer, just back from three years of embedded reporting in Afghanistan and Iraq, and former lover of the anchor, is deeply committed to the fourth estate role of the news in a democracy; and various younger producers and researchers all vying to prove their worth and contribute to a visionary news show), centers the narrative on the Deepwater Horizon oil spill. The drama takes place almost entirely in the newsroom itself, and the tension hinges on the question of whether the news of the explosion on the rig—when it first comes through the news wires—is "big" enough to dominate an entire hour's worth of reporting and analysis, and displace other news of the day. Despite tensions between the incoming and outgoing production team, thanks to some good luck and reliable sources at BP and Haliburton, the team quickly realizes that the Deepwater Horizon story is about much more than a search-and-rescue operation for missing workers, but about to be the worst oil-spill environmental disaster ever. Thanks to their shrewd recognition of the broad public implications of the explosion and spill and their willingness to take risks in covering it, they scoop every other network on the real story and set the tone for the coverage for the days to come. Through the discussion that the journalists have on the implications of the explosion and spill, the viewers learn key facts: that the rig was attempting to drill deeper than ever, that important safety precautions and tests had not been carried out, that the scale of the spill was exponentially bigger than the Exxon-Valdez spill in the Arctic years earlier, that the government had failed to properly monitor and check the rigs in order to hold them accountable to safety and environmental standards, that the company itself had been negligent. In the episode, very few visuals are shown of the disaster itself. The only cue is the image of the burning oil rig visible in the background of the scene on one of the television screens in the office. Hinting at how environmental stories might be the new mainstream, Episode 1 of the first season of *The Newsroom* drives home the vision of journalists working in the public interest in order to expose facts and to hold the powerful to account. The oil spill is understood to be a disaster of such magnitude that it affects all citizens. In this narrative, accountability is understood to be something that corporate and political power share, and journalism plays the crucial watchdog role in exposing them when they fail to act in the public interest.

The Great Invisible is a 2014 documentary directed by Margaret Brown (93 minutes). The film aims to present the hidden story of the disaster, and to trace the long-term effects of the oil spill on the affected communities on the Gulf coastline. Most of the film focuses on the economic and social impact of the spill on the local inhabitants of the areas on the coastline, exploring the major economic challenges the disaster created for people working in the fishing, oyster and shrimp industries, one of the main areas of employment for people in Louisiana and Alabama. Most of the documentary focuses on providing an account of the impact of the oil spill on the economic life of the Louisiana wetlands, the technical aspects of the rig, and the lives of the workers on the rig before it exploded. A number of scenes present interviews with Deepwater Horizon workers who survived the tragedy, allowing them to share in detail how their lives were destroyed by the tragedy on multiple levels: their physical and mental health, economically, socially, and the impact on their relationships.

The documentary also includes scenes from various government enquiries and also from some oil industry events, putting the personal stories of the survivors into the context of the seemingly unstoppable economic machinery of the oil-industrial complex, buoyed by powerful government and economic structures. The film is extremely effective at exploring the detailed social and political aspects of the disaster, and the impacts that it had on the lives of those living in the affected communities, and the brazen abuse of power by the corporations and governments who should not have allowed it to happen.

Deepwater Horizon (97 minutes) is a 2016 major Hollywood blockbuster directed by Peter Berg and starring Mark Wahlberg, Kate Hudson, Kurt Russell, John Malkovich and Gina Rodriguez. This film, as its title makes plain, tells the story of what happened on the oil rig on the fateful day of April 20, 2010. Told from the perspective of one of the oil rig workers, chief electronics technician Mike Williams (played by Wahlberg), the narrative focuses on the day of the explosion, and follows Mike and his colleagues as they interact with visiting BP officials who are on the rig purportedly to hand out an achievement award to the team, but in truth are there to put pressure on the operational team to finalize testing and proceed to the drilling of the extraction well, with no further delays that would have been caused by important safety checks. The story is told from the perspective of the oil rig workers, who are portrayed as honest, good-natured, and hard-working ordinary folk. BP is represented, through its executives visiting the rig, as an evil corporation interested only in profit and neither the well-being of their workers nor the environment.

What these narratives share in terms of their overall orientation to the story of accidental oil spills in general, and the Deepwater Horizon disaster in particular, is the argument that accountability rests with the powerful: the corporations that own and leased the rig and that were prospecting for deep-sea oil, and the government that failed to properly ensure that they were not operating in ways that could damage the public interest or the environmental commons. In their testimony to the congressional inquiry into the spill, it was found that BP's communicative approach was to "stonewall," that is, to deflect attention to miniscule and unimportant details, rather than take liability for the bigger picture (Smithson & Venette, 2013). The huge failure in accountability, both corporate and governmental, is therefore a central narrative theme in popular media narratives about the creation of massive, accidental trashscapes like the Deepwater Horizon oil spill. Popular media texts such as the television show and films discussed here, speak to the broader impact of the event, and the journalistic project of consciousness-raising about issues of public importance through media coverage. While there will always be citizens who will hurry to their local beach to try and help sieve nurdles from the sand, or save the lives of oil-coated birds, it is the huge corporations, propped up and insufficiently regulated by governments, that should be held accountable for their central role in creating the kinds of spectacular trashscapes that are, sadly, becoming increasingly recognizable in the age of the Anthropocene. If we agree that accountability for devastating oil spills rests primarily with the powerful, while of course recognizing that citizens have some power to react and activate in resistance, the question then rises about how the scale of these spectacular disasters is communicated, and the extent to which individual citizens (who are also consumers) are invited to consider their own positionality within the drama of trashscapes, like the BP oil spill of 2010.

READING THE SLICK: SPECTACLE, SCALE, AND THE MONSTROUS

The first four seconds of *The Great Invisible* show the now immediately recognizable aerial footage of the burning oil rig (see fig. 12), which dominated news broadcasts after the explosion. Slightly blurry, and shifting in a manner suggesting that it was taken by an amateur filmmaker from a helicopter, the screen frames a scene of the rig on fire, surrounded by four rescue ships, two of them sending jets of water on to the blaze. The horizon, interrupted by a thick black plume of smoke underscored by a fluorescent orange blaze, cuts the image around a quarter of the way from the top. The rig and ships sit in the next quarter of the image, and the bottom half of the screen is dominated by the smooth, deep blue of ocean surface.

Next, the film cuts to scenes of rig burning at night, the blaze filling the screen, the crackle of the conflagration filling the audio, before cutting to clips of the key political and economic actors, and survivors, speaking in various settings of the disaster, as well as underwater clips of oil spewing from the punctured well shaft. For the majority of the documentary, apart from a few scenes once again of the conflagration in the middle, the focus remains firmly fixed on the people affected by the disaster, including the survivors and the residents of the affected communities. But it is the scenes of the conflagration, and the oil slick that carry a particularly powerful resonance, and that set the tone for the sense of spectacular disaster that are underwritten by the social narrative. Aerial photography of the spill shows rust-brown oil slicking hugely into the blue of the water, underwater shots of the dirty oil pumping into the ocean, and scenes of the rig smoking at dawn, follow swiftly from one

Figure 12. The scene featured in the opening image of *The Great Invisible*. Deepwater Horizon burns while oil gushes into the Gulf of Mexico and ships try fruitlessly to put out the fire. Photograph by US Coast Guard, free use license through Wikimedia Commons.

another as the opening credits roll. The beautiful crystal blue of the ocean is disrupted by the oil slick, thick and rust colored in patches, and dispersing to a fuzzy brown at its edges. It is only through these long shots, the process of zooming out, that the viewer is able to get an abstract sense of quite how much oil spilled into the ocean, and imagine what this immense amount of wasted crude looks like: a devastating spectacle.

In an oil spill as huge as Deepwater Horizon, "the temporal horizons of the disaster zone are, on a number of fronts, difficult to keep in view" (Nixon, 2013: 272). The farthest that we are able to zoom out, when attempting to view massive phenomena on the earth's surface, is to look from the perspective of a satellite. Fig. 13 shows a satellite image of the oil spill, taken and made publicly available by NASA. The image was captured on May 24, 2010. NASA captioned the image as follows:

NASA's Terra Satellites Sees Spill on May 24: Sunlight illuminated the lingering oil slick off the Mississippi Delta on May 24, 2010. The Moderate-

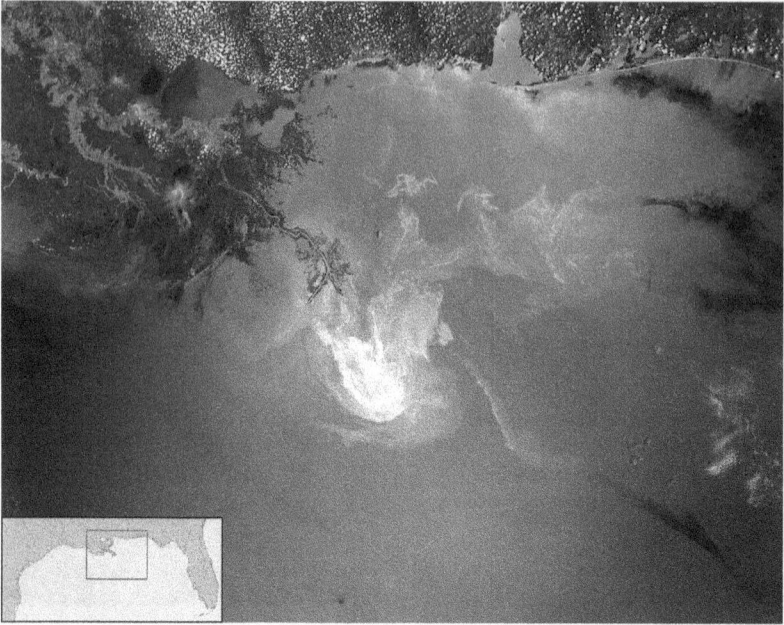

Figure 13. Satellite photo of the oil spill taken by NASA. Available in the public domain. Source: Wikimedia Commons. Image by NASA licensed by Wiki Commons.

Resolution Imaging Spectroradiometer (MODIS) on NASA's Terra satellite captured this image the same day. Oil smoothes the ocean surface, making the Sun's reflection brighter near the centerline of the path of the satellite, and reducing the scattering of sunlight in other places. As a result, the oil slick is brighter than the surrounding water in some places (image center) and darker than the surrounding water in others (image lower right). The tip of the Mississippi Delta is surrounded by muddy water that appears light tan. Bright white ribbons of oil streak across this sediment-laden water. Tendrils of oil extend to the north and east of the main body of the slick. A small, dark plume along the edge of the slick, not far from the original location of the Deepwater Horizon rig, indicates a possible controlled burn of oil on the ocean surface. To the west of the bird's-foot part of the delta, dark patches in the water may also be oil, but detecting a manmade oil slick in coastal areas can be even more complicated than detecting it in the open ocean. When oil slicks are visible in satellite images, it is because they have changed how the water reflects light, either by making the Sun's reflection brighter or by dampening the scattering of sunlight, which makes the oily area darker. In coastal areas, however, similar changes in reflectivity can occur from differences in salinity (fresh versus salt water) and from naturally produced oils from plants. (Michon Scott NASA's Earth Observatory NASA Goddard Space Flight Center)

The image is immediately recognizable as a piece of planet earth. The little green-and-blue map in the bottom-left corner confirms this, by locating and contextualizing it as a portion of the coast in the Gulf of Mexico, indicated by the red square. The satellite image of the oil slick offers an epic extraterrestrial viewpoint—first popularized through the photographing of earth from the moon in 1969—in which humanity, with the help of technology, achieves an extreme long-shot vision of the planet we call home. Very few people actually get to go to space, but through satellite photography we can get a glimpse of the view from up there. Usually the view of the earth from space invites a kind of magnificent reverie from the viewer, as it replaces a sense of locality with one of globality. Seeing the earth as it exists moving through space, a complete and whole sphere carries with it the message not only of its fragility but of how it is the only place that all human beings and living creatures can call home. It was images of the earth from space that contributed to the popularizing of a discourse (though of course not apolitical) that the earth is home to all humanity (Cosgrove, 1994). Fig. 13 speaks to that optimistic and transcendent narrative; through its capturing of the sublime beauty of sunlight reflecting off water. Our sun, our water. But the beauty of the image is quickly evaporated by the detailed discussion of what it is showing. The viewer quickly learns that the beautiful flares of light on the surface of the ocean are in fact slicks of oil, smoothing the surface of the water and thereby reflecting the sun more brilliantly. Underneath that gorgeous reflection untold horrors are taking place: sea creatures are being smothered and suffocated, and oil-slicked death multiplies. What lies in the appeal of seeing the world like so, from above? Is it precisely because stepping back—as far back as our technologies have allowed us to step—means that as viewers we can be spared the miserable detail of what is happening in the precise locality of the surface? The human cost (the lives lost, the injuries, the emotional and psychological traumas suffered by the survivors, the families of the dead, the toll on the rescue workers and those fighting to save wildlife), the cost to fauna and flora, to ocean, beach, wetland and soil is momentarily eclipsed by the brightness in the longest-possible shot of that mess. It is taken from so far away, that the ugliness and misery is obliterated into an abstract scene of light, color and organic shapes—once again the earth that we recognize. The pain and suffering caused by the spill is obscured by the prettiness of reflected sunshine and the lattice of a coastline. Although the satellite and aerial image succeeds in communicating the scale of the oil spill, it also serves to obscure some of its most horrific details.

In contrast, the feature film *Deepwater Horizon* does not spare the viewer in its harrowing account of the human cost of the tragedy, and the terror endured by the survivors. In the opening sequence, the visual narrative takes the viewer under the water below the rig. Offering the perspective of a remote-controlled submarine, the viewer scans the length of pipe stretching from the rig at the surface all the way down to the ocean bed almost four miles blow. The screen is almost entirely dark, and as the seconds tick by shapes become discernible—the line of the pipe, its curved surface, the rivets at internals connecting one piece to another. The soundtrack comprises of inky-sounding submersion noises, inescapably ominous. Most viewers would be well aware how this story ends, having watched the spill, fire, and cleanup operation on television for months in 2010. Because there is a need to create suspense in this narrative even though everyone knows how the story ends, the director has instead worked to introduce tension by leveraging precisely off the viewers' knowing. Opening the film by showing us the pipeline that will—devastatingly—explode and leak within twenty-four hours puts the viewer into a sense of complicity with the pipe, but also introduces a sense of helplessness. We know what will happen and we know that we are powerless to stop it. The only thing to do, then, is to abandon ourselves to the narrative in order to see *how* it happens. After this unnerving opening sequence, which hints at impending doom with that creaking pipeline at its heart, the narrative turns to establishing the characters and their relationships, following Mike as he packs up to leave home for a three-week stint on the rig, and journeys with colleagues and BP executives by helicopter back to their remote place of work, surrounded by only the stunning blue of the ocean.

Once on the rig, catching up again with colleagues, Mike pauses to flip a penny into the ocean (at around 23:30). This coin is a symbol of good luck, and the camera once again dives, following the hapless penny as it plunges into the depths, and descends along the pipeline, down, down, down. We leave the sunny surface, the reassuring hardhats and work overalls worn by the rig workers, their good-natured banter and the familiar blue of our sky, and reenter this strange underwater world, where light is quickly lost and within moments we are in a dark abyss once again, with the shapes of the underwater infrastructure, more familiar now, coming into view. But this time, alongside the pipe infrastructure we remember from the opening scene, as we watch the coin spin and sink, we see something unnerving: bubbles ascending past. This sure sign of the presence of some form of gas in the water is brought to the attention of the viewer, and we know that it signals that something is terribly wrong. But as the scene shifts to a shot of the rig from below, we realize that the workers on the rig above, shielded by the voracious surface of the ocean with its wind-whipped whitecaps and surging waves crashing against the pillars of the rig, have no chance of spotting those telltale bubbles that are so obvious below.

As the film then builds toward the inevitable, scenes play out detailing the internal politics and power plays of the men and woman in charge of the rig, undertaking the negative pressure test in order to ascertain the safety of the well. The narrative positions the BP executives as driven by avarice and ego, who will not allow the working-class men whose job it is to look after the rig to make sure it works as it was supposed to. The workers' good intentions, their hard work, their expertise, is undermined by the arrogance and shortsightedness of the company executives, who did not have the expertise of the technical workers on the rig, and who repeatedly ignored safety concerns raised. As the infrastructure of the rig is aligned to undertake another negative pressure test, the camera dives underwater again, taking us to the pipes, and then inside them. For a few seconds, we see a dark-brown substance surging and rushing within the pipes. This is the first time in the film that the oil itself is visually represented. We get a sense of the extreme pressure under which this substance exists, and we get a hint of the intense power of its movement. While the visuals of the film fetishize the hardware of the rig, its size, and awesome scale and functionality, they simultaneously hint at its impending failure. And while the narrative succeeds in capturing the human error and egoism that inherently causes the deadly failure of the technology, there is also a suggestion that there is a much more powerful force at work, one that ultimately overshadows the authority of human invention and technology. And it is in this visual that the idea of oil as a monstrous beast, ultimately uncontrollable, emerges.

Earlier in the film, Mike has a conversation with his daughter, in which she rehearses a presentation she will give at school about her dad's job. Using a can of coke as a prop, she explains the physics of the oil well: due to the pressure that exists at great depths, when a reserve of oil is punctured, and pressure is placed on that spot, eventually the oil inside will shoot or gush out, sometimes in a spectacular fashion. The little girl says,

That oil is a monster. Like the mean old dinosaurs all that oil used to be. So, for 300 million years these old dinosaurs have been squeezed tighter and tighter and tighter ... because they got miles of earth and ocean pressing down on them. They're trapped. [...] Then dad and his friends make a hole in their roof. And these mean old dinosaurs can't believe it. So, they rush to the new hole, then smack, they run into a big machine that he and his friends have down on the ocean floor called a ... [Mike interjects: blowout preventer] and then they put this stuff called mud that they cram down the straw. The mud's so thick and heavy that it blocks the monsters from coming up.

She concludes her practice presentation by proudly saying that it was her daddy who "tamed the dinosaurs." Oil is a fossil fuel in the sense that it is formed through ancient processes. The suggestion that oil is a kind of untamed prehistoric angry monster is fully realized in the scenes showing the pipeline exploding. When the pipe fails and the pressure builds up to the point that the machinery of the rig can no longer contain it (51:39), there is a sense that the terrifying metaphysical beast that lies in the deep, that cannot be stopped, is trying to push up through the creaking and clanking machinery of the pipe and the well after having made an arduous journey through the ocean floor and miles of water. As mud starts to seep through the floor of the testing room, increasingly unnerving noises are apparent: loud creaking and groaning, the sounds of pressure and something straining to break or erupt. Along with the mounting terror of the workers, the sounds of the "monster" preparing to unleash its fury builds, until suddenly the pipe erupts with tremendous force, hurling the human bodies around like dolls, slamming them into the walls and ceiling of the pump room. The beast has been unleashed— by human folly—and its rage is terrifying. The rest of the film hinges on this moment, and scenes of terror, devastation, and destruction; mud, blood, broken bones, and bodies, follow.

In Peter Hugh's ethnography of oil workers in Trinidad, he reports on how his participants spoke about Deepwater Horizon. The comments of his participants reveal an enthusiasm for oil exploration, for the adventure and excitement of the extraction project.

British Petroleum had done nothing but perforate the caprock, and geological pressure was producing huge volumes [of oil] every day. This is how it comes up, they explained. It seemed beautiful, natural, and inevitable. No

Figure 14. Harrowing scenes in the film *Deepwater Horizon* feature the exploding and burning oil rig against a black night sky and ocean, echoing the kind of visual documented in this photograph of flare-off gas at the site of drilling operations at the Deepwater. Photograph by US Coast Guard Petty Officer 1st Class Matthew Belson, licensed by Wikimedia Commons.

one said as much, but the haemorrhage at the bottom of the sea seemed to prove that oil *should* come up, not that it shouldn't. (Hughes, 2017: 141)

This sense is brilliantly captured in the special effects images created for *Deepwater Horizon*. As the oil and mud erupt through the pipes, it become increasingly obvious that they are forces that cannot be controlled by the machines and human bodies in its way, indeed, these are easily destroyed and wounded by the power of the erupting oil and mud, the "monster." The human bodies that are in the way are crushed and broken by this immense, nameless, faceless power. And the oil monster only builds in its expression of rage, unleashing more fury on the rig and its unlucky workers. In disaster orgy style, the film proceeds from scene to scene of explosion, injury, collapse, destruction, and fire, as the catastrophe rapidly unfolds. For the next fifty minutes, the film chronicles in detail the incredible events—the injuries, the losses of life, the gigantic fireballs and explosions, the collapsing machinery and infrastructure, and the escape attempts of all the survivors on board. As the disaster builds, the narrative increasingly relies on long shots, showing the burning rig dwarfed by the ocean, of the rig burning in the distance. These are juxtaposed with close-up shots in which only fire, flames, or spewing oil fill the frame.

The material aspects of the disaster are communicated in intense visual detail. Of course, the impact on human life takes center stage, but as we know well from the media coverage about the oil spill, the impact of the explosion was much more than the eleven human lives lost, countless injuries and posttraumatic stress of the survivors. The event had major environmental consequences. These are not addressed in *Deepwater Horizon*—barring one short scene when an oil-covered pelican flies into a ship anchored off to the side of the rig after the oil starts spewing. The bird is covered in oil and can't fly, and when it careens into the pilot cabin of the observing vessel, it bashes into all the windscreens until it comes to rest, traumatized, dying, a cipher for the thousands of animals soon to be suffering the same condition.

Some might analyze the presence in the public realm of spectacular images of burning oil rigs and spreading oil spills as a kind of "disaster porn" (Recuber, 2013), in which news agencies profit from providing spectacular, shocking images of news events, usually removed from the everyday experiences of the viewers, hooks them with addictive footage of suffering and disasters happening elsewhere in the world. Although there is certainly an economic motivation for reporting on or narrating highly dramatic and sensational environmental stories, it should not be forgotten that the coverage also provides an opportunity to engage with the social issues at stake. As Lilie Chouliaraki has argued, how distant images of suffering are narrated matters, in terms of how viewers are invited to see themselves as capable of moral action in relation to those who are affected by the suffering (Chouliaraki, 2008, 2013). In the feature film just discussed at length, the viewer is invited to empathize closely with the suffering oil rig workers, betrayed by their employers and the conglomerate of greedy corporations who insisted on drilling despite the dangers, as well as the families of those who lost their lives, those who were physically and mentally scarred for life. But there is little opportunity given to the viewer to feel empathy for the other victims of the disaster: the ocean itself and the many creatures living within it.

To offer a brief point of contrast, in the novel *Sing, Unburied, Sing* by Jesmyn Ward, set in a fictional Louisiana rural town, the character Michael is the father of one of the narrators, a young boy called Jojo. Michael is in prison for drug-related offences, and when time comes for his release, Jojo's mother takes him and his sister upstate to collect Michael. As he reintegrates into Jojo's precarious and spiritually troubled life, we learn more about Michael's background. Before going to jail, Michael worked as a welder on the Deepwater Horizon rig, and was on board when it exploded. Michael and Leonie (Jojo's mother) both have drug problems. It is implied that part of the suffering that Michael is trying to drown in a meth high stems from the massive trauma of what he experienced on Deepwater Horizon. In one scene, where he takes Jojo fishing—"just the boys"—he reveals a rare moment of vulnerability and posttraumatic stress. Michael tells Jojo how he when he was on the rig, he used to watch the dolphins playing in the waves below, seemingly performing for the pleasure of the humans above. And how, when he learned about the baby dolphins washing up dead on Louisiana beaches, poisoned by the billions of gallons of oil spilled into his beloved Gulf, he broke down and wept. Jojo takes the story as a lesson about the spiritual importance of all animals, but for readers it might hint at some of the broader existential and emotional fallout of the spill.

Deepwater Horizon invites a kind of masochistic witnessing of tragedy in all its horrendous glory. Although the close-up scenes of the injured, trapped, and dead humans are incredibly upsetting, when the point of view pulls out to show the rig burning at night, a kind of awful beauty is recognizable. The power of fire, its uncontrollability, being fed by the rich fuel of crude oil surging with an almost mystical power, and the elemental clash of water and flame lends itself to a kind of sublime aesthetic. Human beings are incredibly vulnerable in the face of such powerful natural forces. Our bodies cannot withstand the heat of the flame; our lungs will quickly be filled by saltwater if we are immersed in it, injured. We are breakable. And it is the elemental forces of the earth that can break us. Yet still, we play—as a species—with that fire. We have intentionally come close to danger in our quest to extract resources from underneath the earth; we have taken huge risks in our attempt to conquer nature. But sometimes nature conquers us back. As the oil monster uncurls from its peaceful lair beneath us—provoked by our prodding, our hubris, our arrogance in thinking that we can control the uncontrollable—and works up to unleash the full force of its power on us, the true extent of the natural forces that organize the earth, and our own weakness in response, become visible. And other living creatures, blameless, are the collateral damage.

From the perspective of the film, media narratives about the Deepwater Horizon spill tend to accentuate the scale of devastation as well as the mysterious monstrosity of oil. The impact of the spill is framed as being on workers and citizens, and very little sense of either consumers or consumption comes into the narratives that have been discussed so far. Does this mean that they have nothing at all to do with consumer culture? Discourse analysis often highlights absences: and in the narratives that have been looked at about the Deepwater Horizon oil spill, the link between oil and consumer culture is perhaps the most striking omission. A second monster lurks underneath narratives of the oil spill, this one invisible: consumer society itself.

Up to this point, the discussion has focused on the ways in which the large-scale devastation caused by the Deepwater Horizon disaster was visually communicated in key texts. Next the discussion will turn to a different kind of oceanic waste, the presence of plastic in the world's waters, and how these are visually communicated in two key screen-texts. These two case studies—of oil and plastic trashing the oceans—will be brought together in a critical discussion in the final section of the chapter. Although oil is the driver of consumer capitalism, evocatively represented perhaps by the scene in which the Coca-Cola can stands in for the oil well in an explanation of how drilling happens, it seems almost impossible for popular narratives about the devastation caused by spills to make direct connections between the mythical substance and the ordinary consumption practices of everyday life. This connection is made more easily in narratives about another oceanic trashscape: so-called plastic gyres.

NARRATING THE "GYRE": PLASTICITY, AFFECT, AND DEVASTATION

The oceans are not only the repository for that most awful form of trash, accidentally spilled oil. It is also the end point of many other forms of garbage made from and with oil, most notably plastic items. In recent years, there has been growing public awareness about the problem of plastic in the oceans. The first report on the so-called plastic trash island in the Pacific was published in *Natural History Magazine* in 2003 (Moore, 2003). The author, an experienced sailor, Charles Moore, reports how he and his crew decided to take a "short-cut" across the Pacific Gyre between Hawaii and the American mainland, after completing a yacht race. A gyre is an area of the ocean in which the waters circulate slowly in a clockwise direction, an effect caused by the rotation of the earth and the resultant prevailing winds and ocean currents. Crossing the Pacific gyre in 2003, Moore was shocked to see that, "in the week it took to cross the subtropical high, no matter what time of day I looked, plastic debris was floating everywhere: bottles, bottle caps, wrappers, fragments" (Moore, 2003). At the time, it was estimated that the "patch" of plastic trash was around the size of Texas, and that there were around 3 million tons of plastic waste coagulated in the Pacific gyre. In the seventeen years since this first report on the monumental presence of plastic rubbish in the oceans, the scale of the problem has only gotten worse. A recent report in the *Washington Post* noted that plastic within the "Great Pacific Garbage Patch" is increasing exponentially, with scientists estimating that its size is now three times that of France, and that is actually four to sixteen times larger than originally thought (Mooney, 2018), though it is certainly not visible from outer space as some have sensationally suggested (Parker, 2018). The topic of plastic in the ocean has been addressed by a number of science and environmental journalists, but it has also been brought into the public eye through the activist efforts of a number of environmental organizations, including Ocean Cleanup. According to media reports, humans put 8 million metric tons of plastic into the oceans annually (Mooney, 2015). Trash, mostly plastic, ends up in the oceans by being washed there via city storm drains and river systems. Plastic rubbish has even been discovered in the Mariana Trench, the deepest point in the ocean (Gibbens, 2018). A significant number of media reports highlight the consumer origination of the items floating and photodegrading in the ocean. An *Independent* article about a "tide of plastic rubbish discovered in the Caribbean" notes that it includes cutlery, bags, and bottles (Embury-Dennis, 2017). However, other media reports point out that the majority of the plastic detritus in the ocean is from abandoned fishing gear (Parker, 2018)

Perhaps one of the key things to understand about plastic as oceanic trash, is that is does not biodegrade, it only photodegrades. This means that instead of being reintegrated into organic matter, the way other forms of waste are, plastic can only be broken down by light into smaller and smaller particles, which although progressively smaller fragments, remain polymers. Research has shown that "in a marine environment, polymer molecules are virtually immortal" (Freinkel, 2011: 292). These "micro-plastics" are "still too tough for most anything—even such indiscriminate consumers as bacteria—to digest" (Moore, 2003). The massive trash gyre that exists in the Pacific—as well as in every other ocean gyre on the planet (see Lindemann, 2017)—is comprised of both trillions of fragments of microplastics, which are not visible to the naked eye and larger, visible items such as "ghost nets" (discarded and broken fishing nets) and plastic containers of every shape, size, and color.

Studies have shown that in the plastic-rich trash gyres, for every kilogram of microscopic plankton present (the building block of life in the ocean, and the bottom of the food chain), there are also six kilograms of microplastics present, a "plastic-plankton soup" (Moore, 2003). Whatever creature eats plankton

Figure 15. A sample of floating plastic trash in the ocean. Image reproduced with permission of the Ocean Cleanup Foundation.

also eats microplastics—and the toxic chemicals contained in and attached to them—which are in turn ingested by larger sea creatures all the way up the food chain, and including the many sea creatures that humans eat. Through the epic proportions of waste that humans have produced through industrial production and consumption, we have created a plastic ocean in more ways than one. First, we have produced a situation in which the ocean, and all the life that it contains, is literally being choked by plastic trash. Second, we have created a substance that is indestructible by any known organic process, and as such it is becoming intricately enmeshed with life in the ocean at a molecular level—it is now a plastic-plankton soup, not just plankton, that is the basis of the ocean food chain. And finally, we have created so much trash that the only way to be able to hold the idea of its scale is to think of it as an ocean of trash. We have trash in the ocean, our ocean is "made" of trash, and we have produced oceans and oceans of trash that are now impacting on life in numerous ways. Thus, we could make the argument that plasticity—the key material feature of being moldable into any conceivable shape, which makes this postmodern substance so useful to modern consumer society—needs to be retheorized from the perspective of rubbish. Now the material is remolding our environments, our food chain, and ultimately also human beings. No longer can we take pride in molding the polymers to our own agendas; now we need to recognize, as one *Guardian* writer put it, that as we eat the seafood that has eaten plastic, "the sea is feeding human garbage back to us" (Hoare, 2018).

NGOs are increasingly relying on strategies of visual communication in order to communicate the scale of the plastic trash problem, and to incite viewers to help solve the problem by contributing to their efforts as well as by changing their own consumption habits with regards to plastic. The Ocean Cleanup is one such NGO. Led by a charismatic millennial, Boyan Slat, the organization devotes significant efforts to media campaigns aimed at documenting the scale of the plastic ocean problem and explicating their proposed solutions. There is no scope to explore the latter in too much detail here; instead it is worthwhile focusing on the visual strategies engaged to show how the ocean has become the planetary site in which plastic waste aggregates. One of the first campaigns by the NGO was to get a more accurate sense of the size of the Pacific Trash Gyre between Hawaii and the West Coast of the United States. In order to do this, they chartered a plane able to fly very long distances, and performed systematic aerial photography of representative samples of the ocean. The organization produced a "behind-the-scenes" video of the mission, and also published some of the photography showing the huge floating bits of trash from above, on their website (www.theoceancleanup.com). These images are particularly captivating, showing the abstract shapes of discarded fishing nets and other large detritus suspended in the perfect blue of deep waters (see fig. 16). Putting similar images into a series of long rectangular tiles, the striking mosaic shows a magnificent array of shades of blue, and an equally intriguing series of shapes that confuse scale, and make the viewer wonder, *What's that?* The answer: that is plastic. These are the things in which marine animals are caught and lose their lives, starving, unable to swim and feed. These are the things that, over time, break down into microplastics that will be ingested by the smallest creatures, entering the food chain and eventually, along with their toxins, our own bodies. Plastic, plastic, plastic. Strangely poetic, these pieces of plastic megatrash float suspended in pure electric blue rippled by the wind, carrying a mute message: a new form of unintelligibility now resides in the water.

How then, can these epic ideas about plastic in the ocean be communicated in media forms? And what can their communication invite, in terms of understanding the scale of the problem and potential solutions? A number of documentaries have explored the problem of huge-scale plastic pollution

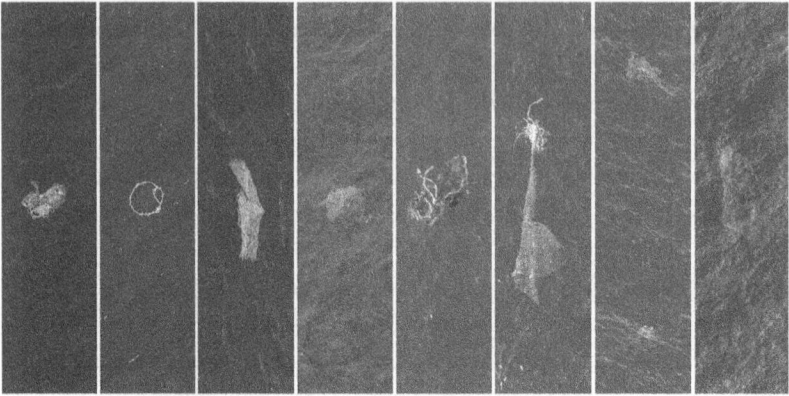

Figure 16. Floating plastic megatrash in the Pacific, as documented from the air. Image reproduced with permission of the Ocean Cleanup Foundation.

in oceans, including *Garbage Island*, a film produced by youth-culture magazine *Vice* (67 minutes, 2008) and *Plastic Paradise*, produced and directed by Angela Sun (57 minutes, 2014). Funded by an NGO called Plastic Oceans, *A Plastic Ocean* (102 minutes, 2016) directed by Craig Leeson, is also a call to action with regards to the "problem" of plastic. The film travels the world, taking viewers from the seas off the coast of Sri Lanka in search of the elusive blue whale (and finding it, but also the extent of plastic pollution in the sea), to the famous trash gyre in the north Pacific to remote islands in the South Pacific, to the Mediterranean, to recycling plants and initiatives in Munich and Manchester. It attempts—and largely succeeds—to show the full extent of the plastic problem, and to introduce viewers to scientific evidence of the pollution and damage being caused by the integration of plastic into the ocean food chain. Such films, along with a variety of photographic and video materials produced by NGOs such as the Ocean Cleanup Foundation, and excellent reporting by science journalists in online newspapers, have worked to introduce a new set of visual material and narratives into the public eye, and to make visible the extent of plastic garbage in the oceans, something that is most likely not visible to most people, who rarely have the chance to see the material detritus floating in our waters for themselves. Such media narratives are activist texts in the sense that they aim to change perceptions and behavior and to connect the bigger problem of plastic trash in the oceans with individuals, communities, and futures. The discussion that follows focuses on the aesthetic strategies of the films, which attempt to capture the uncapturable: the scale and extent of plastic pollution in the ocean.

It might be tempting, now, to see ourselves, inhabitants of the Anthropocene, this new "Eaarth," as in a hell without exit, destined to go down with the planet we mistakenly dubbed a spaceship (as though we were always headed for some other destination, some planet B). (Wallace, 2016: 208)

The imagery of oceans polluted by plastic is difficult to see. It captures the realities of plastic pollution, and offers evidence of the central role that all consumers play therein. Seeing the slow choking of the oceans, and by implication the painful end of many species and environments as we know them, forces viewers to confront an anxiety so primal, a sadness so devastating, that that it becomes difficult to try and name it. Climate change activist Bill McKibben's book, *Eaarth*, published in 2010, catalogs every tiny climate-change related devastation currently befalling the planet, and reminds the reader that humanity is going to have to imagine entirely new ways of living, organizing ourselves, and surviving on this planet that we have fundamentally changed through our own activities. Seeing the oceans—which are typically imagined as untouched wildernesses in which life and biodiversity flourish—being choked with huge floating plastic trash, and worse, understanding how microplastics are integrating themselves into the very food chain, opens a new territory of despair. Recently, media reports about dead whales washing up on beaches, their bellies filled with plastic waste that both choked and starved them, have become more common (Gabbatis, 2018; Nace, 2018; AFP, 2019; Borunda, 2019). As the visual media narrative about oceanic plastic trashscapes enters popular culture, so too does a new type of witnessing, one that forces us to consider, in the most bodily way, our own prospects for survival. Witnessing the trashscape is not an abstract project, we cannot philosophize what it means without introducing our own bodies, as well as the bodies of the many other creatures—both those on which we rely for sustenance, and those we admire as mystically equal, or superior, to us.

The affect of plastic ocean narratives is a visceral, emotional regarding of the boundaries of survival.

Affect is the precursor of emotion, and an attempt to bring the body back in to social theory. [...] it emphasizes the viscerality of experience, suggesting that cognition is not the only way we come to know things. By focussing on sensation and resonance, affect theory allows for the possibility that the body and its capacities matter as much as the brain in how we navigate the world. [...] Because affect theory unseats reason and suggests that the notion of an autonomous subject is a fiction, it points us to the fact that people are animals too, not imbued with qualities that make us different or allow us to rise above nature. [...] Given that affect occurs without language—along the philosophical dividing that policed the boundaries between human and nonhuman—affect theory lets us think with the possibilities of multiple forms of agency, contingent on their interaction with each other. (Rutherford, 2017: 46)

Witnessing the scale of devastation—the strange beauty of the oil slick, the sudden understanding that what is being seen is a giant floating fishing net that spells sure death for turtles, seals, whales, and dolphins, the birds dead from bellies full of colored plastic bits that stay bright as the bones and feathers decompose—is compelling and extremely unsettling. We can no longer be sure of how the earth is our home, or our place in it. When we see the visual evidence—and the invisible evidence made visible by powerful media narratives—we are forced to come face to face with the possibility of our end, not only as individuals and families, but as a species, and a species that has exploited the existence of every other species on the planet for our own benefit, and has carelessly destroyed the quality of life and prospects for survival of almost every other living thing that we claim to value. We do not choose to eat plastic, but it enters our bodies anyway through the other sea life that we eat. Neither do whales and seabirds choose to eat plastic; nor do seals and turtles choose to be caught up in its tangles. The destruction of the ocean, although witnessed on the scale of the gyre, also takes place at the level of the body, both ours and other creatures. Seeing large-scale destructive trash works as a kind of evidence, that in turn puts our own existences—our lives, our pleasures, our experiences, and the experiences of those people we love, as well as those we don't know but claim to care about—into precarity.

Fig. 17 shows a scene from *A Plastic Ocean*, in which director Craig Leeson with scientist Dr. Jennifer Lavers collect and dissect dead albatross chicks found on the beach on Lord Howe Island, a UNESCO World Heritage site. Inside the body of just one lifeless ninety-day-old chick, they find 176 pieces of plastic, which filled up the belly of the little bird, making it impossible to eat anything with nutritional value, leading to death by starvation. Dr. Lavers explains that up to 270 pieces of plastic have been found in some chicks.

What relationship do these two humans, and indeed all those who watch the scene, have to those dead albatross chicks? Should it mean anything to us? Writing in a different empirical context, but still reflecting on the links of asymmetrical responsibilities and rights that bind all animals, including

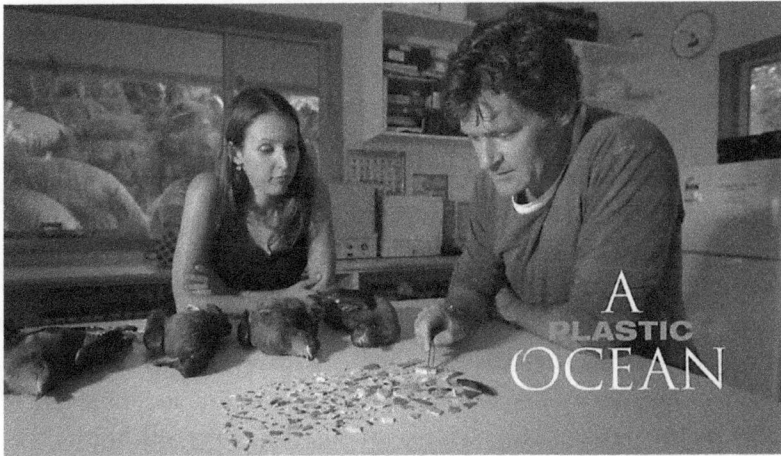

Figure 17. Production still from *A Plastic Ocean*, showing film producer Craig Leeson and scientist Jennifer Lavers examining the plastic found in the bellies of dead albatross chicks. Image reproduced with permission from A Plastic Ocean Foundation.

humans, Donna Haraway comments, "There is no better place to learn such things than in the immersive depths of the earth's oceans" (Haraway, 2008: 263). And in those oceans, now, is plastic, which becomes the new material and moral link between humans and animals. Arguably, media narratives about trash in the oceans force us to think about the link between our own existence and the existence of the other animals with whom we share this planet, and the ecosystems and environments that we all rely on in order to survive. When we see the bodies of birds coated in oil, or decomposing and exposing the persistent plastic within, it invites us to imagine our own bodies covered in oil or filled with plastic. Indeed, the science shows that there are more plastics than ever integrated into our own bodies. To be more specific, the chemicals in plastic "can get into our systems through almost any route— by inhalation, ingestion, or absorption through the skin," and once there have been shown to have effects on the endocrinal system and hormonal balance (Freinkel, 2011: 229). And although we are not coated in oil in the same slowly suffocating, apocalyptic way that the poor pelicans of the Gulf of Mexico were, and we do not suddenly find ourselves with bellies full of sharp shards of disposable lighters and toothbrushes that we thought were food and now leave us no space to eat, we too are surrounded by oil and filled up by the plastic things it fires and makes.

Like the plastic-filled whale, the suffocating bird is a simile for our suffo-cating civilization. This metaphor stands up only so far, because of course the bird is blameless, it did nothing at all to produce the circumstances of its suf-focation. But we—and by "we" I mean all of humankind, though some sectors of that generalization are of course more responsible than others—have cre-ated precisely the conditions of plasticity that now suffocate us. In the images of the oceans-turned-plastic, we are forced to witness how, as Bill McKibben outlines in *Eaarth*, it is no longer a question of how we can save the planet for future generations ("our grandchildren") but how we can work out new ways of surviving right now (McKibben, 2010). To some extent, these questions of affect—how our own bodies, individual and collective, and the bodies of other animals, are impacted by the knowledge that comes with bearing wit-ness to monumental moments of planet-trashing—are still within the realm of the comprehensible. Indeed, a number of science-fiction texts are based on the human tendency to imagine worlds that are crumbling toward a climate apocalypse, or somehow finding ways to rise from its ashes (or more proba-bly, its smoldering trash-mountains and seething plastic-oceans). But what lies beyond comprehensibility?

THE NEW SUBLIME: TRASHSCAPES BEYOND CONSUMER COMPREHENSION

In the trashscapes that have been examined thus far, in which oil slicks and plastic oceans mark a particular version of an apocalyptic future, the figure of the consumer has perhaps been notably absent. We have seen workers and citizens devastated by the oil spill and campaigning against the plastics, but practices of consumption and market exchange have been submerged under other, perhaps more urgent, discourses of corporate accountability, and the material and moral affect of witnessing devastation. In the opening section of this chapter, the tight links between oil and plastic, both molecular and cul-tural, were described. To sum up, oil and plastic are linked not only by the natural environment that they both pollute, and the polymers from which they are comprised, but also in terms of the central role that they play in consum-er economies. Although in the dark slick of toxic oil pumping into the ocean and the terror of the oil-fueled conflagration at its surface it is difficult to rec-ognize the glossy, plastic, object world that surrounds us in late capitalism, in the devastated oceans clogged with plastic trash we can make out the shapes of things that once we purchased, put to our mouths, held in our hands. As the ocean brings together oil and plastic, so too does consumer culture. As such, analyzing how the Deepwater Horizon oil slick was narrated in popular culture is just as central to the project of understanding how waste defines wasteful consumerism today as is exploring narratives of how single-use plastic bottles and disposable lighters and toothbrushes are choking life in saltwater.

> In an age when the media venerate the spectacular, when public policy is shaped primarily around perceived immediate need, a central question is strategic and representational: how can we convert into image and narrative the disasters that are slow moving and long in the making, disasters that are anonymous and that star nobody, disasters that are attritional and of indifferent interest to the sensation-driven technologies of our image-world? How can we turn the long emergencies of slow violence into stories dramatic enough to rouse public sentiment and warrant political intervention, these emergencies whose repercussions have given rise to some of the most critical challenges of our time? (Nixon, 2013: 3)

To a significant extent, the media narratives examined in this chapter have attempted to rouse public sentiment about the "slow violence" of plastic pollution in the oceans, and even the inherently more spectacular damage of the oil spill. The landscapes of devastation wrought by the global industrial economy and its twin, global consumer culture, require us to consider both the aesthetic register of zooming out that captures the immense scale of consumption-driven environmental disaster, and the ethical register that requires us to address, somehow, the anxiety and horror that we feel at witnessing it. The remainder of this chapter argues that trashscapes, as narrated in popular media, take us to the edge of a new form of the sublime.

The idea of the sublime is rooted in western philosophy, and often comprised of attempts to give a language to the experience of natural beauty (Brady, 2013: 184). The sublime does not simply describe a feeling of appreciation or awe at the beauty of nature, but also a kind of "edgy feeling" and an "anxious pleasure" (Brady, 2013: 185) because it is precisely within the beauty of nature that we recognize its immense power—we can surf the waves of the ocean but also quite easily be pummeled and drowned by them, we can hike to the top of a mountain but our bodies may not withstand the altitude, the weather, the fog descending may make us lose our way and fall into a sharp-toothed gorge, and so on. Within our aesthetic adoration of nature is an inherent fear of its awesome power and unpredictability. A crucial component of the sublime is "the combination of negative and positive feeling"—where the negative is associated with our capacities of being overwhelmed and the positive with our appreciation of the immense majesty and beauty of the natural world (Brady, 2013: 192). The sublime is a concept that has been applied not only to natural beauty but also to various productions of the modern and postmodern ages. For example, the production of large-scale fantasy worlds such as Las Vegas, in the United States, have been theorized as producing a "consumer sublime" (Nye, 1996). Building on these ideas of how human activity in both production and consumption have created new landscapes of awe, escapism and anxiety, we can also consider how the scenes of epic trash considered in this chapter interrupt the beauty of nature, and by interrupting it remind us of its awesome, irreplaceable beauty. To what extent can these trashscapes be theorized as a new kind of consumer sublime? In looking at, witnessing, being horrified by the epic trashscapes that humanity has created—and we are all, to some degree or another, implicated in those acts of trash-creation and planet-destruction—we see at once the magnificence of life on our planet and the epic tragedy of our destruction of it.

The ocean comes up often in scholarly writings about the sublime. Philosophers use the ocean to illustrate the idea that there is a kind of expansive majesty available for humans to experience and through that experience to integrate into some kind of abstract knowledge of an awesome beauty more profound than the individual experience can ever be. Paradigmatic of the sublime in a similar way to the star-laden sky, the open expanse of ocean suggests something transcendent, beyond the influence of the human, crossable by us certainly, but not under our power. Media narratives about the ocean trashed by oil and plastic show how waste, produced either in our quest to mine more fossil fuels or in our persistent consumption of plastic, has fundamentally changed the composition of the ocean. In this witnessing of how we are actively polluting and destroying the ocean, how is it still possible to consider the ocean an opportunity to "commune with the divine" (Costelloe, 2012: 192)? Before we trashed the oceans, humans shared an unspoken reverence for the magnificent landscapes of shifting silver-blue, filled with mysterious life and full of an unknowable power. Now, thanks to these new ways of seeing the ocean, and our new long-shot, high-level, up-close visions of it as a place of desecration, oil slicked, plastic-pelleted with waste, with what do we commune? What "divinity" are we able to recognize? Or is it simply our hubris, our own negligence, our own deeply disposable existence? As such, coming face to face with that knowledge and its visualization, what shocks and awes us on a molecular, perhaps unconscious level, is no longer the possibility that we might be overwhelmed by nature but that nature is being overwhelmed by us. Scientist after scientist has proved that humankind has fundamentally altered the functions of the planet. Through burning fossil fuels and pumping carbon into the atmosphere—activities at which oil and plastic are at the heart—we have changed the climate, oceans, and forests.

This new sublime is a situation in which we gain awareness of our own transformative power, our own awesome destructiveness, and the realities of what we have done and are doing to the planet. And trash—the material landscapes of waste that we have created and which we are increasingly, through film, photography, and other forms of popular discourse, forcing ourselves to look at—is the evidence of that new sublime. Trash makes the sublime visible. Rubbish, in its materiality, is a devastating crystallization of awe, of that recognition of being subsumed entirely by a new beast of our own making: the oil monster rising up from the deep, the plastic behemoth at once engulfing living creatures and insinuating its toxins into our endocrine systems.

Some argue that "the sublime, in all its theorizations, is marked by an event or encounter with something so vast that it escapes all attempts to apprehend it fully" (Kainulainen, 2013; Clark, 2015: 185). The extent to which plastic and oil-polluted oceans have become ordinary are precisely the thing that makes trashscapes hard to comprehend. This suggests that the sublime experience that used to constitute witnessing the beauty of the ocean has become fundamentally compromised. But still we recognize the marvelous beauty behind the trash—this is why we are saddened by whales, albatross, and other sea life found dead with bellies of plastic, why we are enraged by yet another day of oil spilled and leaked from a mismanaged exploratory well. What forms of moral action does the new sublime, produced by these media narratives about oceanic destruction and wastage, invite? Although underlying all the images and narratives is a discourse of accountability and, especially in the narratives about plastic waste, direct injunctions to consumers to minimize the amount of disposable plastic they use, in the strategies used to communicate the scale of trashscapes, a sense of spectacle dominates. The gargantuan oil slick is framed as a monster against which we are powerless to struggle, destroying all in its path. The accumulating choke of plastic swirling in ocean gyres fills screens and frames, and fills and kills even the largest, most peaceful and majestic mammal we know: the whale (Gabbatis, 2018). The new sublime takes the beauty of the ocean and through trash turns it into pure awe-and-anxiety at the extent to which the beauty is being compromised. In other words, the trashscape-as-sublime affect "shatters or overwhelms the subject's stability in language, identity and therefore also in society" (Berlant, 2012: 59). How can we give an account of ourselves, as subjects, as consumers, as citizens, when we regard the trashscape in which we are to some extent or another absolutely complicit? Are we overwhelmed, shattered, or do we act? The next chapter attempts to address this question while bringing together the many empirical themes explored in this book so far.

5

Public Objects,
Wasted Subjects,
Uncertain Futures

Where consumer culture is mentioned in relation to the Anthropocene, it is usually in the context of one of the causes of its "great acceleration" (Stoner & Melathopoulos, 2015: 20). Scholarship on the Anthropocene has focused on the ethical, moral, economic, ecological, and philosophical aspects of this phase in human and planetary existence (Zylinska, 2014; Brown & Timmerman, 2015; Clark, 2015; Bonneuil & Fressoz, 2016; Morton, 2016; Wark, 2016; Dellasala & Goldstein, 2017). This book has shown that these aspects cannot be separated from the material and the consumption-oriented and that it is necessary to theorize consumption (and waste) not just as a cause of the Anthropocene but as structures and cultures that suffuse it entirely. Just as we cannot separate the causes of the Anthropocene (unbridled fossil-fueled overproduction and consumption) from its existence, so too can we not separate the moral challenges raised by consumer culture in the current global economic formation from the seemingly petty issues of what we buy and how we dispose of our waste. As Anna Tsing articulates, there are complex webs of entanglements, both material and moral, that are produced by global capitalism, and forging collective methods for navigating these will be the main challenge for making life in the ruins of capitalism (Tsing, 2015: 133). This book has taken a particular methodological approach: exploring how key ideas about trash are made public, and circulate, in media texts. The synthetic and thematic discussions

that have been presented here have inevitably been shaped by my personal experiences, politics and worries (for it is nigh impossible to not become
worried when engaging with the realities of postconsumer waste in the contemporary moment). Nevertheless, I feel confident that this book's discussion
of the different ways in which rubbish is mediated through consumer culture
and the media makes a valuable contribution to scholarship to do with both
waste and consumption. Future research will be required that looks into how
consumers relate to waste, both rubbish they produce themselves and that
they see produced by others, as well as into the extent to which media narratives about the impact of waste on people and planet may influence individual
actions and ethics in relation to waste. In addition to this, ethnographic research exploring the ways in which people produce, live with, and dispose of
waste in relation to consumption will be valuable, in order to provide thick-
er detail for cultures of wasteful consumption, as well as the implications of
consumer waste. The work presented here has allowed for a preliminary set of
understandings to emerge about waste-subjectivity, rubbish-related hedonism,
and the aesthetics of waste, as these are discussed in public media discourses,
but there is huge scope for more detailed exploration of specific case studies
linked to these themes.

This book has shown how, to an extent, trash is a central topic of conversation in the contemporary moment. The problem of rubbish is being addressed
in multiple ways by artists, filmmakers, activists, journalists, and entrepreneurs
around the world, all of whom are contributing to a growing conversation
about the causes of waste, the problems it in turn causes, and different ways
to make rubbish visible again in cultures where it has been removed, ignored,
and denied. As these conversations about waste enter public discourse, they
become part of social and cultural formations. From the perspective of this
book, it may seem as though everyone is talking about rubbish. Of course, this
is not entirely true. One of the shortfalls of focusing on a series of intentionally chosen case studies, as I have done in this book, is the implication that
these case studies stand in for some kind of general truth about the world.
According to the case studies that have been presented here, it may seem that
either incredibly pessimistic or wildly optimistic ideas about trash are in the
mainstream of political thought and popular culture at the moment. Is everyone in the world aware of the huge problem of microplastics in the ocean,
and willing to take drastic action to try and solve it? Probably not: the pre-
ponderance of cosmetic products with "microbeads" on supermarket shelves
suggests otherwise. A quick glance at the ongoing success of thousands of

fast-food outlets in profitable operation in any city, and a rough calculation of how many disposable plastic food items are consequently thrown away on a daily, weekly, monthly basis, will immediately put paid to any suggestion that "most" people are becoming more conscious about the impacts of single-use plastic consumption practices. Similarly, although the discussion of various—many quite innovative and inspiringly creative—approaches to recycling and waste reduction explored in this book may create the idea that everyone in the world is committed to taking responsibility for contributing to collective recycling schemes, I have no evidence to suggest this is true. There is enough litter on the streets of most cities in the world, and not enough recycling bins in a huge number of public places, to remind us that most human beings do not care to take much responsibility for the trash that they produce through consumption, and are not overly fussed about the lack of recycling infrastructure provided in their home towns and cities. The extent to which environmentally aware waste practices are being implemented by consumers, and how the wide diversity of social, political, and economic contextual factors might affect this, is an important area for future research. In the context of the aspirations of economically marginalized people, to enjoy the full pleasures of consumer culture and to have access to the many services and commodities that global north consumer enjoy, the outlook for the growth of ethically minded consumption might seem gloomy. Further, considering the growing inequalities between the rich and poor, it is without a doubt that the majority of human beings on the planet are likely to be more concerned with survival, health, education, and subsistence than their postconsumer waste (modest though that footprint might be). An important issue for future sociological and anthropological research will be to explore how consumer behavior may or may not shift in relation to growing public awareness about environmental problems, including garbage. However, the problem in this line of thinking— that it falls to consumers to minimize their waste regardless of the resources at their disposal—is precisely that responsibility is shifted to individual consumers when indeed, it needs to be collectively handled.

Without coming across as misanthropic or pessimistic to a fault, it might be necessary to consider that most human beings are inherently selfish: that is, they prioritize their own needs and desires, and those of the people that are close to them, over any sense of the anonymous collective. While many people do express a concern for unknown others, such as those who are part of the same religion or nation, at the end of the day economic resources are most likely to be deployed where they are considered most urgently needed and where they are most immediately likely to bear fruit for those deploying them. Consumption and creating waste are simply part of the everyday aspects of lived experience. As Joanna Zylinska writes,

> Any place in the universe I temporally occupy, and from which I build, consume, love and destroy, is never originally and duly mine: I am just a wayfarer through matter's planetary unfoldings and thickenings. There is therefore a story-telling aspect to ethics. (Zylinska, 2014: 93)

I have been reflecting on my own attitudes to post-consumer waste, and my lifestyle regarding it, as I have researched and written this book. To an extent, I have become more aware of my personal role in the web of destruction that is currently being spun around our planet, from the most populated and busy city to the most remote rural location. I have become aware of my personal trash imprint, and how I must take on some sense of guilt and responsibility: I cannot remove myself from the narrative that human beings are destroying the natural world, species and ecosystems in large part through the waste that we produce by the manufacture and distribution of a huge variety of objects and commodities that once consumed and used (whether in the instant it takes to eat a chocolate bar and throw away the wrapper, or in the increasingly fewer years it takes for my laptop to become obsolete and be replaced by another). Unlike Zero Waste Girl, I have not been able to adjust my personal consumption habits in extreme ways in response to my growing understanding about the role that my personal consumption plays in the planetary environmental problems partially caused by the wasteful matrix that is neoliberal production-consumption, and unlike the women of SWaCH and the street-recyclers of Johannesburg, I have not been forced into a situation where the only way I can make a living is by sorting and recycling the rubbish of those wealthier than I. Although I have been inspired to make some small personal changes—such as making ecobricks, choosing a bamboo rather than plastic toothbrush, and remembering to refuse disposable plastic straws that are given to me in restaurants—it is important to question whether these actions are enough to make a real difference. Does the fact that I have not been able to change other behaviors (such as still buying fruit and vegetables packaged in plastic, taking more short-haul flights than strictly necessary, and still relying on a number of products and services powered by fossil fuels) render the other behavior-changes obsolete? What I would like to explore in this concluding chapter is precisely these difficult questions about ethics, subjectivity and agency in relation to consumption and waste, and to think through new ways of theorizing the consuming self that have been provoked by the various public representations of trash formations that have been explored in this book. Therefore, this concluding chapter offers a new set of theoretical orientation points for thinking about the human condition in the current moment in which cultures of rubbish and consumption intersect in increasingly urgent ways, and which are constructed and narrated through various media texts available in the public realm. In short, what remains to be done in this book is to theorize, as Zylinska puts it, the *storytelling aspect* to the ethics of rubbish.

Just as we needed a new vocabulary to define the state of the planet in the age of changes produced by human activity, so, too, do we need a new vocabulary for the changing forms of agency and subjectivity that arise in relation to that. These orientations are unavoidably linked to different questions about consumer culture, precisely because consumption is one of the primary causes for the waste-scapes that are reshaping the planet in visible and invisible ways. In addition to this, consumption is one of the primary social institutions or discourses that shape human subjectivities, be it through the privileges of excess, frugal and careful expenditure aimed at providing for one's self or family, or hopes and aspirations for better lives. If we consider that consumption exists at the interface of human action, inaction and a variety of options for considering and forging moral self-hood and the current structure of the global economy, including its many supposedly "natural" forces that have brought us to this brink, then it follows that questions of consumption need to be brought into the heart of political and philosophical discussions about how we should approach future lives, future selves, and future scenarios for surviving and thriving as a species.

This book has shown that it is impossible to talk about consumption—ever again!—without also considering the waste that it leaves behind. Arguably, because consumption defines human subjectivity, and rubbish defines consumption, rubbish is therefore central to modes of being human in the current moment in world history. What we will do, collectively and individually, with this knowledge is an open question. What follows offers one set of answers thereto, but it is my hope that they will be a significant contribution to ongoing work in cultural studies and critical interdisciplinary work on the sociology and mediation of consumption and capitalism. As one set of starting points for this ongoing critical work, and drawing on existing work by theorists of the environment and consumption, this chapter argues that rubbish needs to be articulated as a public object, that consumer subjectivity requires rearticulation in relation to detritus, and that collective futures will need to be forged in ways that take these two things into account.

RUBBISH: THE MOST PUBLIC OF ALL OBJECTS

Rubbish is the ultimate public object. It becomes the responsibility of village, town, and city governments once it is thrown out by citizens of those places. It litters public places when people drop it on the ground or throw it out of a car window. It collects in the most public of landscapes—our shared natural environments—and washes into the oceans, which exist beyond the imagined and contested borders of coastlines and national fishing zones and are shared by all humans collectively. As much as we cannot ever own, never mind fully know, the oceans, we need to accept that we now share the responsibility for these vast tracts of the planet we call home. This responsibility is not natural or because of some supposed human superiority over other animals, but is the result of the mere fact that it was us who put that garbage into the ocean. When plastic that we manufactured and used ends up in the oceans, littering its seabed or integrated into the food chain and filling the bellies of once-living, now-dying creatures, humans can no longer exist under the illusion that we have thrown that rubbish "away." We have put it somewhere that we cannot often visit, but we still own it, and we have to take responsibility for the new place that we have littered.

If we were to trace the trajectory of a material commodity from private to public, we see that it begins and ends in the public realm, and when passing through conditions of "privateness," we may still be able to make arguments that certain shared conditions of "publicness" remain in play. Many commodities are manufactured from raw materials that are mined, transforming therefore from publically owned materials into those that are appropriated and capitalized on by private actors. As Jo Littler notes, drawing on Arjun Appadurai's theory of the "social life of things" (Appadurai, 1988), recycling is one kind of green consumption that allows us to think critically about how certain commodities and material values cross mental, social, and environmental ecologies, and can complicate ideas of ethical action (Littler, 2008: 111). For example, most smartphones use coltan, which is mined, often by children (Tsing, 2015: 134), in various locations globally, including the Democratic Republic of Congo. During manufacture, the coltan becomes privately owned by the phone manufacturers and integrated into the tech product. It remains privately owned even when introduced into a quasi-public retail display space, although the ideas about it are made public through extensive advertising and communications campaigns. Once the consumer purchases the smartphone, it becomes theirs: once again privately owned. When the phone becomes obsolete, it is usually replaced by a newer model, and the old phone either re-enters the market through secondhand sales, or is thrown away. Whichever fate it meets, it will eventually end up on a rubbish heap or electronics recycling dump, such as the one at Agbogbloshie in Ghana, where once again it becomes public property in some way. Either it is seen as a resource that has its value extracted once again, or it simply sits on the rubbish dump experiencing the slow deterioration brought by time. No longer owned by a particular individual, the discarded smartphone becomes either a public resource or a public problem. "Commodities often finish their lives in salvage operations for the making of other commodities, to be recouped again for capitalism through salvage accumulation" (Tsing, 2015: 134). We could think of the trash-scapes that human beings have created, and which are constantly being mined in different ways for new sources of value through recycling, as assemblages of salvage accumulation (Tsing, 2015: 134), in which those doing the work of salvaging are siloed into separate patches of productivity. There is potential for the entanglements of subjectivity produced by waste to be mobilized into "common cause," because of their existence as "latent commons" (Tsing, 2015: 135) of waste. The public character of garbage requires us to "stretch the notion of the commons" and to seek allies rather than allow alienation to thrive, but also, crucially, to manage our idealism in the process. "Some radical thinkers hope that progress will lead us to a redemptive and utopian commons. In contrast, the latent commons is here and now, amidst the trouble. And humans are never fully in control" (Tsing, 2015: 255). As Litter argues, the ethical potential of recycling is limited both by the other forms of material waste that it produces (such as burning fossil fuels in the transporting or processing of the recycled material) and in terms of how it can be psychologically taxing for individuals to work out when and how to recycle, with or without the support of their governments. The waste-scapes discussed in this book illustrate both this "commons" character of rubbish, and the civic trouble that it causes.

The accumulation of various forms of rubbish in various physical places— like the rubbish dump or ocean, or in the aftermath of leisure pursuits—has produced the most public of problems: the desecration of shared environmental places and resources. No longer owned by anyone specific, rubbish is therefore owned by everyone, and it is imperative that we develop collective dialogues and solutions to deal with it. Media narratives are an important part of this consciousness-raising project. If we consider the natural resources that exist on the planet as communally owned, at least before they are appropriated and extracted by corporate power, then we can see that all of the naturally occurring materials on the planet were (and arguably still are) public in the most original sense of the word. And so too, is rubbish. The trashscapes that are increasingly defining the world around us belong to us all, just as in theory all fresh water on the planet belongs to us all and should be shared by us all, though in practice it is sold as a commodity in bottles by private companies and through pipes by governments (Hawkins, Potter, & Race, 2015). The public character of rubbish needs to be limited, however, by a pragmatic analysis of who created it. Although all human beings in theory have an equal right to the valuable resources buried in various locations under the earth's crust and oceans, not all human beings have had equal opportunity to access, extract, and profit from those resources. Some have protected those opportunities for themselves, denied others the chance to share them, and oppressed and exploited others in pursuit of those privileges and for their own benefit. The entire economic system as we know it is based on this lack of equal opportunity. As Kathryn Yusoff writes, the "Anthropos" in the "Anthropocene" has been coded as universal, but it is not, because it was "organized by historical geographies of extraction, grammars of geology, imperial global geographies, and contemporary environmental racism," such that it is "black and brown bodies" most likely to suffer exposure to toxicity and to be forced to "buffer the violence of the earth" (Yusoff, 2018: 1). Seeing as we have to theorize rubbish as one of the products of this economic system, then we need also to be able to theorize rubbish as something that is born of inequality, and for which, therefore, some more than others bear a greater responsibility. If your housemate throws a huge party when you are out of town, then expects you to clean up the mess when you get home while they sleep off the hangover in bed, you would be justified in feeling angry. Similarly, because one socioeconomic group was the cause of creating an economic system organized around wastefulness, it is extremely unfair to expect those who were marginalized and impoverished by that very same system to clean up the mess. Unsurprisingly, however, this is precisely what is happening. It is the poor, economically precarious who are most likely to have to work with waste—hauling it, sorting it, recycling it, living in close proximity to it.

Elites in the West—who rely more heavily on technology than anyone else on the planet—insist that development and technology are the causes of ecological problems but not their solution. They claim that economic sacrifice is the answer while living amidst historic levels of affluence and abundance. They consume resources on a vast scale, overwhelming whatever meager conservations they may partake in through living in dense (and often fashionable) urban enclaves, driving fuel-efficient automobiles, and purchasing locally grown produce. Indeed, the most visible and common expressions of faith in ecological salvation are new forms of consumption. Green products and services—the Toyota Prius, the efficient washer/dryer, the LEED-certified office building—are consciously identified by consumers as things they do to express their higher moral status. (Shellenberger & Nordhaus, 2011: 25–26)

Although trash is political because it concerns us all, our collective moral orientations toward it need to take into account the inequalities of the economic system that created the problem. Although consumer-driven activists like Zero Trash Girl may be acting from a place of sincerity, their activism exposes the global class politics that arise with rubbish. While the wealthy enjoy the luxury to discard at will—as do the revelers at Glastonbury festival—they are also increasingly able to enjoy the luxury of painstakingly limiting their trash—as do Burners and careful consumers like Lauren Singer—and feeling the moral high ground that comes with such actions. Arguably, although there is only rhetorical value in this position because ultimately their actions are not likely to have much impact on the bigger picture as long as wasteful overproduction remains powerful, while huge populations of aspirational people work toward their imagined utopias of consumer freedom. This said, there is also, arguably, buried beneath the glossy self-branding of Zero Trash Girl's communications, an ethical commitment to an unavoidable truth: that rich, privileged consumers need to take on a disproportionate responsibility for reducing the future scale of waste being produced, and need to invest a disproportionate amount of their own resources, their mental and social ecologies (Guattari, 2005; Littler, 2008), into helping to clean up the legacy of rubbish past that still pollutes the planet. But the individualistic strategies for reducing waste still rely entirely on a consumer economy even if they are adopted on a mass scale by wealthy consumers in the north. While orientations to green consumption are often critiqued as elitist and exposing class privilege (Littler, 2008: 101), an argument can also be made that it is precisely the elites who need to change their behavior. But as long as consumption and its concomitant waste, is theorized as in the realm of the individual, we will mis-recognize the shared, public, nature of rubbish, and the fact that it presents a new commons that somehow needs to be handled collectively, with due rec-ognition given to the inequalities that produced it in the first place, such that while strategies to solve the problem are forged in the public interest, those who bear greater responsibility for creating the trash need to take a bigger share in cleaning it up.

As the various forms of labor linked to recycling that have been explored in this book show, along with the labor that waste produces, new forms of collec-tive labor formations arise. In every city in the world, formal waste collection services are present to some degree or another. This important work that is performed in the service of the public is often undervalued by the rest of soci-ety, and is often also underpaid. When wage disputes arise, refuse workers are in a unique position to make their grievances visible, and indeed, smellable.

In Johannesburg, South Africa, the company contracted to collect waste, Pikitup, experiences regular wage disputes. One of the strategies deployed by the striking workers involves not only not collecting refuse on scheduled days, such that it piles up in unsightly and repellent piles on street corners, but also, when the workers feel particularly frustrated and unheard, in strewing bagged refuse all over the city streets (see fig. 18). It is telling that this form of public protest is constituted by garbage. While it cleverly deploys the ma-terial and political resources available to the striking workers it also makes a powerful point about how important the work that they do is. By leaving the rotting and decomposing trash in the heart of the city, rather than removing it for minimum wage or an unsatisfactory increase, the Pikitup workers were not only reminding the rest of the city's inhabitants how lucky they are to have formal waste removal services, but also how central trash (even in its remov-al) is to our sense of civilization. As Gilles Baro explores in an ethnography of the semiotic landscape of a corporate driven urban improvement district in Johannesburg that discusses the Pikitup strikes, smell and dirt are central to publicly constituted discourses about urban civilization (Baro, 2017: 113–16). The piles of protest trash make a commentary on the work required to keep public spaces clean, in other words how public places are made to feel public through the social contract that citizens take for granted: they pay their taxes trusting that the money will be spent on caring for collective resources, part of which is the removal of rubbish. When that inherently fragile contract is compromised, citizens and workers both are left feeling like the system can-

Figure 18. Striking Pikitup workers spread rubbish on the streets instead of collecting it as usual, in Johannesburg, in March 2016. Photograph by Dr. Gilles Baro, used with permission.

not care for them. The presence or absence of rubbish in shared urban spaces therefore speaks to the presence or absence of shared political processes to manage garbage as a shared public object.

In place of the mirrors (both physical and metaphorical) provided by the retail and advertising landscape of a city, piles of uncollected rubbish offer a new surface for regarding ourselves. As Johannesburg residents made their way through the new trashscape of their city, created intentionally by the striking workers, on their way to the taxi ranks, bus stops, or parking garages, toward work or home, perhaps they were forced to consider on an elemental level the extent to which they were responsible for the rubbish strewn around them. Johannesburgers are known to litter easily and often (Baro, 2017: 111). Perhaps some city residents identified, in those disintegrating piles of dirty materials, the wrapper of a chocolate bar they had recently eaten, or a familiar bundle of a dirty baby nappy that they had tossed in the garbage the day before? Perhaps, but how likely is this? Most of us avoid looking closely at rubbish, repulsed as we are by the things we for which we no longer have a use, which we have redefined as dirty and expelled from our homes and personal spaces. While it is hard to guess whether the trashscape produced anger at the strikers or introspection about whether, or where, to throw the next piece of rubbish one produced, there is no doubt that the Johannesburg Pikitup strikes, momentarily at least, forced a new sense of shared public space as trashed. Although part of the human condition is a refusal to see the self in rubbish, it is precisely that deep compulsion to remove dirt from our lived spaces that often defines our individual and collective identities. Part of the challenge of the current cultural politics of rubbish, on both local and global scales, is that we find ways to face up to the scale and intensity of waste that we are producing collectively, and through that facing up to develop new orientations toward our modes of consumption and disposal. Arguably, we cannot face up to anything if it is not in our faces. It is therefore increasingly important to create media spaces for narratives about rubbish, and to seek ever new ways to engage individuals in new forms of responsible action and reaction, and to cultivate understandings of rubbish as a collective public problem. As such, the discussion now turns to the new modes of seeing the self in relation to garbage that have been exposed through this book's analysis.

HOMO DETRITUS: SUBJECTIVITIES DEFINED BY RUBBISH

As this book has shown, trash is inherently linked to consumption. As such, rubbish politicizes consumption in new and urgent ways that need to be translated into new subjectivities, new forms of agency and new types of public engagement. So-called ethical consumption is not enough because of the complex overlaps between social, mental and environmental ecologies (Littler, 2008): it is certainly now necessary for new forms of collective action in relation to commodities, consumption, and consumer cultures to emerge. Consuming less is one approach, but arguably this is a form of enclave politics (Littler, 2008: 108) that might not feel relevant to most human beings, especially those who have historically been excluded from and exploited by the global consumerist economy. Can we throw consumption (the baby) out with the trash (bathwater)? Consumption is meaningful to all human beings in different ways, and we need to integrate an understanding and appreciation of how it is meaningful into radically new ways of providing for our needs and desires, without creating mountains of waste in the process. Key to this emergence of new collective strategies for saving ourselves from the bitter end promised by the wastefulness of our current situation is creating space for new ways to imagine the Self, which in turn requires new narratives of consumer identity. This book has explored a number of trash-defined subjectivities that are being represented in the public realm. These media narratives create space for viewers to reconsider their own identities and positionalities, and to imagine different ways of living in relation to consumption and waste.

Particularly powerful are the creative interventions of artists who work with rubbish. By redefining trash as a medium for their works, these artists are making a statement both about the excess of rubbish in the social and natural world, and about the new possibilities for communication, reflection, and dialogue that are created through it. Through their "waste-work" artists are reminding us of the materiality of trash, but also about how human communication can take place through various modalities, including the modality of trash. What does it mean for the constitution of the subject that communication can now occur precisely through the materials that we try to remove from our lives? The new materialities of our world—one in which it will be more likely that we will scale mountains of rubbish than actual mountains peaks, or swim and sail through oceans filled with more microplastics than microplankton—force us to reconsider the very essence of our being. Whereas throughout history, human subjects have defined ourselves in relation to the natural world around us, and considered ourselves at once part of a natural system and to some extent apart from, or dominant over it, how can we consider our place in this new world, that looks and feels very different to the one that humans first evolved out of and into?

It has been argued that Homo sapiens is now evolving into Homo deus: that we are inventing "godlike" attributes for ourselves, in our ongoing scientific quest to prolong life, and beat death, famine, and disease though technological innovation (Harari, 2016). To whatever extent this may be true, we may also need to consider the possibility that we are evolving into subjects defined by the waste that we create and are forced, by virtue of the closed system that is our planet, to live among, in one way or another, for the rest of time (our bodies decompose, plastic does not). While it may be "chilling and thrilling" (Adams, 2016) to imagine ourselves as the new God, it may be more important to rather consider our future as one defined by an altogether less sexy, more pragmatic version of ourselves: Homo detritus. Human beings defined not by knowledge, or the power of creation, but by the traces they leave on the environment around them. Humans as the mess they create. Some commentators suggest that humans might not survive the next shift, thanks to our own hubris and destructiveness. If we shift the conception of ourselves from the inherently egoistic angle of seeing ourselves as Homo deus, in which we consider ourselves the pinnacle of existence in the known universe, and instead learn to take some responsibility for the impact that we have had and may continue to have, perhaps then we can find a more moral orientation for our collective and individual existences. Homo detritus will need to learn not only to live with our waste now, but to find clever ways to survive alongside it in the future, on the new Eaarth (McKibben, 2010).

It is clear from the various case studies examined in this book that there are already in existence many human subjects who are shaped and defined by trash. Most obvious perhaps, are those whose work is organized around trash. The informal recycling workers in cities around the world: those who haul handcarts filled to the brim with the household trash of their rich neighbors, those who pick by hand through the trash dumps looking for electronics that can be dissembled and melted down, those who eke out a financial survival by seeing and extracting new forms of value from the items discarded by others. To the extent that one's work defines self-identity, we could then say that these waste-workers are trash-subjects. Of course, this is not an absolute identity—work is for many people merely a means to an end, and personality, family, religion, sexuality, leisure, and politics play equally important, if not more important, roles. But we cannot avoid the fact that more and more individuals, in the new, often toxic and precarious economies that are being created by the mountains of trash that the old economy created, are being forced to take on work involving rubbish, and that this in turn means that labor itself, and its role not only in the production of value but also in the production of selfhood, needs to be rethought. Once again it bears emphasizing that the types of waste-work created by the Anthropocene are predicated on historical injustices: "The disposal of waste mobilizes a new frontierism in the designation of sacrifice zones within and beyond national borders that aggregates environmental harms with anti-Blackness" (Yusoff, 2018: 77); some waste-workers' lives and well-being are considered, by the abstract operations of capital and the entitlement of those who are privileged by it, disposable (Yusoff, 2018: 77). Waste-work is therefore always raced and classed, and cannot be separated from the inequalities that forged the Anthropocene.

Rubbish forces us to rethink how consumption operates in our productions of self. The closer we are to rubbish, or the closer rubbish comes to intersecting with our lived experiences (including through the media narratives that we consume), the more urgent become questions about wasteful/l subjects. Up to this point, consumer culture theory has been limited to articulating the many ways in which various forms of aspiration and accumulation contribute to the construction of individual and group identities. To what extent do new orientations toward rubbish also operate in this way? As this book has shown, waste-work has not only forged new laboring subjects, who are forced through economic marginalization to do the dirty waste-work for privileged groups not willing to do it for themselves, but it has also forged new narratives of empowerment, agency and an eco-conscious orientation toward consumption. Both of these narratives are shaped by race, class, and gender and cannot be seen as moral outside of existing, intersectional relations of power. Trash requires work: it must be eliminated through conscious choices to produce less of it, and it also needs to be sorted and recycled and redeployed in creative ways to meet a variety of human needs, from the creative and expressive to the survivalist. The central question for consumer-citizens in the current moment is, are we willing to do this work, both material and moral? The privileged are currently alienated from their waste, they outsource it and have it removed from sight as efficiently as possible. What will it take for consumers to once again get in touch with a real sense of their own individual pollution footprints? Media narratives are one part of this picture, but alone they cannot be expected to create behavior change. Some form of collective political action is also required, which should include resistance from those oppressed and marginalized by consumer culture and waste-work. The extent to which this will happen is partially dependent on individual consciousness changes. And this in turn is partially dependent on the socioeconomic context in which individuals live. And this, as is painfully apparent, is wildly unequal.

We have seen that trash work—the ugly, dirty, smelly and unpleasant up-close and personal kind of work that removes and sorts trash—is the work of the poor. Middle- and upper-class consumers—such as the iconic Zero Trash Girl and festivalgoers worldwide—are more likely to engage with trash from the more abstract vantage point of waste reduction and ethical shopping, that is, putting their mental ecologies before the social and environmental ecologies (Guattari, 2005; Littler, 2008), and denying that they intersect. Creatives find and use rubbish and repurpose it into beautiful and politically engaging artworks—this too is a kind of privilege afforded usually by the socioeconomic safety net of middle-classness. It is important to not discount the significance of "small actions and pleasures" that can serve to stretch the "moral sense of the possible" (Hawkins, 2006: 90; Littler, 2008: 114). Although the rich create more waste, the poor do more work to clean it up. We see here a very clear sense in which identity politics takes shape in the age of the Anthropocene. As

Timothy Morton argues, theories of the Anthropocene are organized around the idea that the human race is responsible for the massive and terrifying geological, climate, and ecological changes that we are witnessing. What this really means, he points out, is that "*white* humans" are responsible (Morton, 2016: 15). Why is it that "whites go unmarked" in the theory of the Anthropocene? The devastation currently unfolding is the product of "Western humans, mostly Americans" (Morton, 2016: 15)—so why should it be the responsibility of all humans to try and fix it? As economies in the global south are being driven by their governments towards the neoliberal industrial model, and the common sense idea that everyone deserves equal access to consumption-centered lifestyles, will new forms of responsibility evolve alongside the expansion of the consumer-capitalist model? This said, the assumption that Morton makes that all other humans in the world are intent on mimicking the American model is misplaced. There is more to forms of consumption in the global than merely trying to "catch up" or emulate with the west (Iqani, 2016; Dosekun, 2019). Although there might be some hope in the idea that as the West gets more eco-conscious in their modes of production and consumption, the global south might catch up on or leapfrog these efforts, this idea also undermines the full agency that global south governments and individuals exercise in their own economic and ecological decision-making. Always constrained in significant ways by the limitations of the global and national socioeconomic systems in which they exist, marginalized subjects nevertheless are always able to make choices that matter, and exercise their agency in ways that are directed at improving their circumstances. The women of the SWaCH waste collective in Pune are a case in point. Their ownership of their labor is inspiring—but it begs the question of whether, in a more equal world—they would choose to do the work that they do. If all people, including the rich and privileged, produced less waste and took responsibility for sorting and distributing their own recycling, perhaps the SWaCH waste-pickers would be able to make other life choices, imagining that they had access to the social and economic resources to do so? Would middle-class rubbish-responsibility free them, or strip them of a much-needed source of income? Is it possible to imagine and collectively forge a world in which human beings are not forced—by themselves or others—to define their subjectivities in relation to waste?

The different iterations of Homo detritus revealed by the media narratives explored in this book show how material culture continues to exert huge influence over subjectivity. Rubbish provokes a new dialectical link between subject and object, which defines consumer culture but also individual and collective ethics in relation to consumption. It also forces—and this is the question taken up by the next section—a reconsideration of the relationship of humanity with the idea of the future. While consumer culture has always explicitly and implicitly promised continued growth and improvement of life through consumption, narratives about rubbish suggest a different scenario.

THE BEAUTY OF SAYING GOODBYE: SELF, OTHER, PLANET

The various media narratives about rubbish, and the new surfaces for communication and expression produced by rubbish in the natural and social worlds, lift up a new specter. The very real possibility that the human race may not survive, in its current form, the ecological disaster that it has itself produced, looms behind every narrative about consumption and garbage. Although some caution that we should "love our monsters" and avoid sensationalist, apocalyptic hype (Shellenberger & Nordhaus, 2011), it is hard to avoid the vision of destruction that is captured by images that show the scale of waste spilled in environments suffering the slow violence (Nixon, 2013) of ecological destruction. Even pictures that optimistically show attempts to re-imagine how we use trash invite viewers to contemplate the wholeness of the earth, and to consider our deep reliance on it, and equally, our precariousness when nature, on which we rely for survival, is threatened. Media narratives about immense trashscapes—the oil spill, the plastic ocean, the ever-growing and intentionally unseen garbage dumps on the edge of every city—are material evidence of the massive changes humanity (specifically, those who hold power within human societies) have made to our planet in the past century. Coming face to face with this evidence is at best sobering and at worst terrifying, because in that witnessing we have to make choices about whether or not we believe or understand what we are seeing. This form of seeing and affect has been theorized in this book as the new sublime. In some ways, the mountain of trash may be a sight more attuned to touching the terror of the sublime than the peak of Sagarmatha, because in the former mountain we can see the full ugliness of what humanity when driven by capitalism is collectively capable of, while the former simply encourages us to indulge egoistic fantasies of conquering a summit. Who will climb the mountain of trash that we have collectively produced, and plant a flag in it to call it theirs? Seeing the world from afar can invoke a sense of the sublime: that complex mix of awe, appreciation, and terror. Consider the satellite photograph of the Maldives Islands (fig. 19). As seen from a NASA satellite, the archipelago is visible as a string of pale aqua-colored rings. Most of the islands are atolls, that is, ring-shaped coral reefs. At only six and a half feet above sea level, these coral reefs are delicate protuberances from the depth of the ocean around it. The atolls only just break the surface to meet the light of the sun, thereby creating the perfect conditions for rich and abundant sea life in their shallows. This contrast is clear in the satellite photograph: the deep ocean is dark blue in hue, and the shallows of the coral reefs pop out in luminescent aqua, slender crusts of white beach sand barely visible. With scattered white clouds between the satellite and the surface of the sea adding an ethereal, feathery texture, and the sunlight reflecting brightly off the surface of the ocean elsewhere in the image, the overall result is a mesmerizing scene, almost abstract. We observe breathlessly the immense beauty of our "blue planet."

The presence of these islands in the middle of the wild deep Indian Ocean seems almost miraculous: from the midst of a saltwater wilderness, these little crescents of fertility and beauty have risen over millions of years, allowing warm aqua waters to punctuate the deep cool of the unknowable depths around them. Within the magnificence of the image, the breathtaking invitation to appreciate the wild filigree of the natural world, is a sense of ethereality. The ringed coral atolls appear so fragile that they might disappear at any moment, sucked back under the surface by suboceanic, tectonic forces, or conversely submerged under rising waters. The sense that this is possible is based, of course, not on wild fantasy or imagination but on the reality of peer-reviewed science, which confirms again and again, with ever more dire calculations, that due to climate change and the melting of glaciers and Arctic and Antarctic ice, ocean levels will rise. Are rising. The Maldives is the most threatened by climate change of all islands nations (Gagain, 2012). Within my lifetime, we may witness the first climate refugees fleeing that very archipelago, and see a satellite image of the exact same geolocation in which those delicate tracings of life, coral and sand emerging from the shapeless ocean are no longer visible. Disappeared below the surface. Perhaps the only section of the Maldives that might still be visible from outside our atmosphere in a few decades time will be Rubbish Island, towering forty two and a half feet higher above sea level than every other atoll in the archipelago. Within the beauty of the image, therefore, there exists also a deep sense of loss, an awareness of impending destruction by the rubbish choking the oceans, and the carbon emissions choking the atmosphere.

What do we do with the conflicting messages carried by the image? How do we hold the affect it produces? At once, we find ourselves breathlessly in

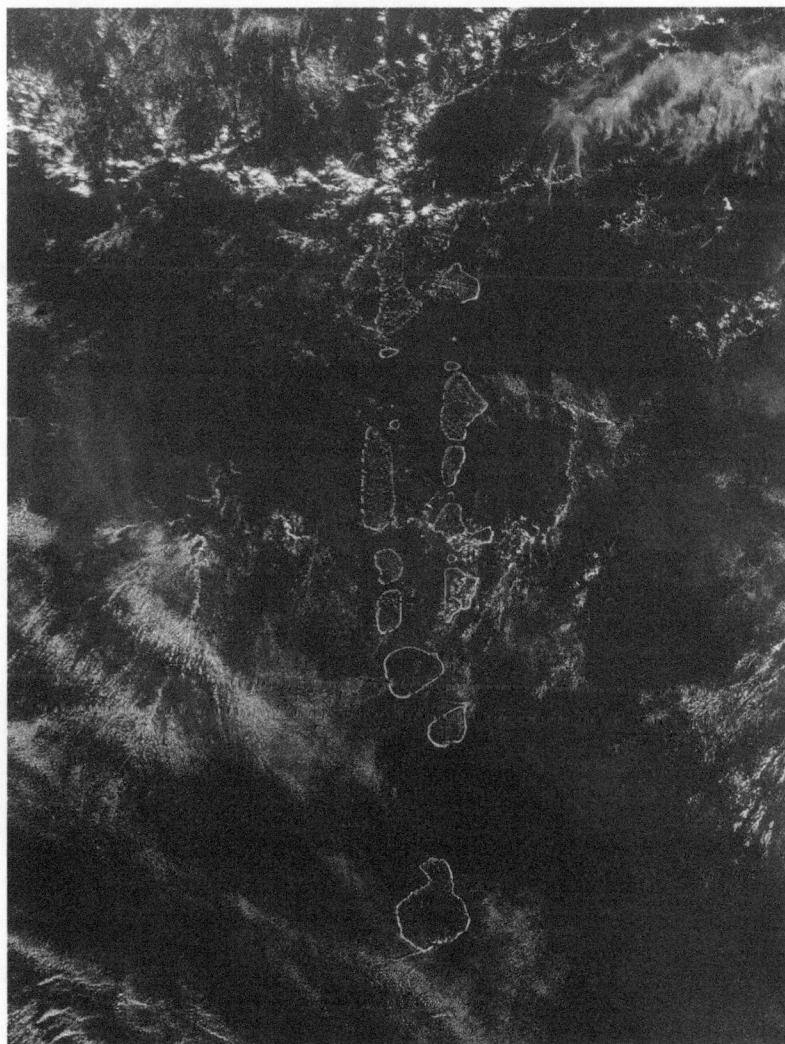

Figure 19. The Maldives as seen from space. Image from NASA in the public domain.

love with the beauty of our planet and shocked by the knowledge that we are destroying it (and the life that it sustains). How do we square these two entirely contrasting senses, these two different and difficult pieces of knowledge provoked by the image? As most climate scientists are reminding us, against the willful ignorance and backpedaling of most governments, we are beyond the point of no return (Oreskes, 2004; Wallace-Wells, 2019). Despite the heroic efforts by many environmental activists to educate people about reducing rubbish imprints and to clean up the oceans, corporate actors continue to produce and sell disposable products regardless of the consequences. As such, it is hard to look at an image like the one under consideration without feeling nostalgic—for a beauty that will be imminently gone, that we may not be able to save despite our best efforts. Is it then, simply a matter of being able to say goodbye to the world that we used to think we lived in, which very shortly we may not be living in, and which the next generation will almost certainly not be living in at all (McKibben, 2010)?

It is striking that aerial photography is a significant mode of communication in the media project of narrating the scale of the trash problem. As the discussion in chapter 3 showed, sometimes the point of view needs to be lifted out of the spaces we are most accustomed to inhabiting—eye level, just a little way above the ground—in order for us to get a clearer sense of the bigger picture. Sometimes we need to zoom out to get a sense of what the accumulation of two hundred thousand people's trash dropped on the floor looks like. Similarly, it is nigh impossible to comprehend the scope of a massive oil slick, or the huge pieces of plastic garbage that float in the ocean, unless we look at them from above, taking a bird's-eye view, tragically, as those same birds are grounded and coated in oil, belly-full of plastic, slowly dying. These new perspectives, gifted to us through technologies of flight and photography, force us to rethink our relationship to the environment. Just as the famous photograph of earth from space widely disseminated in the 1960s contributed to new ideas of the earth as one (Cosgrove, 1994), so too do images recording the planetary scale of littering require new public conversations about our relationship to the planet and our responsibilities related to cleaning up the messes we, collectively, have made and still are making.

The affect of the spectacular aerial images that have been described and theorized in this book—the mix of awe at the beauty of the world and terror at knowing we are destroying it, and that it is almost impossible to reverse that destruction—should not be misinterpreted as misanthropy, or a prioritization of animals and natural environments over human beings. Some might argue that worries about species going extinct, with rain forests being destroyed, with climate change, are middle-class concerns. It is sometimes pointed out that white middle-class people care more about trying to stop rhino poaching than they do about homelessness and hunger in their own cities, that they are more likely to spend money on eco-conscious products than they are to pay their domestic workers a living wage, that they will shed tears when they see images of sea turtles trapped in floating plastic waste but turn a blind eye when they witness police violence against young black men (indeed, who will routinely call the police on black people legitimately occupying certain spaces, while shedding tears about the plastic-trapped turtle). How do we square the absolute legitimacy of this critique—that many well-off, middle-class people show little compassion or care for their suffering fellow humans—with the validity of the bigger picture of ecological devastation that we are witnessing? Working with the ideas of Félix Guattari, Jo Littler argues that part of the problem is a general unwillingness to see mental, social, and environmental ecologies as deeply interrelated, and the strategic disconnection between the social and the ecological that has, arguably, been produced by the operations of capitalism and neoliberalism. The ecological is not separate from the social and mental but in fact permeates every aspect of life (Littler, 2008: 103). We could return to the argument that because the global middle- and upper-classes are historically the group responsible for the creation of extractive and destructive global capitalism, they should bear a bigger responsibility for trying to fix the problems it has created. But this argument falls short of a deeper level of humanism that is required in order to marry the concerns of inequality, poverty, and injustice with the concerns of the survival of the species as a whole. The goals of forging a more sustainable, less wasteful and rubbish-conscious relationship with the world we inhabit and the goals of working toward more equity, justice, and reciprocated care among humans should not be mutually exclusive. That they are put into competition with one another is evidence of the shortsighted perspectives of both groups arguing that the environment is more important and those arguing that humans are more important. Is it impossible for us to treat one another and the environment with the respect that both deserve? Indeed, if we learn one, should the other not surely follow?

These questions are perhaps idealistic. To start with a reflection on the extent to which consumer subjectivity is now as defined by rubbish as it is by the brands and commodities that people consume, and to end with a grand philosophical musing on whether individuals care more about the environment or suffering humans, might seem a stretch. But both problems are rooted in the injustices of capitalism. Is there enough moral substance in material culture to allow us to effectively ruminate on the most existential question animating the human condition at present? I would argue, I have argued, yes. The existing scholarship that allows us to understand how material culture defines identity and lived experience can extend to understanding how the materiality of rubbish equally, if not more so, defines identities and lived experiences.

Furthermore, the presence of rubbish as the most public of objects forces us to consider how material formations of waste are inherently political, both in the sense that they integrate with and extend existing social inequalities and in the sense in which they demand collective action, structures, and solutions in order to find ways of controlling the rubbish, rather than being controlled and overwhelmed by it. These social and political dimensions of trash—which we have learned about through examining media narratives about it—are inherently linked with its epic ecological dimensions. As such, media narratives about rubbish teach us both about the Self and its true opposite, not Other but Planet. Rubbish shapes us as individuals as well as the material dimensions and conditions of Earth. It teaches us about how we relate to one another through forms of selfishness, exploitation, and wastefulness, and reminds us to consider how our needs and desires translate not only into our own regimes of fulfillment and pleasure but also into structures that may injure other people and external environments. It is hard to think about rubbish, after the analytical explorations that we have achieved in this book, and not think about the future of our planet and how it has been compromised by human activities. In other words, there is a conceptual progression between consumption, trash, and big ethical questions to do both with inequality and ecology.

IMAGINING ANOTHER WORLD: CONSUMPTION WITHOUT WASTE?

At the time of writing, *National Geographic* magazine published a special issue titled "Planet or Plastic?" (June 2018). In the special feature, various articles examine different aspects of the problem of plastic pollution. Featured on the website as well as the Instagram page (which has almost 90 million followers), the material examines the lives of trash pickers at a Mumbai garbage dump, artworks created from trash found in the bellies of dead albatrosses, and gives advice on how readers can reduce their own plastic consumption. The special feature includes well-researched writing, and excellent photography documenting plastic at all of its points in the cycle, including powerful visuals of production, retail, recycling, and disposal. As a particularly influential media brand, with huge reach across the English-speaking world, it is arguably quite positive to see *National Geographic,* and by extension mainstream media, turn their attention to the problem of plastic. In line with this trend, more high-profile celebrities are starting to speak out against plastic use, often in tandem with environmental NGOs like Greenpeace, who are trying to raise awareness about the role consumers can play in reducing trash and pressuring companies, through their consumption choices, to act differently. As this book has shown, there is arguably more public dialogue about the problem of trash than ever before. As discourses about the links between rubbish and consumption become more normalized, and stronger arguments are made about the need for behavior change, it is worth asking the question: can we imagine consumption without rubbish? And if we cannot imagine consumption without rubbish, then what does this mean for everything that we currently understand about inequality, aspiration, identity, and neoliberal culture? If waste has been missing from the critical scholarly analyses of these items, then this book has sounded the call not only for making closer connections between theories of waste and theories of consumption, but also for integrating perspectives gleaned from engaging with the materiality of rubbish into the big questions that animate our engagement with the social and natural world.

Some might argue that the question of whether consumption can be re-engineered to exclude waste is obsolete, because consumption without waste cannot be imagined until we imagine a consumer economy that *produces* without waste. There is a problem of overproduction in the world. There are too many disposable things being manufactured and sold in the world. There are too many products manufactured with built-in obsolescence, precisely so that they will fail or break within a couple of years, forcing their owners to replace them (Littler, 2008: 106). There are too many plastic items being manufactured, full-stop. There are too many items that are designed in order to be used once or twice and then thrown away. But as we have seen, there is no "away." Every piece of rubbish goes somewhere: to a dump, the ocean, a recycling plant, or beautiful artwork if we are lucky. Until the problems of excess that are rooted in production are solved, we are doomed to staying a wasteful, overconsuming global society.

> The only true response to the ecological crisis is on a global scale, provided that it brings about an authentic political, social and cultural revolution, reshaping the objectives of the production of both material and immaterial assets. Therefore this revolution must not be exclusively concerned with visible relations of force on a grand scale, but will also take into account molecular domains of sensibility, intelligence and desire. (Guattari, 2005: 28)

The call for revolution contains within it a pessimistic outlook: it considers corporate power almost absolute, and sees consumers as simply responding to the supply that is pumped out from factories around the world, working in tandem with sophisticated branding and marketing efforts aimed at convincing us that we need rubber ducks, widget spinners, new smartphones and mp3 players, new sneakers, new clothes, plastic flowers, plastic everything. Megastores and warehouses in cities all over the world are stocked floor-to-ceiling with products that need to be sold. Will all these items be sold, and how soon will they need to be replaced? Of course, consumers are not mindless zombies who simply dance on the demand of the big corporations that want to sell them things. Consumers are also citizens (Canclini, 2001), and they consistently make intentional, informed, and careful choices about what they acquire and how they spend their money. History has shown that it is possible for consumer boycotts to contribute to political change (Smith, 1987). Middle-class consumers refusing to buy sugar from plantations using slave labor in the eighteenth century helped to raise awareness about the evils of slavery (Mintz, 1986), and middle-class consumers in the 1980s who boycotted fruit exported from South Africa arguably contributed to the struggle to end Apartheid. On their own these actions were certainly not enough to bring about an end to some of the miseries of racist oppression, but it would also not be fair to characterize them as meaningless. If enough consumers across the globe choose to not buy plastic products, could it contribute to a shift in production priorities and values?

The framework of ethical consumption allows us to think about more ecologically and morally sounds ways of fulfilling our desires and needs, without contributing to the exploitation of labor, the torture of animals, the pollution of the oceans. As proponents of ethical consumption argue, it is possible to enjoy chocolate or coffee without contributing to the exploitation of the workers on the farms that grow the beans, and it is possible to choose ways of consuming those pleasurable things without adding to the trash in the ocean, for example, by buying a reusable bamboo coffee mug instead of taking a disposable polystyrene cup. But as Jo Littler cautions, ethical consumption and even anticonsumerism activism tends to center the individual as the locus of change (even when aggregated into collective action), which can be problematic especially when the solutions offered are "individualistic channels of new forms of commerce" (Littler, 2008: 18). It is important to ask about the extent to which such choices merely serve to make consumers feel better about themselves (Littler, 2008: 107), and the extent to which they actively contribute to a cultural shift that may change structures of power permanently. In the current moment, mainstream political and economic systems based on slavery are hard to imagine. Though of course slavery is not fully eradicated now, it might have been hard to imagine that it ever would be in 1780. Perhaps, with enough determination and communicative effort from activists to raise awareness about the deep connections between consumption and the environment, in a hundred years human beings will find themselves living in a culture where it is unimaginable that we throw trash in the oceans, or even on the streets outside our homes.

This book has explored and theorized the multiple meanings of garbage and waste in contemporary global media culture. Across the diversity of case studies—ranging from individual social media narratives about recycling, to works of fine art created using trash, to press coverage about tropical island tourism and entertainment festivals, and feature-length films and documentaries about oil spills and plastic pollution—are a number of important cross-cutting concerns. On one level is the aesthetic of trash, and how different materialities of waste are often narrated in a large-scale format through reference to the idea of the spectacle. On another level is the different ways in which individual subjectivity is brought into (and left out of) media narratives, sometimes suggesting that individual action on a small scale can contribute to dealing with the global, public problem of waste, other times that it has no place in any solution. This tension between the macro and micro, the societal and the personal, the global and the local is a key feature of how rubbish is narrated in popular culture.

To what extent is the long-shot, aerial-view pictorial form one that prioritizes spectacle over an invitation to ethical action? When we see large-scale disasters from afar, we may be successfully educated in understanding the scope of the problem. We see the millions of plastic beer cups dropped on the floor at Glastonbury, and we might think, people are messy and selfish. But we might still take that single-use cup when we buy beer at the next festival we attend. We see the miles-wide oil slick staining the Gulf of Mexico, and we might think, oil corporations are evil, irresponsible scum. But we still fill our cars with petrol and complain when the prices go up. We see the trash island rising out of the Maldives, and we might think, tourists really need to pay more attention to how much rubbish they create and leave behind. Yet we still plan our next holiday. But to what extent do the long-shot visual records of trashscapes invite us to consider some form of ethical action in response to that understanding? Arguably, it is very difficult to imagine forms of action in response to the overwhelming scale of the problem. What could one person do, to clean up the oil slick, or capture the giant bits of plastic flotsam? How could one person help pick up all the litter at Worthy Farm (and then where would they put it)? Faced with the sense of impossibility, many viewers might feel helpless and useless, and come to a subconscious conclusion that nothing can be done. Lilie Chouliaraki writes about how certain media texts invite certain ethical responses from viewers (Chouliaraki, 2008). In the context of media coverage about suffering distant others, she concludes that the narrative form that is most likely to urge viewers to action (be it signing a petition, donating money, or volunteering time) is one that portrays the suffering other as a fully human subject, with whom the viewer can identify. And the form of media coverage least likely to inspire action is the type that portrays the suffering as an abstract adventure (Chouliaraki, 2006b). When the global problem of garbage is portrayed as an abstract spectacle, from afar, arguably a form of distance is produced, through which the viewer may struggle to identify any personal impact. Of course, other narrative forms may counter the sense of alienation and helplessness produced by the spectacular images. Personal narratives of agency, activism, and creativity offer opportunities to relate to the stories on offer, and make it more likely that the viewer will consider forms of action in their own lives, or recalibrations of their own ideas and belief systems. This might explain why Zero Trash Girl is so popular on social media. Seeing artists collaboratively create inspiring public monuments using plastic bottles, or seeing partygoers talk about an ethic of leaving no trace: these media narratives create opportunities for education and identification. In examining the transformative possibilities of media narratives offering new ways of thinking about the links between consumption and rubbish, it will be important for future research to consider the extent to which spectacular imagery can both educate and alienate, as well as the extent to which identity-centered narratives can both inspire and desensitize. Audience-oriented studies may help in shining a brighter light on the complex processes of behavior change that might be required to square the motivations behind the actions linked to both consumption and environmentalism.

What then, are the different scales of political possibility evident in contemporary forms of consumption, once rubbish is taken into account? The most optimistic media narratives are those organized around forms of individual or collective action in relation to garbage. In narratives such as the ongoing diary of Zero Trash Girl, and the self-controlled narrative about the SWaCH collective, we see arguments being made respectively that careful, ethical consumption can help to reduce unnecessary garbage, and that careful, ethical forms of self-organized labor can at once create forms of sustainable income and effective forms of disposal and recycling. As such, analysts should continue to ask, when is political agency affirmed and invited through media narratives about rubbish, and when is it denied? It is no accident that individualism comes up as a main lens through which rubbish-related action is defined. If consumption is individualized by neoliberal culture, so then it follows that cultures of disposal are also individualized by it. But individual actions are not enough: they need to be girded by collective as well as political efforts and contribute to a building of a critical mass of consumer demands that should, hopefully, challenge and shift production norms. Media narratives about recycling all too often focus on individualism, suggesting that the benefit is to be gained in individual moral orientations (feeling like a good or better person), rather than in accumulative, collective culture shifts. While much media coverage about epic trashscapes implies that some consumers are morally deficient (those who abandon their once-used tents at Glastonbury, those who thoughtlessly throw plastic bottles in the hotel trash can in the Maldives), there are increasingly narratives that shine a spotlight on neoliberal structures and corporate power. Arguably, it is profit-based and privately owned institutions that are responsible for producing the mountains of waste that are increasingly coming to define the geography and climate of the planet.

> The basic problem that we faced was that carbon carried no price—coal and gas and oil companies could pour it into the atmosphere for free, which undercut every effort at conservation or renewable energy. The industry lobbied and donated and schemed endlessly to maintain that special break. No other business can put its trash out for free. (McKibben, 2013: 140)

How can citizens make business pay, both in retrospect and going forward, for all the years that they have been putting their trash out for free? This question should animate future research and activism. Media narratives focusing on the terrifying trashscapes of oil spills and plastic pollution take care to identify and expose the responsibilities of corporations for the devastation that they have wrought. But what opportunities for collective action and response do they invite? Viewers of *Deepwater Horizon* may finish the film feeling angry with BP for the scale of environmental devastation and human suffering that they caused, but what then do they do with those feelings? How can that impotent rage be converted into ethical action? This is not to suggest that it is the responsibility of media texts to force or produce action, but to consider the extent to which the discursive work being done in the texts allows for, or invites, moral responses of a certain kind. Do they make us feel helpless or able to act?

These will be important questions for future analyses of media narratives about rubbish and consumption, and indeed for studies on social and environmental activism considering the role of media discourses. In the contemporary neoliberal global political-economy, freedom is defined as the "freedom to consume," and it has come to mean the "freedom to waste" (Hawkins, 2006: 29). This book has shown how that "freedom to waste" is discursively constructed in relation to the agencies and actions linked to various form of recycling, various forms of pleasurable and hedonistic consumption, and in relation to epic spills and messes created by powerful corporations and abetted by powerful governments. As this chapter has explored, these case studies have brought up deep existential questions about how human subjectivity is increasingly defined by waste, how public worlds are increasingly shaped by trash, and what both of those mean for how we theorize, and feel about, the future of existence and the planet. As such, therefore, the most pressing issue for any future research that might be inspired by the work done in this book, is whether and how consumer culture will be able to evolve to define a new kind of freedom, the freedom to find pleasure and meaning in material culture, while crucially also minimizing its devastations.

Adams, T. 2016. "Homo Deus: A Brief History of Tomorrow by Yuval Noah Harari Review—Chilling." *The Observer*. September 11. http://www.theguardian.com/books/2016/sep/11/homo-deus-brief-history-tomorrow-yuval-noah-harari-review [Accessed May 15, 2018].

Adams, W. H. 2012. *On Luxury: A Cautionary Tale, A Short History of the Perils of Excess from Ancient Times to the Beginning of the Modern Era.* Washington, DC: Potomac Books.

AFP. 2019. *WATCH | Dead Whale in Philippines Had 40kg of Plastic in Stomach.* https://www.timeslive.co.za/news/world/2019-03-20-watch—dead-whale-in-philippines-had-40kg-of-plastic-in-stomach/ [Accessed 2019, May 15].

Afrika Burn. 2018. "Guiding Principles." https://www.afrikaburn.com/about/guiding-principles"[Accessed June 7, 2018].

Alexander, P., Ceruti, C., Motseke, K., Phadi, M., and Wale, K. 2013. *Class in Soweto.* Pietermaritzburg, South Africa: University of Kwazulu Natal Press.

Alfreds, D. 2018. *Here's How Much Plastic Every South African Uses—and the Number Is Shocking.* https://www.news24.com/Green/News/heres-how-much-plastic-every-south-african-uses-and-the-number-is-shocking-20181004 [Accessed April 11, 2019].

Anderson, A. 2014. *Media, Environment and the Network Society.* London: Palgrave Macmillan.

Anderson, B. 2000. *Doing the Dirty Work?: The Global Politics of Domestic Labour.* London and New York: Palgrave Macmillan.

Anonymous. 2017. *Pills, Thrills and Bellyaches: Glastonbury Ain't What It Used to Be.* http://www.independent.co.uk/arts-entertainment/music/features/pills-thrills-bellyaches-a7802536.html [Accessed May 4, 2018].

Appadurai, A. 1988. *The Social Life of Things: Commodities in Cultural Perspective.* Cambridge, UK: Cambridge University Press.

Atkinson, D., and Ingle, M. 2016. "Growing Like a Magic Mushroom: AfrikaBurn

Festival in the Tankwa Karoo." *African Journal of Hospitality, Tourism and Leisure* 5(2).

Atlas Obscura. 2018. *Thilafushi: the "Rubbish Island."* http://www.atlasobscura.com/places/thilasfushi-the-rubbish-island [AccessedMay 7, 2018].

Baker, K. 2015. *As This Year's Glastonbury Closes the Big Clean Up Begins.* http://www.dailymail.co.uk/news/article-3142856/As-year-s-Glastonbury-closes-big-clean-begins.html [Accessed June 7, 2018].

Barnett, C., Cloke, P., Clarke, N., and Malpass, A. 2010. *Globalizing Responsibility: The Political Rationalities of Ethical Consumption.* Chichester, UK: John Wiley & Sons.

Baro, G. 2017. "The Language of Post-apartheid Urban Development: The Semiotic Landscape of Marshalltown in Johannesburg." Johannesburg, South Africa: University of the Witwatersrand.

Bauman, Z. 2004. *Wasted Lives: Modernity and Its Outcasts.* Cambridge, UK: Polity.

Baviskar, A., and Ray, R. 2011. *Elite and Everyman: The Cultural Politics of the Indian Middle Classes.* New Delhi, India: Routledge.

BBC Cornwall. 2019. "Recycled Plastic to Make Glastonbury Arena." *BBC.com.* May 9. https://www.bbc.com/news/uk-england-cornwall-48213844 [Accessed May 30, 2019].

Belle, N., and Bramwell, B. 2005. "Climate Change and Small Island Tourism: Policy Maker and Industry Perspectives in Barbados." *Journal of Travel Research* 44(1):32–41. DOI: 10.1177/0047287505276589.

Bennett, T., Savage, M., and Savage, P., and S. M., Silva, E. B., Warde, A., Gayo-Cal, M., and Wright, D. 2009. *Culture, Class, Distinction.* London: Routledge.

Berlant, L. 2012. *Desire/Love.* New York: punctum books.

———. 2016. "The Commons: Infrastructures for Troubling Times." *Environment and Planning D: Society and Space* 34(3):393–419.

Beyer, J., Trannum, H. C., Bakke, T., Hodson, P. V., and Collier, T. K. 2016. "Environmental Effects of the Deepwater Horizon Oil Spill: A Review." *Marine Pollution Bulletin* 110(1):28–51. DOI: 10.1016/j.marpolbul.2016.06.027.

Blight, G. 2014. "The World's Biggest and Most Dangerous Dump Sites—Interactive." *The Guardian.* October 6. http://www.theguardian.com/global-development/ng-interactive/2014/oct/06/world-biggest-most-dangerous-dump-sites-interactive [Accessed May 31, 2018].

Boebert, E., and Blossom, J. M. 2016. *Deepwater Horizon.* Boston, MA: Harvard University Press.

Böhm, S. 2015. "Stop Blaming India and China for the West's 300 Years of Destroying the Environment." https://qz.com/562417/stop-blaming-india-and-china-for-the-wests-300-years-of-destroying-the-environment/ [Accessed June 7, 2018].

Bonner, P. L., and Segal, L. 1998. *Soweto: A History.* Johannesburg: Maskew Miller Longman.

Bonneuil, C., and Fressoz, J.-B. 2016. *The Shock of the Anthropocene: The Earth, History and Us.* London: Verso Books.

Boo, K. 2012. *Behind the Beautiful Forevers: Life, Death and Hope in a Mumbai Slum.* London: Portobello Books.

Borunda, A. 2019. *This Pregnant Whale Died with 50 Pounds of Plastic in Her Stomach.* https://www.nationalgeographic.com/environment/2019/04/ dead-pregnant-whale-plastic-italy/ [Accessed May 15, 2019].

Bostrom, A., Walker, A. H., Scott, T., Pavia, R., Leschine, T. M., and Starbird, K. 2015. "Oil Spill Response Risk Judgments, Decisions, and Mental Models: Findings from Surveying U.S. Stakeholders and Coastal Residents." *Human and Ecological Risk Assessment: An International Journal* 21(3):581–604. DOI: 10.1080/10807039.2014.947865.

Bowen, F. 2014. *After Greenwashing: Symbolic Corporate Environmentalism and Society.* Cambridge: Cambridge University Press.

Brady, E. 2013. *The Sublime in Modern Philosophy: Aesthetics, Ethics, and Nature.* Cambridge, UK: Cambridge University Press.

Britton, L. M. 2016. *Shangri La—A Look at the Best Bits of the Weirdest Glastonbury Area–NME.* https://www.nme.com/photos/shangri-la-a-look-at-the-best-bit s-of-the-weirdest-glastonbury-area-1407394 [Accessed May 30, 2019].

Brosius, C. 2012. *India's Middle Class: New Forms of Urban Leisure, Consumption and Prosperity.* London: Routledge.

Brown, K. R. 2013. *Buying into Fair Trade: Culture, Morality, and Consumption.* New York: NYU Press.

Brown, P. G., and Timmerman, P. 2015. *Ecological Economics for the Anthropocene: An Emerging Paradigm.* New York: Columbia University Press.

Canclini, N. G. 2001. *Consumers and Citizens: Globalization and Multicultural Conflicts.* Minneapolis: University of Minnesota Press.

Carlsen, J., and Butler, R. 2011. *Island Tourism: Sustainable Perspectives.* Cambridge, MA: CABI.

Carrier, J. G., and Luetchford, P. 2012. *Ethical Consumption: Social Value and Economic Practice.* Oxford, UK: Berghahn Books.

Chen, K. K. 2012a. "Artistic Prosumption: Cocreative Destruction at Burning Man." *American Behavioral Scientist* 56(4):570–95. DOI: 10.1177/0002764211429362.

Chen, T.-P. 2012b. "Hong Kong Cleans Up Massive Plastic Spill." https://blogs.wsj. com/chinarealtime/2012/08/06/hong-kong-cleans-up-massive-plastic-spill/ [Accessed June 11, 2018].

Chikarmane, P. 2016. "Public Space, Public Waste, and the Right to the City." *NEW SOLUTIONS: A Journal of Environmental and Occupational Health Policy.* 26(2):289–300. DOI: 10.1177/1048291116652689.

Chouliaraki, L. 2006a. "Towards an Analytics of Mediation." *Critical Discourse Studies* 3(2):153–78. DOI: 10.1080/17405900600908095.

Chouliaraki, L. 2006b. *The Spectatorship of Suffering.* London: SAGE Publications.

———. 2008. "The Media as Moral Education: Mediation and Action." *Media, Culture & Society* 30(6):831–52.

———. 2013. *The Ironic Spectator: Solidarity in the Age of Post-Humanitarianism.* London: John Wiley & Sons.

Clark, T. 2015. *Ecocriticism on the Edge: The Anthropocene as a Threshold Concept.* London: Bloomsbury Publishing.

Comaroff, J., and Comaroff, J. L. 2012. "Theory from the South: Or, How Euro-America Is Evolving toward Africa." *Anthropological Forum* 22(2):113–31. DOI: 10.1080/00664677.2012.694169.

Connett, P. 2013. *The Zero Waste Solution: Untrashing the Planet One Community at a Time.* White River Junction, VT: Chelsea Green Publishing.

Cosgrove, D. 1994. "Contested Global Visions: One-World, Whole-Earth, and the Apollo Space Photographs." *Annals of the Association of American Geographers* 84(2):270–94. DOI: 10.1111/j.1467-8306.1994.tb01738.x.

Costelloe, T. M. 2012. *The Sublime: From Antiquity to the Present.* Cambridge, UK: Cambridge University Press.

Couldry, N. 2000. *The Place of Media Power: Pilgrims and Witnesses of the Media Age.* London: Routledge.

Couldry, N. 2010. *Why Voice Matters: Culture and Politics after Neoliberalism.* London: SAGE.

Crang, M., Hughes, A., Gregson, N., Norris, L., and Ahamed, F. 2012. "Rethinking Governance and Value in Commodity Chains through Global Recycling Networks." *Transactions of the Institute of British Geographers* 38(1):12–24. DOI: 10.1111/j.1475-5661.2012.00515.x.

Cubitt, S. 2005. *Eco Media.* New York: Rodopi.

Dant, T. 1999. *Material Culture in the Social World.* London: McGraw-Hill Education (UK).

Datta, P. B., and Gailey, R. 2012. "Empowering Women through Social Entrepreneurship: Case Study of a Women's Cooperative in India." *Entrepreneurship Theory and Practice* 36(3):569–87. DOI: 10.1111/j.1540-6520.2012.00505.x.

Dellasala, D. A., and Goldstein, M. I., eds. 2017. *Encyclopedia of the Anthropocene.* Amsterdam: Elsevier.

DeLuca, K. M. 2012. *Image Politics: The New Rhetoric of Environmental Activism.* London: Routledge.

DNews. 2012. *Oil Giant to Pay for Hong Kong Nurdle Spill.* https://www.seeker.com/oil-giant-to-pay-for-hong-kong-nurdle-spill-1765918020.html [Accessed April 3,2018].

Dodds, R., and Graci, S. 2012. *Sustainable Tourism in Island Destinations.* London: Routledge.

Dorling, D. 2015. *Inequality and the 1%.* London: Verso.

Dosekun, S. 2019. *Fashioning Postfeminism: Spectacular Femininity and Transnational Culture.* Champaign: University of Illinois Press.

Douglas, P. M. 2013. *Purity and Danger: An Analysis of Concepts of Pollution and Taboo.* London: Routledge.

Downes, R. 1992. "What Have We Made of the Landscape?" *Art Journal* 51(2):16–19. DOI: 10.2307/777385.

Du Gay, P. 1996. *Consumption and Identity at Work.* SAGE.

Ellis-Petersen, H. 2017. "UK Music Industry Gets Boost from 12% Rise in Audiences at Live Events." *The Guardian.* July 9. http://www.theguardian.com/music/2017/jul/10/uk-music-industry-gets-boost-from-12-rise-in-audiences-at-live-events [Accessed May 4, 2018].

Embury-Dennis, T. 2017. *Tide of Plastic Discovered Floating off Coast of Idyllic Caribbean Island Coastline.* http://www.independent.co.uk/news/world/americas/plastic-rubbish-tide-caribbean-island-roatan-honduras-coast-pollution-a8017381.html [Accessed June 11, 2018].

Estrin, J. 2009. "Behind the Scenes: Woodstock Memories." https://lens.blogs.nytimes.com/2009/07/30/behind-8/ [Accessed May 30, 2019].

Evans, B. 2018. *The Aftermath: Mardi Gras Trash at 620 Tons and Counting.* https://www.nola.com/politics/index.ssf/2018/02/mardi_gras_trash_beads_clean_u.html [Accessed June 8, 2018].

Evans, J. 2015. *Maldives Island Swamped by Rising Tide of Waste.* https://www.ft.com/content/29399966-e80b-11e4-9960-00144feab7de [Accessed April 21, 2018].

Ewen, S. 2008. *Captains of Consciousness: Advertising and the Social Roots of the Consumer Culture.* New York: Basic Books.

Fagan, A. 2006. "Buying Right: Consuming Ethically and Human Rights." In *Human Rights and Capitalism: A Multidisciplinary Perspective on Globalisation.* J. Dine and A. Fagan, eds. Northampton, MA: Edward Elgar Publishing, 115–41.

Feigenbaum, A. 2012. "Concrete Needs No Metaphor: Globalized Fences as Sites of Political Struggle." *Ephemera: Theory and Politics in Organization* 10(2):119–133.

Ferrell, J. 2006. *Empire of Scrounge: Inside the Urban Underground of Dumpster Diving, Trash Picking, and Street Scavenging.* New York: NYU Press.

Finch, J., and Smithers, R. 2006. "Too Much Packaging? Dump It at Checkout, Urges Minister." *The Guardian*, November 14. http://www.theguardian.com/business/2006/nov/14/supermarkets.ethicalliving [Accessed June 3, 2018].

Flinn, J., and Frew, M. 2014. "Glastonbury: Managing the Mystification of Festivity." *Leisure Studies*, 33(4):418–33. DOI: 10.1080/02614367.2012.751121.

Frayne, D. 2015. *The Refusal of Work: The Theory and Practice of Resistance to Work.* London: Zed Books.

Freinkel, S. 2011. *Plastic: A Toxic Love Story.* Boston: Houghton Mifflin Harcourt.

Freud, S. 2015. *Civilization and Its Discontents.* Peterborough, Ontario: Broadview Press.

Freytas-Tamura, K. de. 2018. "Plastics Pile Up as China Refuses to Take the West's Recycling." *New York Times*, January 11. https://www.nytimes.com/2018/01/11/world/china-recyclables-ban.html [Accessed January 16, 2018].

Gabbatis, J. 2018. *A Sperm Whale Has Died after Swallowing 29 Kilos of Plastic Waste.* https://www.independent.co.uk/environment/plastic-pollution-killed-sper m-whale-dead-spain-beach-bags-blue-planet-a8293446.html [Accessed June 13, 2018].

Gabrys, J. 2013. *Digital Rubbish: A Natural History of Electronics.* Ann Arbour: University of Michigan Press.

Gagain, M. 2012. "Climate Change, Sea Level Rise, and Artificial Islands: Saving the Maldives' Statehood and Maritime Claims through the Constitution of the Oceans." *Colorado Journal of International Environmental Law and Policy* 23:77.

Gibbens, S. 2018. *Plastic Bag Found at the Bottom of World's Deepest Ocean Trench.* https://news.nationalgeographic.com/2018/05/plastic-bag-mar iana-trench-pollution-science-spd/ [Accessed June 11, 2018].

———. 2019. *Newborn Hawaii Beach Is Already Polluted with Tiny Pieces of Plastic.* https://www.nationalgeographic.com/environment/2019/05/newborn-h awaii-beach-already-polluted-with-plastic/ [Accessed May 31, 2019].

Gill, R. 2008. "Culture and Subjectivity in Neoliberal and Postfeminist Times. *Subjectivity*" 25(1):432–45. DOI: 10.1057/sub.2008.28.

Gilmore, L. 2010. *Theater in a Crowded Fire: Ritual and Spirituality at Burning Man.* Berkeley: University of California Press.

Gilmore, L., and Proyen, M. V. 2005. *AfterBurn: Reflections on Burning Man.* Albuquerque: University of new Mexico Press.

Glastonbury Festival, P. G. 2018. *Glastonbury Festival—Camping.* http://www. glastonburyfestivals.co.uk/information/accommodation/camping/ [Accessed June 7, 2018].

Goldman, R. 1996. *Sign Wars: The Cluttered Landscape of Advertising.* New York: Guilford Press.

Gopal, M. 2013. Ruptures and Reproduction in Caste/Gender/Labour. *Economic and Political Weekly* 48(18):91–97.

Gössling, S. 2001. "The Consequences of Tourism for Sustainable Water Use on a Tropical Island: Zanzibar, Tanzania." *Journal of Environmental Management* 61(2):179–91. DOI: 10.1006/jema.2000.0403.

———. 2003. *Tourism and Development in Tropical Islands: Political Ecology Perspectives.* Northampton, MA: Edward Elgar.

Graf, H. 2016. *The Environment in the Age of the Internet: Activists, Communication, and the Digital Landscape.* Cambridge, UK: Open Book Publishers.

Greer, J., and Bruno, K. 1998. *Greenwash: The Reality Behind Corporate Environmentalism.* Montevideo, Uruguay: IBON Foundation Incorporated, Third World Network.

Guattari, F. 2005. *The Three Ecologies.* London: Bloomsbury Academic.

Guido, G. 2009. *Behind Ethical Consumption: Purchasing Motives and Marketing Strategies for Organic Food Products, Non-GMOs, Bio-fuels.* Bern, Switzerland: Peter Lang.

Haenn, N., Harnish, A., and Wilk, R. 2016. *The Environment in Anthropology: A Reader in Ecology, Culture, and Sustainable Living* (2d ed.). New York: NYU Press.

Hall, E. J. 2004. *Recycling*. New York: KidHaven Press.

Hall, S. 1997. *Representation: Cultural Representations and Signifying Practices*. London: SAGE.

Hampton, M., and Jeyacheya, J. 2013. *Tourism and Inclusive Growth in Small Island Developing States*. London: Commonwealth Secretariat.

Harari, Y. N. 2016. *Homo Deus: A Brief History of Tomorrow*. London: Random House.

Haraway, D. 2008. *When Species Meet*. Minneapolis: University of Minnesota Press.

Harrison, R., Newholm, T., and Shaw, D. 2005. *The Ethical Consumer*. London: SAGE.

Harshey, S., and Sharma, P. 2016. "Making Waste Matter: Reimagining Urban Renewal and Advocating for Women Waste-Pickers' Right to a Dignified Livelihood." In *Land, Labour and Livelihoods*. Palgrave Macmillan, Cham. 263–83. DOI: 10.1007/978-3-319-40865-1_13.

Haviland, C. 2011. "'Rubbish Island' Is 'Overwhelmed.'" *BBC News*. December 8.http://www.bbc.com/news/world-asia-16072020 [Accessed May 7, 2018,].

Hawkins, G. 2006. *The Ethics of Waste: How We Relate to Rubbish*. Rowman and Littlefield.

Hawkins, G., and Muecke, S. 2003. *Culture and Waste: The Creation and Destruction of Value*. New York: Rowman & Littlefield.

Hawkins, G., Potter, E., and Race, K. 2015. *Plastic Water: The Social and Material Life of Bottled Water*. Boston, MA: MIT Press.

Hoare, P. 2018. "Microplastics in Our Mussels: The Sea Is Feeding Human Garbage Back to Us." *The Guardian*, June 8. http://www.theguardian.com/environment/shortcuts/2018/jun/08/microplastics-in-our-mussels-the-sea-is-feeding-human-garbage-back-to-us [Accessed June 11, 2018].

Hoffman, A. J., and Jennings, P. D. 2011. "The BP Oil Spill as a Cultural Anomaly? Institutional Context, Conflict, and Change." *Journal of Management Inquiry* 20(2):100–12. DOI: 10.1177/1056492610394940.

Honey, M., and Hogenson, S. 2017. *Coastal Tourism, Sustainability, and Climate Change in the Caribbean, Volume I: Beaches and Hotels*. New York: Business Expert Press.

Hook, G .D., Lester, L., Ji, M., Edney, K., Pope, C. G., and Does-Ishikawa, L. van der. 2017. *Environmental Pollution and the Media: Political Discourses of Risk and Responsibility in Australia, China and Japan*. London: Routledge.

Hughes, D. M. 2017. *Energy without Conscience : Oil, Climate Change, and Complicity*. Durham, NC.: Duke University Press.

Humes, E. 2013. *Garbology: Our Dirty Love Affair with Trash*. Reprint ed. New York: Avery Publishing Group.

Hutchinson, K. 2015. "Glastonbury 2015 after Dark—Ravers Seek Unbridled Dance

Hedonism." *The Guardian*. June 28. http://www.theguardian.com/music/2015/ jun/28/glastonbury-2015-after-dark-ravers-dance-silver-hayes-shangri-la [Accessed May 4, 2018].

IB Times. 2014. *Rio Carnival Leaves City in Mess with Smelly Trash all Over* [photos]. https://www.ibtimes.co.uk/rio-carnival-leaves-city-mess-smelly-trash-all-over-photos-1439074 [Accessed June 8, 2018].

Inhabitat Staff. 2019. "Ecobricks Transform Plastic Trash into Reusable Building Blocks." https://inhabitat.com/ecobricks-transform-plastic-trash-into-reusable-building-blocks/ [Accessed February 19, 2019].

Iqani, M. 2012. *Consumer Culture and the Media: Magazines in the Public Eye*. London: Palgrave Macmillan.

———. 2016. *Consumption, Media and the Global South: Aspiration Contested*. London: Palgrave Macmillan.

Iqani, M., and Knoetze, F. 2017. "Art" Durban: Somatosphere." http://somatosphere. net/2017/12/art.html.

Jensen, D., McBay, A., and Keith, L. 2011. *Deep Green Resistance: Strategy to Save the Planet*. New York: Seven Stories Press.

Johnson, B. 2013. *Zero Waste Home: The Ultimate Guide to Simplifying Your Life by Reducing Your Waste*. New York: Simon and Schuster.

Jucan, I. B., Parikka, J., and Schneider, R. 2019. *Remain*. Minneapolis: University of Minnesota Press.

Kainulainen, M. 2013. "Saying Climate Change: Ethics of the Sublime and the Problem of Representation." *symploke* 21(1):109–23.

Kapferer, J.-N. 2017. "Managing Luxury Brands." In *Advances in Luxury Brand Management*. London: Palgrave Macmillan, Cham. 235–49. DOI: 10.1007/978-3-319-51127-6_11.

Kilby, P. 2013. "Waste Recycling and the Household Economy: The Case of the Pune Waste-Pickers' Response to the Changing 'Rules of the Game.'" In *The Global Political Economy of the Household in Asia*. Palgrave Macmillan, London. 211–26. DOI: 10.1057/9781137338907_14.

Knappett, C. 2011. *Thinking Through Material Culture: An Interdisciplinary Perspective*. Philadelphia: University of Pennsylvania Press.

Knapton, S. 2017. "Paradise Lost: Hotels Bury Waste Plastic in the Sand to Keep Tourists Happy." *The Telegraph*, March 20. https://www.telegraph.co.uk/science/2017/03/20/paradise-lost-hotels-bury-waste-sand-keep-tourists-happy/ [Accessed May 7, 2018].

Kolbert, E. 2014. *The Sixth Extinction: An Unnatural History*. New York: Henry Holt and Company.

Korst, A. 2012. *The Zero-Waste Lifestyle: Live Well by Throwing Away Less*. Emeryville, CA,: Ten Speed Press.

de Kort, Y. A.W., McCalley, L. T., and Midden, C. J. H. 2008. "Persuasive Trash Cans: Activation of Littering Norms by Design." *Environment and Behavior* 40(6):870–91. DOI: 10.1177/0013916507311035.

Kozinets, R. V. 2002. "Can Consumers Escape the Market? Emancipatory Illuminations from Burning Man." *Journal of Consumer Research* 29(1):20–38. DOI: 10.1086/339919.

Krol, C. 2019. *Arcadia Spider Team Share First Official Glimpse of "Pangea" for Glastonbury Festival 2019*. https://www.nme.com/news/music/arcadi a-team-share-first-glimpse-of-pangea-for-glastonbury-festival-2019-2489653 [Accessed May 30,2019].

Kuppinger, P. 2018. "Waste and Garbage in the City: A Case Study from Cairo, Egypt." In *Urban Life: Readings in the Anthropology of the City.* G. Gmelch and P. Kuppinger, eds. Long Grove, IL: Waveland Press. 431–43.

Lavery, C. 2017. "Drift." In *Somatosphere*. Durban: Somatosphere. http://somat osphere.net/2017/12/drift.html [Accessed June 8, 2018].

Lehmann, L. V. 2015. "The Garbage Project Revisited: From a 20th Century Archaeology of Food Waste to a Contemporary Study of Food Packaging Waste." *Sustainability* 7(6):6994–7010. DOI: 10.3390/su7066994.

Lehmann, S., and Crocker, R. 2013. *Designing for Zero Waste: Consumption, Technologies and the Built Environment*. London: Routledge.

Lekakis, E. 2013. *Coffee Activism and the Politics of Fair Trade and Ethical Consumption in the Global North: Political Consumerism and Cultural Citizenship*. London: Palgrave Macmillan.

LeMenager, S. 2014. *Living Oil: Petroleum Culture in the American Century*. New York: OUP USA.

Lepawsky, J. 2014. "The Changing Geography of Global Trade in Electronic Discards: Time to Rethink the E-waste Problem." *Geographical Journal* 181(2):147–59. DOI: 10.1111/geoj.12077.

Lewis, T., and Potter, E. 2013. *Ethical Consumption: A Critical Introduction*. London: Routledge.

Lindemann, K. 2017. *Scientists Confirm the Existence of Another Ocean garbage Patch*. https://www.researchgate.net/blog/post/scientists-confirm-the-exi stence-of-another-ocean-garbage-patch [Accessed March 27, 2018].

Littler, J. 2008. *Radical Consumption: Shopping for Change in Contemporary Culture*. London: McGraw-Hill Education.

Looney, R. E. 2012. *Handbook of Oil Politics*. London: Routledge.

MacBride, S. 2011. *Recycling Reconsidered: The Present Failure and Future Promise of Environmental Action in the United States*. Boston, MA: MIT Press.

Machin, D., and Leeuwen, T. V. 2007. *Global Media Discourse: A Critical Introduction*. London: Taylor & Francis.

MacRae, G. 2012. "Solid Waste Management in Tropical Asia: What Can We Learn from Bali?" *Waste Management & Research* 30(1):72–79. DOI: 10.1177/0734242X10386138.

Mamphitha, D. 2012. "The Role Played by Subsistence Waste Pickers in Recycling." Dissertation. University of Pretoria. https://repository.up.ac.za/ha ndle/2263/26322 [Accessed June 5, 2018].

Manga, J. 2003. *Talking Trash: The Cultural Politics of Daytime TV Talk Shows*. New York: NYU Press.

Mardi Gras. 2017. *"After glitter comes the litter"*: 20 *Vintage Mardi Gras Trash Photos*. http://www.mardigras.com/news/2017/02/after_glitter_comes_the_litter.html [Accessed June 8, 2018].

Marsh, S. 2019. "Glastonbury Festival Bans Plastic Bottles." *The Guardian*. February 27. https://www.theguardian.com/music/2019/feb/27/glastonbury-festi-val-bans-plastic-bottles [Accessed May 29, 2019].

Matheson, D. 2005. *Media Discourses*. London: McGraw-Hill International.

Mattelart, A. 1991. *Advertising International: The Privatisation of Public Space*. London: Taylor & Francis.

Mayoux, L. 1995. "Alternative Vision or Utopian fantasy?: Cooperation, Empowerment and Women's Cooperative Development in India." *Journal of International Development* 7(2):211–28. DOI: 10.1002/jid.3380070203.

McCracken, G. D. 1990. *Culture and Consumption: New Approaches to the Symbolic Character of Consumer Goods and Activities*. Bloomington: Indiana University Press.

McCurdy, P. 2017. "Bearing Witness and the Logic of Celebrity in the Struggle over Canada's Oil/Tar Sands." In *Carbon Capitalism and Communication*. London: Palgrave Macmillan, Cham. 131–45. DOI: 10.1007/978-3-319-57876-7_11.

———. 2018. "From the Natural to the Manmade Environment: The Shifting Advertising Practices of Canada's Oil Sands Industry." *Canadian Journal of Communication* 43(1). DOI: 10.22230/cjc.2018v43n1a3315.

McElvaney, K. 2014. *Ghana's e-waste magnet*. https://www.aljazeera.com/indepth/inpictures/2014/01/pictures-ghana-e-waste-mecca-2014130104740975223.html [Accessed June 5, 2018].

McKibben, B. 2010. *Eaarth: Making a Life on a Tough New Planet*. New York: Macmillan.

———. 2013. *Oil and Honey: The Education of an Unlikely Activist*. New York: Macmillan.

McVeigh, K. 2018. *Huge Rise in US Plastic Waste Shipments to Poor Countries Following China Ban | Global Development | The Guardian*. https://www.theguardian.com/global-development/2018/oct/05/huge-rise-us-plasti c-waste-shipments-to-poor-countries-china-ban-thailand-malaysia-vietnam [Accessed February 19, 2019].

Melosi, M. V. 2016. "Fresh Kills: The Making and Unmaking of a Wastescape." *RCC Perspectives* (1):59–66.

Meyer-Arendt, K., and Lew, A. A. 2016. *Understanding Tropical Coastal and Island Tourism Development*. London: Routledge.

Miller, D. 1994. *Material Culture and Mass Consumption*. London: Blackwell.

———. 2010. *Stuff*. Cambridge, UK: Polity.

———. 2013. *Consumption and Its Consequences*. London: John Wiley & Sons.

Minter, A. 2016. *The Burning Truth Behind an E-Waste Dump in Africa*. https://www.

smithsonianmag.com/science-nature/burning-truth-behind-e-waste-dum
p-africa-180957597/ [Accessed June 5, 2018].

Mintz, S. W. 1986. *Sweetness and Power: The Place of Sugar in Modern History*.
London: Penguin Books.

Mitchell, T. 2011. *Carbon Democracy: Political Power in the Age of Oil*. London: Verso
Books.

Momsen, J. H. 2003. *Gender, Migration and Domestic Service*. London: Routledge.

Mooney, C. 2015. "Humans Are Putting 8 Million Metric Tons of Plastic in the
Oceans—annually." *Washington Post*, February 12. \https://www.washingto
npost.com/news/energy-environment/wp/2015/02/12/humans-ar
e-putting-8-million-metric-tons-of-plastic-in-the-oceans-annually/ [Accessed
April 3, 2018].

———. 2018. *Plastic within the Great Pacific Garbage Patch Is 'Increasing
Fxponentially,' Scientists Find. Washington Post*. https://www.washingtonpost.
com/news/energy-environment/wp/2018/03/22/plastic-within-the-great-p
acific-garbage-patch-is-increasing-exponentially-scientists-find/?utm_ter
m=.ea277b5c9c0b [Accessed March 27, 2018].

Moore, C. 2003. "Trashed: Across the Pacific Ocean, Plastics, Plastics, Everywhere."
Natural History. (November).

Morgan, S. 2009. *Waste, Recycling and Reuse*. London: Evans Brothers.

Morton, T. 2013. *Hyperobjects: Philosophy and Ecology after the End of the World*.
Minneapolis: University of Minnesota Press.

———. 2016. *Dark Ecology: For a Logic of Future Coexistence*. New York: Columbia
University Press.

Murray, R. L., and Heumann, J. K. 2009. *Ecology and Popular Film: Cinema on the
Edge*. Albany: SUNY Press.

Nace, T. 2018. *Yet Another Dead Whale Found with Pounds of Plastic in Its Stomach*.
https://www.forbes.com/sites/trevornace/2018/11/26/yet-another-dead-whal
e-found-with-13-pounds-of-plastic-in-its-stomach/#7799ac566af5 [Accessed
May 15, 2019].

Nagle, R. 2014. *Picking Up: On the Streets and Behind the Trucks with the Sanitation
Workers of New York City*. New York: Farrar, Straus and Giroux.

Nava, M., Blake, A., MacRury, I., and Richards, B. 2013. *Buy This Book: Studies in
Advertising and Consumption*. London: Routledge.

Neville, B., and Villeneuve, J. 2012. *Waste-Site Stories: The Recycling of Memory*.
Albany, NY: SUNY Press.

Newlands, M. 2018. *Environmental Activism and the Media: The Politics of Protest*.
New York: Peter Lang AG International Academic Publishers.

Nixon, R. 2013. *Slow Violence and the Environmentalism of the Poor*.Cambridge, MA:
Harvard University Press.

Nye, D. E. 1996. *American Technological Sublime*. Boston, MA: MIT Press.

O'Dougherty, M. 2002. *Consumption Intensified: The Politics of Middle-Class Daily
Life in Brazil*. Durham, NC: Duke University Press.

Oliphant, R. 2017. "Bali Declares Rubbish Emergency as Rising Tide of Plastic Buries Beaches." *The Telegraph*. December 28. https://www.telegraph.co.uk/news/2017/12/28/bali-declares-rubbish-emergency-rising-tide-plastic-buries-beaches/ [Accessed May 9, 2019].

Oreskes, N. 2004. "The Scientific Consensus on Climate Change." *Science* 306(5702):1686–86. DOI: 10.1126/science.1103618.

Oyake-Ombis, L. 2018. *How Nairobi Can Fix Its Serious Waste Problem*. http://theconversation.com/how-nairobi-can-fix-its-serious-waste-problem-92443 [Accessed March 20, 2018].

Pájaro, F. de. 2015. *Art Is Trash*. Barcelona, Spain: Promopress.

Parikka, J. 2015. *A Geology of Media*. Minneapolis: University of Minnesota Press.

Parker, L. 2018. *The Great Pacific Garbage Patch Isn't What You Think It Is*. https://news.nationalgeographic.com/2018/03/great-pacific-garbage-patch-plastics-environment/ [Accessed June 11, 2018].

Parra, F. 2004. *Oil Politics: A Modern History of Petroleum*. London: I. B.Tauris.

Peake, L. 2011. *When the Party's Over*. https://resource.co/article/Think_Tank/When_party%E2%80%99s_over [Accessed June 7, 2018].

Pearse, G. 2012. *Greenwash: Big Brands and Carbon Scams*. Collingwood: Black Inc.

Pew Research Center. 2010. "A Different Kind of Disaster Story. http://www.journalism.org/2010/08/25/oil-spill-was-very-different-kind-disaster-story/ [Accessed March 23, 2018].

Pickerill, J. 2010. *Cyberprotest: Environmental Activism Online*. Oxford: Oxford University Press.

Press, A. L., and Williams, B. A. 2010. *The New Media Environment: An Introduction*. Wiley-Blackwell.

Rathje, W. L. 1984. "The Garbàge Decade." *American Behavioral Scientist*. 28(1):9–29. DOI: 10.1177/000276484028001003.

———. 2004. "A Manifesto for Modern Material Culture Studies." In *Material Culture: Critical Concepts in the Social Sciences*. V. Buchli, ed. New York: Routledge, 402–8.

Rathje, W. L., and Murphy, C. 2001. *Rubbish!: The Archaeology of Garbage*. Tucson: University of Arizona Press.

Recuber, T. 2013. "Disaster Porn!" *Contexts* 12(2):28–33. DOI: 10.1177/1536504213487695.

Redmon, D. 2014. *Beads, Bodies, and Trash: Public Sex, Global Labor, and the Disposability of Mardi Gras*. New York: Routledge.

Reich, J. W., and Robertson, J. L. 1979. "Reactance and Norm Appeal in Anti-Littering Messages." *Journal of Applied Social Psychology* 9(1):91–101. DOI: 10.1111/j.1559-1816.1979.tb00796.x.

Reid, D. 2014. *Toxic Legacy of E-waste in Ghana*. https://www.bbc.com/news/av/technology-26239741/making-a-living-from-toxic-electronic-waste-in-ghana [Accessed June 5, 2018].

Reuters. 2018. *East African Plastic Manufacturers Step-up Recycling after China Ban |*

Africanews. http://www.africanews.com/2018/09/18/east-african-plastic-ma
nufacturers-step-up-recycling-after-china-ban// [Accessed February 19, 2019].

Robinson, D. R. 2015. *Music Festivals and the Politics of Participation*. Farnham, UK:
Ashgate Publishing.

Robinson, J. 2009. Interview with the Organisers of Woodstock Festival. August
12. https://www.telegraph.co.uk/culture/music/rockandpopfeatures/6017442/
Interview-with-the-organisers-of-Woodstock-Festival.html [Accessed June 8,
2018].

Rogers, H. 2006. *Gone Tomorrow: The Hidden Life of Garbage*. New York: New Press.

Rose, N. S. 1990. *Governing the Soul: The Shaping of the Private Self*. London:
Routledge.

Roy, A. 2016. "The Saint and the Doctor." In *Annihilation of Caste: The Annotated
Critical Edition*. B. R. Ambedkar, ed. London: Verso, 11–179.

Rust, S., Monani, S., and Cubitt, S. 2015. *Ecomedia: Key Issues*. London: Routledge.

Rutherford, S. 2017. "A Resounding Success? Howling as a Source of Environmental
History." In *Methodological Challenges in Nature-Culture and Environmental
History Research*. J. Thorpe, S. Rutherford, and L. A. Sandberg, eds. Abingdon,
UK: Taylor & Francis, 43–54.

Safina, C. 2011. *A Sea in Flames: The Deepwater Horizon Oil Blowout*. New York:
Crown/Archetype.

Samson, M. 2009. Wasted Citizenship? Reclaimers and the Privatised Expansion of
the Public Sphere. *Africa Development* 34(3–4). DOI: 10.4314/ad.v34i3-4.63525.

———. 2015. "Accumulation by Dispossession and the Informal Economy—
Struggles over Knowledge, Being and Waste at a Soweto Garbage Dump."
Environment and Planning D: Society and Space 33(5):813–30. DOI:
10.1177/0263775815600058.

Samuelson, M. 2018. "Beach." In *Somatosphere*. Durban: Somatosphere. http://s
omatosphere.net/2018/01/beach.html [Accessed June 8, 2018].

Scanlan, J. 2005. *On Garbage*. London: Reaktion Books.

Scheyvens, R., and Momsen, J. 2008. "Tourism in Small Island States: From
Vulnerability to Strengths." *Journal of Sustainable Tourism* 16(5):491–510. DOI:
10.1080/09669580802159586.

Schlanger, Z. 2018. *China's Ban on Plastic Recycling Imports Means the World Will
Have 111 Million Metric Tons of Extra Plastic to Deal with by 2030—Quartz.*
https://qz.com/1310240/chinas-ban-on-plastic-recycling-imports-means-th
e-world-will-have-111-million-metric-tons-of-extra-plastic-to-deal-wit
h-by-2030/ [Accessed February 19, 2019].

Schultz, P. W., Bator, R. J., Large, L. B., Bruni, C. M., and Tabanico, J. J.
2013. "Littering in Context: Personal and Environmental Predictors
of Littering Behavior." *Environment and Behavior* 45(1):35–59. DOI:
10.1177/0013916511412179.

Seegert, N. 2014. "Dirty, Pretty Trash: Confronting Perceptions through the
Aesthetics of the Abject." *Journal of Ecocriticism* 6(1):1–12.

Sentime, K. 2011. "Profiling Solid Waste Pickers: A Case Study of Braamfontein—Greater Johannesburg." *Africanus* 41(2):96–111.

Shangri-la. 2017. *Shangri-la | Glastonbury—Official Website*. http://www.sha ngrilaglastonbury.co.uk/ [Accessed May 30, 2019].

Shellenberger, M., and Nordhaus, T., eds. 2011. *Love Your Monsters: Postenvironmentalism and the Anthropocene*. Oakland, CA.: Breakthrough Institute.

Sibley, C. G., and Liu, J. H. 2003. "Differentiating Active and Passive Littering: A Two-Stage Process Model of Littering Behavior in Public Spaces." *Environment and Behavior* 35(3):415–33. DOI: 10.1177/0013916503035003006.

Silverstein, K. 2014. *The Secret World of Oil*. London: Verso Books.

Silverstone, R. 1999. *Why Study the Media?* London: SAGE.

——. 2005. "The Sociology of Mediation and Communication." In *The Sage Handbook of Sociology*. C. Calhoun, C. Rojek, and B. Turner, eds. London: SAGE. 188–207.

——. 2013. *Media and Morality: On the Rise of the Mediapolis*. London: John Wiley & Sons.

Sivaperuman, C., Velmurugan, A., Singh, A. K., and Jaisankar, I. 2018. *Biodiversity and Climate Change Adaptation in Tropical Islands*. London: Academic Press.

Slater, D. 1997. *Consumer Culture and Modernity*. London: Wiley.

Smart, B. 2010. *Consumer Society: Critical Issues and Environmental Consequences*. London: SAGE.

Smith, J. 2017. "This Is What Happens to all the Tents Left Behind at Glastonbury." *Somerset Live*. May 12. http://www.somersetlive.co.uk/whats-on/music-nigh tlife/what-happens-tents-left-behind-56851 [Accessed May 4, 2018].

Smith, N. C. 1987. "Consumer Boycotts and Consumer Sovereignty. *European Journal of Marketing* 21(5):7–19. DOI: 10.1108/EUM0000000004694.

Smith, B. D., and Zeder, M. A. 2013. "The Onset of the Anthropocene. *Anthropocene* 4:8–13. DOI: 10.1016/j.ancene.2013.05.001.

Smithson, J., and Venette, S. 2013. "Stonewalling as an Image-Defense Strategy: A Critical Examination of BP's Response to the Deepwater Horizon Explosion." *Communication Studies* 64(4):395–410. DOI: 10.1080/10510974.2013.770409.

Somerville, M. 2015. "Why Lauren Singer, the 'Zero Trash Girl,'" Is My Crush of the Month. *The Guardian*. October 13. http://www.theguardian.com/env ironment/2015/oct/13/lauren-singer-zero-trash-girl-green-eco-friendly-living [Accessed June 4, 2018].

Starbird, K., Dailey, D., Walker, A. H., Leschine, T. M., Pavia, R., and Bostrom, A. 2015. "Social Media, Public Participation, and the 2010 BP Deepwater Horizon Oil Spill." *Human and Ecological Risk Assessment: An International Journal* 21(3):605–30. DOI: 10.1080/10807039.2014.947866.

Starosielski, N., and Walker, J. 2016. *Sustainable Media: Critical Approaches to Media and Environment*. New York: Routledge.

Steele, J. 2015. "Sculpting with Fire: Celebrating Ephemerality at AfrikaBurn 2015 in the Tankwa Karoo, South Africa." *South African Journal of Art History* 30(3):187–200.

——. 2017. "Yggdrasil, the Tree of Life at AfrikaBurn 2017 in Tankwa Karoo, South Africa. *South African Journal of Art History* 32(2):161–73.

Steffen, W., Crutzen, P. J., and McNeill, J. R. 2007. "The Anthropocene: Are Humans Now Overwhelming the Great Forces of Nature." *AMBIO: A Journal of the Human Environment*. 36(8):614–621. DOI: 10.1579/0044-7447(2007)36[614:TAAHNO]2.0.CO;2.

Still, C. 2015. *Dalits in Neoliberal India: Mobility or Marginalisation?* London: Routledge.

Stoner, A. M., and Melathopoulos, A. 2015. *Freedom in the Anthropocene: Twentieth-Century Helplessness in the Face of Climate Change*. London: Palgrave Pivot.

Strasser, S. 1999. *Waste and Want: A Social History of Trash*. New York: Henry and Holt.

Su, S. 2018. *Zero Waste: Simple Life Hacks to Drastically Reduce Your Trash*. New York: Skyhorse Publishing.

Swartz, S. 2009. *The Moral Ecology of South Africa's Township Youth*. London: Palgrave Macmillan.

Thill, B. 2015. *Waste*. New York: Bloomsbury Publishing USA.

Thomlinson, N. 2013. "Sustainability Is Destroying the Earth." http://dgrnewsservice. org/civilization/ecocide/sustainability-is-destroying-the-earth/ [Accessed June 4, 2018].

Tsing, A. 2015. *The Mushroom at the End of the World: On the Possibility of Life in Capitalist Ruins*. Princeton, NJ: Princeton University Press.

Veltmeyer, H., and Bowles, P. 2014. "Extractivist Resistance: The Case of the Enbridge Oil Pipeline Project in Northern British Columbia." *The Extractive Industries and Society* 1(1):59–68. DOI: 10.1016/j.exis.2014.02.002.

Vergine, L. 1997. *Trash, from Junk to Art*. Berkeley, CA: Gingko Press.

——. 2007. *When Trash Becomes Art: TRASH Rubbish Mongo*. Berkeley: Skira.

Viljoen, K., Blaauw, P., and Schenck, R. 2016. "'I would rather have a decent job': Potential Barriers Preventing Street-Waste Pickers from Improving Their Socio-Economic Conditions." *South African Journal of Economic and Management Sciences* 19(2):175–91. DOI: 10.17159/2222-3436/2016/v19n2a2.

Walker, R. 2018. "Leaving Lost Vagueness: How Glastonbury Left Bohemia Behind." *The Observer*. April 28. http://www.theguardian.com/music/2018/apr/28/ leaving-lost-in-vagueness-glastonbury-pioneers-hedonism-documentary [Accessed May 4, 2018].

Walker, A. H., Pavia, R., Bostrom, A., Leschine, T. M., and Starbird, K. 2015. "Communication Practices for Oil Spills: Stakeholder Engagement during Preparedness and Response." *Human and Ecological Risk Assessment: An International Journal* 21(3):667–90. DOI: 10.1080/10807039.2014.947869.

Wallace, M. 2016. *Risk Criticism: Precautionary Reading in an Age of Environmental Uncertainty*. Detroit: University of Michigan Press.

Wallace-Wells, D. 2019. *The Uninhabitable Earth: A Story of the Future*. London: Penguin UK.

Wark, M. 2016. *Molecular Red: Theory for the Anthropocene*. London: VERSO.

Weberman, A. J. 1980. *My Life in Garbology*. New York: Stonehill.

Whiteley, G. 2010. *Junk: Art and the Politics of Trash*. London: I. B.Tauris.

Wiesner, M. E. 2013. *Early Modern Europe, 1450–1789*. Cambridge, UK: Cambridge University Press.

Wikipedia. 2018a. *Deepwater Horizon*. In *Wikipedia*. https://en.wikipedia.org/w/index.php?title=Deepwater_Horizon&oldid=829392351 [Accessed March 22, 2018].

——. 2018b. *Deepwater Horizon* explosion. In *Wikipedia*. https://en.wikipedia.org/w/index.php?title=Deepwater_Horizon_explosion&oldid=826033481 [Accessed March 22, 2018].

——. 2018c. *Deepwater Horizon Oil Spill—Wikipedia*. https://en.wikipedia.org/wiki/Deepwater_Horizon_oil_spill [Accessed March 22, 2018].

Williams, L. 2015. *Why You're about to Start Eating Tiny Pieces of Plastic Coated in Toxins*. http://www.independent.co.uk/news/uk/hundreds-of-thousands-of-tiny-plastic-pellets-infest-british-beaches-a6681581.html [Accessed April 3, 2018].

Willoughby, N. G., Sangkoyo, H., and Lakaseru, B. O. 1997. "Beach Litter: An Increasing and Changing Problem for Indonesia." *Marine Pollution Bulletin* 34(6):469–78. DOI: 10.1016/S0025-326X(96)00141-5.

Woodward, I. 2007. *Understanding Material Culture*. London: SAGE.

Yusoff, K. 2018. *A Billion Black Anthropocenes or None*. Minneapolis: University of Minnesota Press.

Zallio, M., and Berry, D. 2017. "Design and Planned Obsolescence: Theories and Approaches for Designing Enabling Technologies." *Design Journal* 20(sup1):S3749–61.

Zylinska, J. 2014. *Minimal Ethics for the Anthropocene (Critical Climate Change)*. Detroit: Michigan Publishing.

* 9 7 8 1 4 3 8 4 8 0 1 8 3 *